# A Renaissance in Harlem

# A
# RENAISSANCE
# IN HARLEM

*Lost Essays of the WPA, by
Ralph Ellison, Dorothy West, and
Other Voices of a Generation*

*edited by*

## LIONEL C. BASCOM

*An Imprint of HarperCollinsPublishers*

HarperCollins books may be purchased for educational, business, or sales promotional use. For information, please write: Special Markets Department, HarperCollins Publishers Inc., 10 East 53rd Street, New York, NY 10022.

A hardcover edition of this book, with the title *A Renaissance in Harlem: Lost Voices of an American Community,* was published in 1999 by Avon Books.

First Amistad edition published 2001.

*Designed by Kellan Peck*

The Library of Congress has cataloged the hardcover edition as follows:
A renaissance in Harlem : lost voices of an American community /
edited by Lionel C. Bascom. —1st ed.
p.     cm.
Compiled with manuscripts from the Library of Congress,
Manuscript Division, WPA Writer's Project Collection, 1936–1940.
1. American literature—Afro-American authors. 2. Afro-Americans—New York (State)—New York Literary collections. 3. American literature—New York (State)—New York. 4. Harlem (New York, N.Y.)—Literary collections. 5. Harlem Renaissance Literary collection. 6. American literature—20th century. 7. Harlem Renaissance—Sources.   I. Bascom, Lionel C.
PS508.N3R46   1999                                99-33449
810.8'0896073—dc21                                CIP

ISBN 0-380-79902-2 (pbk.)

01 02 03 04 05  ❖/RRD  10 9 8 7 6 5 4 3 2

This collection is dedicated to my brother Chuck, my sister-in-law Sylvia, my cousin Alfred, and friends Ricky, Vego, Dickie, Mack, Lil, Heavy, Peanut, and all the other characters I knew in Harlem who raised me. We marveled at the speeches we heard Malcolm X give and were equally amused by the tall tales Mack seemed to invent at will.

# ACKNOWLEDGMENTS

I offer special thanks to my agent Jane Dystel and her dedicated staff who labored over this project for months before anyone began calling it a book. The organization, layout and flow of what sometimes became an unwieldy text can be credited to Charlotte Abbott and Stephen S. Power, the editors at Avon Books who brought measured and careful eyes to this work. Together, we were all caretakers of these precious stories these writers found in everyday people.

The staff in the Folklife Center at The Library of Congress offered tireless professional assistance. Likewise, librarians Vijay Nair, JoAnne Elpern and Lorraine Furtick at Western Connecticut State University never failed to respond to my numerous queries and requests. They all helped me wade through layers of bibliographies, searching for the Harlem you will ultimately discover in this book.

I'd also like to extend my thanks to include my wife Ginger and my daughters for allowing me the privilege of telling them these stories day in and day out for months while I was discovering the extent of these archives.

To my colleagues Professors John Briggs and Kristen Nord, I'd like to say thank you for listening to my endless questions about style and form. I am truly grateful for all of this generous assistance.

# CONTENTS

## PART 3   PUSHCARTS, THURSDAY GIRLS, AND
## OTHER WORKERS

## PART 4 UPTOWN GODS, KINGS, AND OTHER
## SPIRITUAL ENTITIES

## PART 5   PEOPLE, PLACES, AND THINGS

# A Renaissance in Harlem

# INTRODUCTION

## History from the Ground Up

A few years after America slipped into the Great Depression, a significant social experiment got under way. In the 1930s, government policy makers conceived and launched an ambitious scheme they hoped would both lift the spirits of and provide weekly paychecks for thousands of unemployed Americans. Financed through the New Deal programs of Pres. Franklin D. Roosevelt, the government created a jobs program commonly known as Works Progress Administration, or the WPA. It was the largest public relief project ever attempted, and it employed people to sweep streets; build roads, bridges, and parks across America; and much more.

Under the WPA, a smaller controversial program called the Writer's Project employed some sixty-five hundred writers in twenty-six states. WPA writers fanned out in neighborhoods of towns and cities all across America with a tantalizing assignment: record the personal histories of the people they found. They recorded more than ten thousand stories and were planning to publish them in a series of comprehensive anthologies. Most never made it into print.

A significant number of the people interviewed lived in various African-American communities. These recorded remembrances inadvertently created a huge, untapped canon of black history. One of those places where people told their stories was in Harlem. Coincidentally, just a few years before a handful of WPA writers arrived in Harlem, this section of upper Manhattan had just been recognized by social observers as the black capital of the world. The period would become widely known as the Harlem Renaissance. It was touted mainly as the most significant black cultural revival in our history and was promoted by a very small band of intellectuals who had migrated to Harlem along with thousands of ordinary folks who flocked there too.

While these men and women promoted the art and literature they created in Harlem between 1924 and 1929, the Renaissance they are credited with starting was much more than an intellectual movement.

If you rely on traditional markers, the Harlem renaissance was an explosion of creative activity that began sometime in the early 1920s and abruptly ended in 1929. A revival of historical proportions did occur in Harlem. But what happened in Harlem and when was quite different from the publicity surrounding it that would make a few men and women famous.

The artistic "renaissance" in Harlem is thought to have begun sometime after the start of Prohibition in 1920, and to have declined after the stock market crash in 1929 hurled the country into economic chaos. But Harlem's revival probably began much earlier and lasted much longer than previous historians have indicated.

There were many landmarks early in the twentieth century indicating that Harlem was a mecca for African-Americans of the time. Some of them are the artistic achievements made by the blacks who came to Harlem. But Harlem's revival was made possible by many factors, including a series of unrelated events that occurred throughout America, not just in the close-knit circle of black intellectuals usually credited with Harlem's renaissance.

When the all-black 369th U.S. Army Regiment returned to New York after World War I, it marched uptown to Harlem on February 19, 1919. In the same month, the first black man to earn a Ph.D. from Harvard, W. E. B. DuBois, organized the first Pan African Congress in New York.

In other parts of America, social conditions prompted large numbers of black people to leave their rural homes in the South in search of better lives. Many headed for New York, fleeing the aftermath of race riots over segregation, employment discrimination, and equal rights issues that broke out in several cities, most notably Washington, D.C.; Charleston, S.C.; Chicago; Knoxville; and Omaha, between June and September of 1919.

Another important but much smaller phenomenon was also being recognized at this time: that there was a prolific expression of black creativity. Writer Claude McKay published his novel, *Spring in New Hampshire*, in 1920. DuBois published his book *Darkwater*. In the same year, playwright Eugene O'Neill's black drama, *The Emperor Jones*, opened at the Provincetown Playhouse starring Charles Gilpin. The following year, performers Josephine Baker and Florence Mills appeared in Eubie Blake's *Shuffle Along*, the first American musical revue written and performed by African-Americans. There were many other creative projects that were either launched in Harlem or created by artists who lived and worked in Harlem during this time.

In 1923, the National Urban League launched *Opportunity: A Journal of Negro Life*. By this time several collections of black poetry had been published for the first time, while a stream of fiction by black authors was making its way into mainstream bookstores for the first time in history.

In the fall of the same year, *The Chip Woman's Fortune* by Willis Richardson opened, making it the first dramatic play by a black writer to appear on Broadway. The Cotton Club, a raucous supper club, opened in 1923 also, and whites began flocking to it and many other places uptown.

By this time, a self-help movement started by Jamaican immigrant Marcus Garvey was in full swing. Garvey was almost a king of Harlem, as you will see in one story in this collection. A real estate magnate who owned large tracts of Harlem property by 1919, Garvey also founded the Black Star Shipping Line and was selling thousands of shares of stock to black people uptown where he was worshipped as a black emancipator and visionary.

Harlem was a magical, transforming place then, and this was especially true for the disenfranchised who came to New York in search of greater opportunity.

The spiritual, social, and literary fervor that raced through Harlem during these years could be called the greatest period of self-discovery in African-American history after the Civil War and before the start of the Civil Rights era of the 1960s.

It was in the midst of this changing climate that a small band of black men and a few women began a public relations campaign to promote what they called the "New Negro" movement. It was a movement born in the minds of the city's black intelligentsia, not an idea that most of the people who lived in Harlem ever heard of or embraced. Nevertheless, the Harlem renaissance and the birth of this New Negro were inextricably mingled. In the intervening years, this cadre from the New Negro movement would be given all the credit for the larger, more sweeping social renaissance that took place in Harlem while they were there.

Consequently, the birth of Harlem's renaissance is sometimes mistakenly thought to be a dinner held at the Civic Club on March 21, 1924, sponsored by *Opportunity* magazine, the media arm of the black intelligentsia of Harlem. These intellectuals included founders of the National Association for the Advancement of Colored People, the National Urban League, and independent scholars like DuBois, James Weldon Johnson, and Howard University Professor Alain Locke. This group anointed a handful of writers and poets as the soliders of Harlem's artistic renaissance, but their work seems to be the only evidence widely used to show that a bigger renaissance had occurred in Harlem. It was this self-appointed cabal that became the voice of Harlem and what had been happening there for decades before and after their arrival. They had used Harlem's growing popularity as a unique opportunity to do what reconstruction after the Civil War had not done—create a positive public image of blacks as thinking, creative human beings in American society. It was a noble effort. In their widely read essays, novels, plays, and newspaper articles, this well-meaning group set out to kill pernicious stereotypes of black folks.

Foremost among them was scholar Alain Locke. A philosophy professor who had once taught at Howard, Locke had degrees from Harvard and Oxford and he had studied in Berlin. He would later be known as the "father of the Harlem renaissance," for the publicizing and writing about a small group of people who were believed to represent all of Harlem's people, but who, in fact, did not. Futher, as the editor of a popular magazine at the time *Survey Graphic*, he would help shape the image of Harlem's renaissance as an intellectual movement, not one spurred on by ordinary people who populated Harlem in unprecedented numbers.

Locke solicited articles for what became known as the "Harlem Number," an issue of the magazine that came out in 1925. It was devoted to the demographic changes in Harlem that transformed it into a mostly black and Latin part of the city. Locke was able to attract some of the best-known writers and thinkers of the time for this task. These included DuBois, who was then editor of the NAACP's *Crisis* magazine and the author of *Souls of Black Folks*, a monumental work on black life, culture, and race relations. The issue also contained pieces by James Weldon Johnson, author of the highly acclaimed *Autobiography of an Ex-Colored Man*; Arthur A. Schomburg, a member of the revered American Negro Academy; novelist Walter F. White; anthropologist Melville J. Herskovits, and writer Konrad Bercovici, author of *Around the World in New York*.

In sharply different pieces, these writers and thinkers set out to describe a phenomenon they had discovered in Harlem as it was still unfolding. In the magazine, they correctly identified the social and economic forces that swept hordes of poor black and Spanish-speaking people in great numbers into this section of upper Manhattan.

According to Locke:

> *Numerically smaller than either [the westward expan-*
> *sion or the European immigration to the United States]*
> *the volume of migration [to Harlem] is such nonetheless*
> *that Harlem has become the greatest Negro community*
> *the world has known. The special significance that*
> *stamps it as the sign and center of the renaissance of a*
> *people lies, however, layers deep under the Harlem that*
> *many know but few have begun to understand.*
>
> *A railroad ticket and a suitcase, like a Baghdad car-*
> *pet, transport the Negro peasant from the cotton-field*
> *and farm to the heart of the most complex urban civiliza-*
> *tion. Here in the mass, he must and does survive a jump*
> *of two generations in social economy and of a century*
> *and more in civilization.*

To New Yorkers, and probably to the rest of the world, they noted, Harlem was merely a "rough rectangle of common-place city blocks that was "unaccountably full" of black people. It was much more, as the writers whose work you will read in this collection discovered years after historians said this renaissance had ended.

The *Survey Graphic* authors noted:

> *Another Harlem is savored by the few—a Harlem*
> *of racy music and racier dancing, of cabarets famous*
> *or notorious according to their kind of amusement . . .*
> *which draws the connoisseur in diversion as well as the*
> *undiscriminating sightseer. This Harlem is the fertile*
> *source of the shuffling and rolling and running wild*
> *reviews that establish themselves season after season*
> *in downtown theaters. It is part of the exotic fringe of*
> *the metropolis.*

This Harlem, Locke said, was a race capital no less vital than other capitals of the world.

*Harlem has the same role to play for the New Negro as Dublin has had for the New Ireland or Prague for the New Czechoslovakia.*

*The tide of Negro migration, northward and cityward, is not fully explained as a blind flood started by the demands of war industry . . . by the pressure of poor crops coupled with increased social terrorisms in certain sections of the South and Southwest. Neither labor demand, the boll-weevil [an insect which decimated cotton crops] nor [terrorists like] the Ku Klux Klan is a basic factor . . . The wash and rush of this human tide . . . is to be explained primarily in the terms of a new vision of opportunity, of social and economic freedom of a spirit to survive, even in the face of an extortionate and heavy toll, a chance for the improvement of conditions.*

*With each successive wave, the movement of the Negro migrant becomes more and more like that of the European waves at their crests, a mass movement towards the larger and the more democratic change— in the Negro's case a deliberate flight not only from countryside to city, but from mediaeval America to modern.*

Ironically, Locke himself was not from Harlem and never took up permanent residence there. Nevertheless, as its ambassador, he served as an interpreter of the literature being written in and about Harlem for the downtown editors who were suddenly interested in publishing it. Rather than tell the stories that could be heard on any Harlem street, or in its parks and playgrounds, Locke and his cohorts deliberately opted for more elite narratives they hoped would further the goals of the "New Negro" movement. This was ironic for a man who clearly seemed to understand that Harlem's revival had been started by and would continue to be fueled by the common people, not the intellectuals, Locke wrote,

*One of the most characteristic symptoms of this [movement by the masses] is the professional man himself migrating to recapture his constituent after a vain effort to maintain [himself] in some southern corner which for years back seemed an established living and clientele. The clergy man following his errant flock, the physician or lawyer trailing his clients, supply the true clues. In a real sense, it is the rank and file who are leading and the leaders who are following. A transformed and transforming psychology permeates the masses.*

After expressing this deep understanding of what had really happened in Harlem, it becomes truly paradoxical that he and other influential intellectuals used this people's movement born in the womb of slavery and its aftermath to promote New Negro causes.

Any creditable "record of fifty years of freedom requires that the Negro today be seen [in ways] other than the dusty spectacles of past controversy. The day of the 'aunties, uncles and mammies' are gone. Uncle Tom and Sambo have passed on. The popular melodrama [of the past] has about played itself out, and it is time to scrap the fictions, garret of bogeys and settle down to a realistic facing of the facts," Locke wrote.

"The Negro too, for his part, has idols of the tribe to smash," Locke said. "He must know himself and be known for precisely what he is . . . Sentimental interest in the Negro has ebbed. We used to lament this as the falling off of our friends; now we rejoice and pray to be delivered from self-pity and condescension. In art and letters, instead of being wholly caricatured, he is being seriously portrayed well and painted . . ."

To DuBois, for example, this meant [promoting] high cultural forms rather than vernacular expressions and stories set in Strivers Row instead of Lenox Avenue cabarets," says Steven Watson in his book, *The Harlem Renaissance: Hub of African-American Culture 1920–1930.* Writer Countee Cullen echoed DuBois's lament in a 1928 edition of *Opportunity.*

He said, "Decency demands that some things be kept secret; diplomacy demands it. The world loses respect for violators of this code."

Among Harlem's elite, that code was apparently strictly enforced and violators were threatened with intellectual banishment. This code would safeguard the pristine image of uptown life created by those writers who were embraced by the white New York publishing houses; the books and stories they wrote would ultimately become the canon of all modern black literature and of a renaissance that occurred in Harlem. As celebrated as this writing was, it did not present a comprehensive portrait of Harlem or its people.

As scholars who studied this period in later years would begin to notice, authentic black storytelling tended to come from the experience of ordinary people, not intellectuals. And, this kind of folk story was almost always associated with an implied ignorance the black intelligentsia had come to Harlem to escape, not embrace. To elevate these common stories to the level of literature, black intellectuals believed, merely perpetuated old images. This was especially true in instances where dialect played a prominent part in the narrative.

"No sane observer, however sympathetic of the new trend, would contend that the great masses are articulate as yet," Locke wrote in the *Survey Graphic* issue. "The challenge of the new intellectuals among them is clear . . . to interpret the aspirations of these new immigrants."

Decades later, modern scholars would comment on this attitude, which may have been prevalent.

"The past haunted many writers of the Harlem Renaissance and folk tradition embarrassed them," wrote University of Illinois Prof. Leonard Diepeveen in a 1986 issue of *American Literature*.

"Many Black writers found their political, social and cultural history distasteful. As a movement, the Harlem Renaissance deliberately tried to break with past social injustices and past misrepresentations of the race. This unofficial literary program of the Harlem Renaissance tended to break completely with folk tales . . . [which] did not seem to promote the type of art the Harlem Renaissance wanted. The association of folk tales with these aspects of the cultural heritage created a new set of [image] problems.''

Less than a decade after the "Harlem Number" of the *Survey Graphic* appeared, the nation fell into a serious economic depression. It was in those years between 1929 and the early 1940s that out-of-work writers were rescued by the New Deal Democrats who created the WPA Writer's Project. By the late 1930s the New York Project writers had generated a comprehensive body of more than four hundred narratives. Scores of these stories were written about the same Harlem Locke's so-called renaissance writers had talked about ten years earlier. When you compare the literature popularized during the period with stories like those in this collection, a glaring number of omissions in both style and content immediately becomes apparent. The well-known literature contributed by Locke's stable of Harlem writers seems to be exclusively patterned after European literary subjects and styles. In sharp contrast, the WPA stories from Harlem express more earthy black tales about life uptown as some of the same writers saw it in all economic and social groups. This casts Harlem and the era that made it famous in a different light from what is generally assumed. The WPA writers dug deep and emerged with textured, often eloquent portraits of the same kind of people who had first given *Survey Graphic* a reason to write about Harlem—migrants, house cleaners, washer women, and unemployed farmers in search of better lives.

Unwittingly, the architects of the New York City Writer's Project had saved an important piece of history about Harlem. It is preserved in this collection but was almost lost again in the 1940s when the WPA folded. When the WPA programs were unceremoniously ended on the eve of America's participation in World War II, these manuscripts were shelved and nearly destroyed or lost.

The resurrection of these stories casts a new and deserved

light on a literary tradition that was woefully incomplete without it. One of the era's most famous participants and its harshest critic was Zora Neale Hurston. Born in the all-black community of Eatonville, Florida, around 1891, Hurston published seven books, numerous short stories, plays, and magazine articles in the thirty years between 1930 and the 1960s when she died. Posthumously, she has been hailed as one of the great American novelists of the twentieth century and became most famous for her 1937 novel, *Their Eyes Were Watching God.*

In 1997, nearly forty years after she died in obscurity, *The New Yorker* bestowed Hurston with a notable review. This upscale weekly took up the merits and weaknesses of Hurston's book in an unusually long critique in the February 17 issue that year. In it, critic-at-large Claudia Roth Pierpont could have been talking about Hurston's narrative to sum up the possible significance of the WPA stories in this book and what they might say about Harlem's renaissance.

In a scene in the novel, Hurston describes a gathering of people on their porches at sundown in Eatonville:

> *It was a time to hear things and talk. These sitters had been tongueless, earless, eyeless conveniences all day long. Mules and other brutes had occupied their skins. But now, now the sun and the boss man were gone, so the skins felt powerful and human. They became lords of sounds and lesser things. They passed notions through their mouths. They sat in judgment.*

Hurston could have been talking about the WPA stories in this collection and WPA writers like her who had collected them.

Pierpont uses this passage to emphasize the importance of ordinary voices in telling the larger story of people and their culture.

The deliberate decision by the architects of Harlem's most famous period to ignore this fact did not go unnoticed by Hurston. Hurston had been recruited by the editors of *Opportunity* magazine to come to New York in the 1920s to share a literary prize with a young Dorothy West.

While West was hailed as a promising member of this cadre of Harlem writers, Hurston would eventually become the era's problem child. Not only did Hurston refuse to adopt their exclusionary code of silence when it came to folklore about simple folks, she often criticized it.

A startling example of this is found in an obscure file of *American Mercury* magazine, sandwiched in among Hurston's varied and eclectic public domain works at the Library of Congress. *American Mercury* was a widely circulated magazine edited by media critic and essayist H.L. Mencken. The folder contains a typeset article entitled "You Don't Know Us Negroes," By Zora Neale Hurston." Scrawled across the top of this long piece is the hand-written word "kill," indicating the article had been pulled just prior to publication, which had been slated to be printed some time in 1934. "Not printed. I don't remember why," an anonymous writer said on top of the piece in a handwritten note.

It is a blistering attack on the very literature that became a cornerstone of Harlem's renaissance. She said the widely touted black writing published between the years 1924 and 1934 offered poor imitations of Negro life and cultures at a time when readers clamored for reality-based fiction and stories. We just don't live like that, she said bluntly.

"The decade just past was the oleomargarine era of Negro writing," Hurston said. "Oleomargarine is the fictionalized form of butter. And so the writings that made out they were holding a looking-glass to the Negro had everything in them except Negroness."

According to Hurston's estate, "You Don't Know Us Negroes" was never published.

Historian Nathan Irvin Huggins, in critiquing the New Negro movement and the renaissance writers, points out the fallacy of ignoring these ordinary voices. The New Negro movement failed, Huggins said, "because the intellectuals who defined it became mimics of whites, wearing clothes and using manners of sophisticated whites, earning the epithet 'dicty niggers' from the very people they were supposed to be championing.''

In his book *Harlem Renaissance* Huggins said, ''the decade of the 1920s seems to have been too early for blacks to have felt the certainty about native culture that would have freed them from crippling self-doubt . . . that is why the art of the Renaissance was so problematic, feckless, not fresh, not real. The lesson it leaves us is that the true Black Renaissance awaits Afro-Americans' claiming their . . . nativity.'' But Huggins must be talking about the literature that was promoted by proponents of this New Negro, not the sometimes gritty, real stories the people in this WPA Writer's Project collection are telling.

When interest in the music, literature, and the quaint art being produced in uptown circles waned after 1929, intellectual life in Harlem was declared dead.

However, by simply examining the wealth of WPA narratives in scattered archives in both New York and Washington, one can conclude that it is unlikely that Harlem's awakening was confined to the four years between 1924 and 1929 usually reserved for it.

Harlem's so-called renaissance most likely began long before the healthy literary and social life was noticed in the *Survey Graphic* article. The driving forces behind the varied activities that made Harlem so vibrant in the twentieth century were sparked by the massive migration of black people from the rural South and the Caribbean. When these seekers from far-flung corners of the world began filling the vacant but plentiful housing Harlem had to offer, these railroad porters, domestic house cleaners, former tenant farmers, and immigrants brought their music, their literature, and their stories with them uptown to Harlem.

Their stories about daily life uptown are still a vital part of the literature and music of Harlem. As told by the WPA writers,

these tales leave an important legacy for us today. Between
1934 and 1939, then unknown African-American writers recruited to join the WPA Writer's Project took advantage of a
unique opportunity to write the topical history of Harlem. Inadvertently, they created a narrative snapshot of black America's
unofficial capital city during one of its most important historical periods.

The stories these fledgling writers collected were commis-
sioned by the administrators of the WPA. In cities, towns, and
neighborhoods across America, they recorded folklore of all
kinds and shaped it into the stories that make up this collection.
They created a rare picture of life on Harlem streets, in its
beauty parlors, markets, apartments, and hospital waiting
rooms. Together, these portraits help create a lasting image of
this still vibrant community, and more important, give us a
glimpse of an American community that has seldom been seen
by outsiders.

The WPA hired aspiring writers such as Ralph Ellison, who
came to New York from the Tuskegee Institute. Joining Ellison
were two Columbia University students: Dorothy West, who had
come from Boston to study journalism in New York; and Zora
Neale Hurston, a Florida native who came to Columbia initially
to study anthropology.

The assignment the Writer's Project tackled was to collect
the stories of the Americans they met. The New York writers
apparently distinguished themselves as unique stylists by the way
they shaped the narratives they collected.

This did not go unnoticed by ambitious colleagues in other
states. In Illinois, for example, writers like Richard Wright, Saul
Bellow, Studs Terkel, Jack Conroy, and Nelson Algren, were
encouraged to follow their example, according to WPA memos.

Washington administrators asked all of its writers to explore
and consider using narrative styles that were pioneered in New
York. These writers tried to fully characterize the people they
encountered on street corners and in public parks by using stark
realism. WPA memos and correspondence encouraged all writ-

ers to create what are sometimes called "slice-of-life" profiles of the communities they covered.

The work of Ellison, Hurston, West, and the other writers in this collection were all written in the late 1930s, which suggests that Harlem's golden era existed well beyond 1929. While none of the stories in this collection are fictional in the strictest sense of the word, many of them are literary versions crafted by writers who struggled to accurately tell the stories they found in creative ways. They often used the techniques of fiction, such as setting scenes, using realistic dialogue, or incorporating flashbacks.

The significance of these narratives was noted during the period by the WPA Writer's Project administrators. These included John A. Lomax at the Library of Congress and Benjamin A. Botkin. Botkin and Lomax were both folklorists and said they wanted stories that not only related what people said, but also they wanted the stories to reflect a point of view and the way the people expressed it.

"The narratives were meant to reflect the ordinary person's struggle with the vicissitudes of daily living," Library of Congress folklorists in Washington have said, looking back on the importance of the WPA work. At the time, Botkin said, "The collected lore and narratives were to be used as the basis for anthologies which would form a composite and comprehensive portrait of various groups of people in America." He said the entire body of material provides the raw content for a broad [look at] both rural and urban life, interspersed with accounts of traditions of ethnic groups; customs regarding planting, cooking, marriage, death, celebration, recreation, and a wide variety of [experiences]. Library of Congress officials said, "The quality of collecting and writing lore varies from state to state, reflecting the skills of the interviewer-writers and the supervision they received."

"We were poor ourselves and these people were, if anything, poorer, so I was very close to them," WPA writer Betty Burke said in a statement used by the Library of Congress to introduce these archives to researchers. "I understood every word they said with all my heart," she said.

Like characters of some Charles Dickens novel, the backdrop for these stories from Harlem was a mostly poor but vital American community that had become largely black and Latino. Among the stories in this collection, you'll find: Ralph Ellison's profile of what is probably the first appearance of his most unforgettable character in a piece simply called "Eddie's Bar". This narrative with a Pullman porter is most likely the prototype for the protagonist for the famous novel he would later write, *Invisible Man*.

Vivian Morris, an obscure but prolific writer, collected a wide array of Harlem stalwarts that even Dickens would have envied. In this anthology, she profiles street hookers, washer women, and swing dancers, and documents stunning historical remembrances by the people she encountered, including one from Marcus Garvey, the would-be king of Harlem.

As a testament to the significance these stories held for the writers who collected them, many of these interviews became the raw material for later works of important fiction. Passages in Nelson Algren's book, *A Walk on the Wild Side*, are from his WPA interviews with a Chicago prostitute. WPA writer Mari Thomas collected stories from granite carvers in Vermont. Her novel, *Like Lesser Gods*, was based on her WPA work in that state. Likewise, Sam Ross worked for the WPA's Illinois Writer's Project in Chicago. His novel, *Windy City*, borrows heavily from the jazz stories Ross wrote for the WPA. As you will see, Ralph Ellison roamed Harlem, interviewing all sorts of people whose words found their way into his landmark novel.

Despite this seemingly sacred mission, political forces opposed to the use of federal money for WPA projects moved against New Deal Democrats. They began rattling their political sabres to kill the WPA in the late 1930s as Adolph Hitler marched through Europe. By the fall of 1939, all new funds for WPA projects had dried up. According to federal records, the WPA was effectively dead by the time America entered the war.

Thousands of the WPA manuscripts were never published.

While some of these narratives were shelved, others were lost, destroyed, or distributed to various libraries and state archives. As a body of work, most of these stories would be stored away and left virtually untouched for decades. The Harlem manuscripts suffered this same fate.

This collection brings together more than forty-five stories written by the many different WPA writers who worked in Harlem. While some like Ellison eventually won worldwide acclaim and joined some of the most accomplished writers in America, most, like Vivian Morris, remained obscure, invisible men and women despite the literary promise of their work. The stories you are about to read are further evidence that there was a renaissance in Harlem, one that may have been completely missed by some of the intellectuals who first coined the phrase.

The kind of people Hurston chose as characters in her great novel, *Their Eyes Were Watching God*, tell stories of ordinary people from an ordinary perspective. In doing so, *New Yorker* critic Pierpont said, "the powerless become lords of sounds, the dispossessed rule all creation with their tongues. It was out of this last, irreducible possession that the Jews made a counterworld of words, the Irish vanquished England, and Russian poetry bloomed thick over Stalin's burial gounds. And in a single book one woman managed to suggest what another such heroic tradition, rising out of American slavery, might have been—a literature as profound and original as the spirituals."

In winding up this long look back at Hurston's book, Pierpont then refers to the literary life of the first African-American woman to be credited with writing a volume of poetry, saying ". . . what might have existed if only more of the words and stories had been written down decades earlier . . . if only Phyllis Wheately had not tried to write like Alexander Pope, if only literate slaves and their generations of children had not felt pressed to prove their claim to the sworn civilities?"

Quiet as it's been kept, there were other voices in Harlem like Hurston's who resisted the overpowering urge to show they could write like Defoe, Dickens, or De Quincey. In the 1930s, they heard the voices of ordinary people and told their stories. WPA writers found choirs of ordinary people singing their songs throughout America.

One of those songs was sung by men and women who created a people's renaissance in Harlem. And these are their fictions.

# PART 1

# Two Harlems

# MINSTREL SHOW

Harlem, like any other large community in America, was diverse and multifaceted. But the variety that could be found in Harlem was too often edited out of most published anthologies about this part of New York during the Harlem renaissance.

Zora Neale Hurston's complaints about the stories she saw being published by her colleagues were well known uptown, and she was not alone. Langston Hughes, a luminary of the era who would become one of America's most respected writers, was softer on but no less critical of his colleagues than Hurston.

Hughes himself wrote about the real Harlem in his book *The Big Sea*. After the gay 1920s, Hughes said the 1929 stock market crash left an imprint on all Americans. Blacks and whites found themselves swept away by an economic tidal wave that rocked the nation. This event ended a period of great optimism in America and sent all Americans racing toward the back-to-work policies of the Works Progress Administration. In *The Big Sea*, Hughes characterized the good and bad times Harlemites saw:

*White people began to come to Harlem in droves. For several years they packed the expensive Cotton Club on Lenox Avenue. But I was never there, because the*

*Cotton Club was a Jim Crow club for gangsters and monied whites. They were not cordial to Negro patronage, unless you were a celebrity like (dancer) Bojangles. So Harlem Negroes did not like the Cotton Club and never appreciated its Jim Crow polity in the very heart of their dark community, nor did ordinary Negroes like the growing influx of whites toward Harlem after sundown, flooding the little cabarets and bars where formerly only colored people laughed and sang, and where now the strangers were given the best ringside tables to sit and stare at the Negro customers—like amusing animals in a zoo.*

*The Negroes said, "We can't go downtown and sit and stare at you in your clubs. You won't even let us in your clubs." But they didn't say it out loud—for Negroes are practically never rude to white people. So thousands of whites came to Harlem night after night, thinking the Negroes loved to have them there, and firmly believing that all Harlemites left their houses at sundown to sing and dance in cabarets, because most of the whites saw nothing but the cabarets, not the houses.*

*I was there. I had a swell time while it lasted. But I thought it wouldn't last long. (I remember the vogue for things Russian, the season the Chauve-Souris first came to town.) For how could a large and enthusiastic number of people be crazy about Negroes forever? But some Harlemites thought the millennium had come. They thought the race problem had at last been solved through Art plus (entertainer) Gladys Bentley. They were sure the New Negro would lead a new life from then on in green pastures of tolerance created by Countee Cullen, Ethel Waters, Claude McKay, Duke Ellington, Bojangles, and Alain Locke.*

*I don't know what made any Negroes think that— except that they were mostly intellectuals doing the*

*thinking. The ordinary Negroes hadn't heard of the
Negro Renaissance. And if they had, it hadn't raised
their wages any.*

WPA writer Levi Hubert captured a similar sentiment. After
white socialites read the Harlem issue of *Survey Graphic*, they
began to swarm uptown to see this black renaissance first hand.
In this WPA piece, Hubert offers a more biting perspective.

# Whites Invade Harlem

*Levi Hubert*

In the late 1920s, the only American black to get a Rhodes scholarship at Oxford came to Harlem to gather material for the now famous Harlem issue of the *Survey Graphic* magazine. Alain Leroy Locke was immediately hailed as the discoverer of artistic Harlem.

The whites who read that issue became aware that in Harlem, the largest black city in the world, there existed a group interested in the fine arts, creative literature, and classical music. So, well-meaning, vapid whites from downtown New York came by bus, subway, or in limousines, to see for themselves these black people who wrote poetry and fiction and painted pictures.

Of course, said these pilgrims, it couldn't approach the creative results of whites, but as a novelty, well, it didn't need standards. The very fact that these blacks had the temerity to produce so-called art, and not its quality, made the whole fantastic movement so alluring. The idea being similar to the applause given a dancing dog. There is no question of comparing the dog to humans; it needn't do it well . . . merely to dance at all is quite enough.

So they came to see, and to listen, and to marvel; and to ask, as an extra favor, that some spirituals be sung.

Over cups of tea, Park Avenue and Central Park West

went into raptures over these geniuses, later dragging rare
specimens of the genus Homo Africanus downtown for exhibition before their friends.

Bustling, strong-minded matrons in Sutton Place, on
The Drive, even on staid Fifth Avenue, sent out informal
notes and telephonic invitations.

"There will be present a few artistic blacks. It's really the
thing. They recite with such feeling, and when they sing—
such divine tones. Imagine a colored person playing De-
bussy and Chopin."

At every party, two or three bewildered blacks sat a bit
apart, were very polite when spoken to, and readily went
into their act when called upon to perform. The hostess
would bring each newly arrived guest over to the corner,
and introductions invariably followed this pattern.

"I do so want you to meet Mr. Hubert. He writes the
nicest poetry. Something really new. You simply must hear
him read his Harlem Jungle tone-poem . . . such insight,
such depth . . . so primitive, you know, in a rather exalted
fashion." These faddists spread abroad the new culture,
seized every opportunity to do missionary work for The
Cause.

"Believe me, the poor dears are so trusting, so childlike,
so very, very cheerful, no matter what their struggles or sor-
rows. They tell me their most popular hymn is something
about 'You Can Have the World, Just Give Me Jesus.' Isn't
that simply wonderful? Such faith, such naïveté. They're
simply unique."

These women, blessed with money and a modicum of
brains, transformed average blacks with anemic souls into
glittering shiny-faced personages. Julius Bledsoe became
Jules. Dave Fountain gave a recital before a countess on
swanky Sutton Place, and a day later his calling cards read
David La Fountaine. Marc D'Albert plays classical selections ever so much better than Marcus Albert.

News that Harlem had become a paradise spread rapidly,

and from villages and towns all over America and the British West Indies there began a migration of quaint characters, each with a message, who descended upon Harlem, sought out the cafés, lifted teacups with a jutting little finger, and dreamed of sponsors. A literary magazine called *Fire!* sprang up briefly.

Wallace Thurman was one of Harlem's chief literary figures. He became most famous as author of *Blacker the Berry* and *Infants of the Spring*—his roman à clef about Harlem literary figures. Thurman lived among them in quarters at a rooming house at 237 West 136 Street, which Zora Neale Hurston called "Niggerati Manor." It was here that Thurman is said to have financed and published *Fire!*, a quarterly journal of black arts that published a single issue before it folded, deeply in debt.

It was called *Fire!*, according to Langston Hughes, because "it would burn up a lot of the old, dead conventional Negro-white writers and artists." The first and only issue of *Fire!* contained illustrations by Aaron Douglas and Bruce Nugent; poetry by Hughes and Countee Cullen; and fiction by Hurston, Thurman, and Nugent.

Ironically, hundreds of unsold copies of *Fire!*, whose first edition cost about one thousand dollars to produce, burned in a fire. Thurman, whose checks and income "were constantly being attached and . . . seized" for the next four years to pay for the magazine's printing, once told Langston Hughes, "*Fire!* is certainly burning me."

Thurman's *Blacker the Berry*, which exposed the hypocritical attitudes of blacks who enthusiastically proclaim the value and uniqueness of their black heritage while at the same time displaying a preference for light skin and white features, was met with a plethora of disapproval among black critics who felt that it merely diluted their attempts to gain acceptance.

Harlem's millionairess, A'Lelia Walker, whose mother made her fortune with kink-no-more [hair] preparations, about this time became imbued with the desire to aid struggling artists. She set aside a floor of her town house at 208 West 136 Street to be used as a studio for art exhibits, poetry recitals, and musicales. Countee Cullen suggested Dark Tower as the name for this shrine of Harlem art, and both he and Langston Hughes had poems inscribed on the walls.

I came from the foothills of Pennsylvania to sit humbly in this temple while Thurman, Leigh Whipper, Sonoma Tally, Augusta Savage, Eric Waldron, among others, basked in the sunshine of public appreciation.

Naturally some good came from this fraternizing. Thurman not only had three books published, but became an editor at Scribners. Her white friends secured a second scholarship for Augusta Savage when she was denied the first because of her color. Countee Cullen went to Paris, where he wrote *The Black Christ*, conceded by critics to be his best effort. Langston Hughes was acclaimed as the first black to bring a genuine contribution to American literature. Gordon Taylor, an ex-Pullman porter [railroad sleeping car attendant], rushed his *Born to Be* into print; Eric Waldron brought out a book, then returned to Brooklyn to muse and ponder. Claude McKay was living in France at the time, but he, too, sent over the manuscript of *Home to Harlem*. Eugene Gorden vented his spleen in several publications, while George S. Schuyler wrote the first satire, *Black No More*.

It was the golden age for black writers, artists, and musicians. Study groups were held in cafés, furnished railroad flats, even the language of the nation was enriched by Harlem colloquialisms, and the curious habit of "passing" for white was brought out into the open in discussions. Whites, hearing for the first time of light-skinned blacks crossing the line into the white world, eyed their neighbors suspiciously when they came to Harlem and were seated near other whites.

The question was, Did these other whites come to Harlem as visitors or were they obeying the call of their kind? Even downtown the uneasiness persisted. Did the brunette woman on the fourth floor have a pedigreed ancestry, or was she on vacation from Harlem? Could one tell for certain who was whom by fingernails, or slant of eye, or by wavy hair? Then the fad for sun tan and even mahogany shades struck the town and no one knew the answer.

In the employees' room of an exclusive Fifth Avenue shop a notice was tacked on the wall. It contained an admonition to be careful not to offend customers by confusing them with blacks. It seems that an old and favored customer had been given the bum's rush because she had been mistakenly sized up as a black trying to pass for white.

But The Dark Tower was the focal point of contact between the downtowners and Harlem's noveau literati. Hurston called them Niggerati. One Sunday evening there was a poetry reading. It provided, according to the master of ceremonies, an opportunity "for those of us with artistic inclination and talent to be stimulated to increased endeavor." He started the proceedings off with some rhymed classical similes. So it was a relief when a brown-skinned, plump-waisted, soft-voiced girl stood up and read a poem ending with "He left me with but my maiden name."

A tall, studious-appearing man lamented that the youth of today must be ashamed of their past, for there could be no other reason for the absence of dialect in their poems. He became offended when another black confessed that the only black dialect he had ever heard was spoken by Al Jolson or some other corkface artist.

A sudden hush fell on the room as a strident voice from the rear began clamoring. The vibrant tones, compelling and forceful, caused everyone to turn his head and view the possessor of such a voice. They saw a tall, robust girl with flaxen hair, and heard her say, "Two years ago I left Russia in search of people who would express the newer poetry. I have traveled through England and there all I heard was stilted, artificial phrases which mean nothing. The English are blind, they are unable to face life. They shut their eyes to facts which primitive peoples accept freely.

"I have been in America six months. Here, too, I am disappointed. Here also, the poets write about the head only. I want to hear the poetry of the hips. Hemingway calls Walt Whitman an exhibitionist in print. Surely Whitman, if anyone, lived unafraid and unwhipped by life; and that was because he had the proper slant on things.

"Perhaps here in Harlem you will catch the secret of rhythmic poetic expression. If you do you will have captured an inkling of the unattainable.

"Centuries ago African artists made phallic images. Today, in Harlem, your poets should write of the hips and of the victory which belongs eternally to women. Then you'll be writing of life as it actually is."

Before the group could break out in excited comment, she gathered her wrap about her shoulders, nodded imperiously to her escorts, and lumbered away, her heavy hips revealed beneath a tight-fitting, red velvet gown.

*December 12, 1938*

# PART 2

# Lost Manuscripts

# VISIBLE MEN

Writer, editor, and critic Ralph Waldo Ellison initially wanted to be a musician. A native of Oklahoma City, Oklahoma, Ellison drifted east, then north to Harlem in the 1930s. Except for brief stints like the time he spent as a merchant marine, he remained close to Harlem until he died in 1994, living in the same Riverside Drive apartment adjacent to Harlem for more than forty years.

Eventually, Ellison would emerge in his own lifetime as one of the most influential American authors of the twentieth century. This accomplishment is all the more remarkable when you consider that Ellison wrote only one published novel—*Invisible Man*—and just a handful of short stories.

Born in 1914, he craved education and worked his way east to Tuskegee Institute in Alabama, the college founded by Booker T. Washington. After studying music from 1933 to 1936, Ellison migrated north to New York where he met writer Richard Wright who gave Ellison the opportunity to write for a magazine Wright edited at the time. Ellison also joined the federal Writer's Project arm of the WPA at Wright's urging. It was during these years that he began shaping the anonymous character whose invisibility would make Ellison one of the most visible writers in American history.

Working for the WPA, Ellison used the opportunity to experiment with the American language he was hearing on the streets of Harlem.

"I would tell some stories to get people going and then I'd sit back and try to get it down as accurately as I could," he later recalled.

In an interview about his Writer's Project days, Ellison said he began to experiment with ways of capturing the sound of black speech that he would later refine in his novel *Invisible Man*.

"I tried to use my ear for dialogue to give an impression of just how people sounded. I developed a technique of transcribing that captured the idiom rather than trying to convey the dialect through misspellings," he said.

In one interview with a Pullman train porter, Ellison captured the cadence of this man's speech in a monologue called "Eddy's Bar" in which he declares "ahm in New York, but New York ain't in me." This refrain was later borrowed for *Invisible Man*.

Published in 1952, *Invisible Man* won the National Book Award for fiction that year. The central narrative of the novel's anonymous protagonist echoes the feelings of actual people Ellison met and interviewed in Harlem between the years 1937 and 1939, preserved in manuscripts in the Library of Congress archives.

Like Ellison's nameless character, the people Ellison interviewed complained of being involuntarily invisible in a country that viewed blacks through the lenses of social stereotypes. In a 1965 interview published in the *Iowa Review*, Ellison delves into the genesis of *Invisible Man*.

"Why do I live always close to other Negroes?" Ellison muses. "Because I have to hear the language. My medium is language, and there is a Negro idiom, in fact, there are many Negro idioms in the American language. I have to hear that sound in my ears, I have to," he emphasized. "A place like Harlem . . . has an expressiveness about it which is almost Elizabethan. Things are revealed in speech in the streets. There's a

lot of humor and the language is always feeding back to the past;
it's throwing up wisdom, it's throwing up patterns and I never
know but when I'm going to hear something . . . in the street
which is going to be the making of some piece of fiction that
I'm trying to write."

The five Ellison manuscripts in the Library of Congress collection are presented in the chapters that follow. In each of
them, it is clear that Ellison had already learned to listen and
to absorb the varied voices of those he interviewed. Each was
black, but each spoke distinctly different versions of American
English. Invisible in different ways, each character in these
monologues complains of being among the unseen. They are also
part of that often invisible genesis of a novelist's work that
emerges in polished fiction.

# Eddie's Bar

## *Ralph Ellison*

It was customary for each WPA article to be prefaced with details about the people these writers interviewed, where the interview took place, and any other details related to the narratives. So on April 30, 1939, Ralph Ellison walked through the front door of Eddie's Bar on St. Nicholas Avenue near West 147 Street. It was about eight o'clock, still early, but already there were a few people drinking at the bar of this modernistic looking tavern. The green walls sported a marine design abruptly interrupted by the loud red imitation leather booths and bar stools scattered throughout. Mirrors were everywhere, making it hard to distinguish the size of the room immediately.

Edging his way toward a man standing near the back, Ellison began talking to him. He was a Pullman porter from Florida. In the background, a fancy jukebox plated with a bronze metal frame played a brassy big band tune. They sat in the back where waiters dressed in green served food and drinks to the customers sitting all around them. He took down the following monologue.

Ahm in New York, but New York ain't in me. You understand? Ahm in New York, but New York ain't in me. What do I mean? Listen. I'm from Jacksonville. Been in New York twenty-five years. I'm a New Yorker! But I'm in New York an New York ain't in me. Yuh understand?

Naw, naw, yuh don't get me. Whut do they do. Take Lenox Avenue. Take Seventh Avenue. Take Sugar Hill! Pimps. Numbers. Cheating these poor people outa whut they got. Shooting, cutting, backbiting, all them things. Yuh see? Yuh see whut Ah mean? I'm in New York, but New York ain't in me! Don't laugh, don't laugh. Ahm laughing but Ah don't mean it; it ain't funny. Yuh see. I'm on Sugar Hill, but Sugar Hill ain't on me.

Ah come here twenty-five years ago. Bright lights. Pretty women. More space to move around. Son, if Ah had-a got New York in me Ahd a-been dead a long time ago. What happened the other night. Yuh heard about the shooting up here in the hill. Take that boy. Ah knowed im! Anybody been around this hill knows [him and] they know he went fo a bad man.

What'd he do? Now mind yuh now, his brother's a bigshot. Makes plenty money. Got a big car an' a fine office. But he comes up on this hill tearin' up people's property if they don't pay him protection. Last night he walks into this wop's place up the street 'n tries to tear it up. Now yuh know that's a bad man. Canna tear up the wop's place. Well, he stepped out the door 'n a bunch of them wops showed up in a car, tried to blow 'im away. He had too much New York. Ahm in New York, yuh see? But New York ain't in me! Hell yes, He went 'n got too much New York, yuh understand what Ahm tryin' to tell yuh?

Ah been in New York twen-ty-five years! But Ah ain't never bothered nobody. Ain't never done nothin to nobody. Ah ain't no bad fellow. Shore, ah drink. I like good whiskey. Ah drinks, but ah ain't drunk. Yuh think Ahm drunk. Ah don't talk drunk, do Ah? Ah drinking 'n Ah got money in mah pockets. But Ah ain't throwing ma money away. Hell, Ah talking sense, aint Ah? Yuh heard me way in yonder didn't yuh? Yuh came to me, heard me. Ah didn't have to come after yuh, did Ah? If Ah hada been talking foolishness, yuh wouldn't a paid me no mind. Hell, Ah know Ahm right. Ah got something to say. Ah got something to say 'n Ah aint no preacher neither. Ahm drinking. Ah likes to drink. It's good for mah stomach.

Good whiskey's good for anybody's stomach. Look at the bottle: Mount Vernon! Good whiskey. Whut did the saint say? He said a little spirits is good for the stomach, good to warm the spirit. Now where did that come from? Yuh don't know, yuh too young. Yuh young Negroes don't know the Bible. Don't laugh, don't laugh. Look here Ah'll tell you something: "Some folks drinks to cut the fool. But some folks drinks to think. Ah drinks to think."

*May 10, 1939*

# Colonial Park

## *Ralph Ellison*

About a month later, the USS submarine *Squalus* (US-192) sank during sea trials. The accident left twenty-six American sailors dead. Thirty-three crew members survived. There were several other naval accidents involving submarines around this same time.

These accidents and the greatest sea tragedy in maritime history—the sinking of the *Titanic*—were part of another conversation Ellison would have in a sprawling park in the shadows of Sugar Hill and [St. Nicholas Avenue] a month after the *Squalus* went down.

Here, Ellison interviews another anonymous elderly man from Virginia. They met in Colonial Park where they were surrounded by playing children not far from Edgecome Avenue and West 150 Street where Ellison lived at the time.

"It's too bad bout them two submarines," the man says, assuming his listener followed the news.

"They can experiment an everything, but they cain't go but so far. Then God steps in. Them fellows is trying to make something what'll stay down. They said they'd done done it, but look what happened. Take back in 1912. They built a ship called the *Titanic*. Think they built it over in England; I thinks that was where it was built. Anyway, they said it couldn't sink. It was for all the big rich folks; John Jacob Astor, all the big aristocrats. Nothing the color of this," he said, rubbing the dark brown skin of his arm, "could git on the boat. Naw suh! Didn't want nothing look like me on it. One girl went down to go with her madam and they told her she couldn't go. They didn't want nothing look like this on there. They told the madam 'You can go, but she cain't.' The girl's madam got mad and told em if the girl didn't go, she wasn't going. And she didn't neither. Yes suh, she stayed right here.

"Well, they got this big boat on the way over to England. They said she couldn't sink—that was man talking. It was so big they tell me they was elevators in it like across yonder in that building. Had the richest folks in England, almost ready to dock, and it ups an hits a iceberg, and sank! That was the boat they said was so big it couldn't sink. They didn't want nothing look like this on it; no suh! And don't you think that woman wasn't glad she stuck by that girl. She was plenty glad.

"Man can only go so far. Then God steps in. Sho they can experiment around. They can do a heap. They can even make a man. But they cain't make him breathe. Why the other day I was down on 125th Street and 8th Avenue. They got one of them malted milk places. Well suh, they got a cow on the counter. It looks like a real cow. Got hair. I was standing there looking and the dog gone thing moved its head and wagged its tail; man done even made a cow. But, they had to do it with electricity.

"God's the only one can give life. God made all this, and he made it for everybody. And he made it equal. This breeze and these green leaves out here is for everybody. The same sun's shining down on everybody. This breeze comes from God and man cain't do nothing about it. I breathe the same air old man Ford and old man Rockerfeller breathes. They got all the money and I aint got nothing, but they got to breathe the same air I do.

"Man cain't make no man. Less see now: This heahs nineteen-hundred-and-thirty-nine. For 1,900 years, man's had things his way. He's been running the world to suit himself. It's just like your father owned that building over there and told you you could live in it if you didn't do certain things. And then you did what he told you not to. And he finds it out and says, 'Go on, you can have the whole building, I won't have nothing else to do with it. You can turn it upside-down if you want to.' Well, that was the way it was in the world. Adam and Eve sinned in the Garden and God left the world to itself. Men been running it like they want to. Rich folks, they done took all the land. They got all the money. Men down to the City Hall making $150,000 dollars a year and nothing like this," he said, touching his arm again, "caint even scrub the marble floors or polish the brass they got down there. Old man Ford and J. P. Morgan got all that money and folks in this park caint even get on relief," he said, using the common term for what would later be known as welfare.

"But you just watch: the lawd made all men equal and pretty soon now it's gonna be that way agin. I'm a man. I breathe the same air old man Ford breathes cause God made man equal. God formed man in his own image. He made Adam out of the earth; not like this concrete we sitting on, but out of dirt, clay. Like you seen a kid making a snowman. He'll git him a stick and make the arms. And he'll get another stick and make for his neck; and so on, just like we got bones. That was the way God made man. Made him outa clay and in his own image.

"That was the way he made Adam. One drop of God's blood made all the nations in the world; Africans, Germans, Chinamen, Jews, Indians; all come from one drop of God's blood. God took something outa Adam and made woman, he made Eve. The preachers tell a lie, and say it was his rib. But they have to lie I guess. They didn't do nothing but sit back in the shed and let you do all the work anyway. But

God went into Adam and took something out and made
Eve. That's the Scriptures; it said he took something. I cain't
remember the exact words, but it said he took something
and it didn't say nothing bout no rib. Eve started having
children. Some of 'em was black and some of 'em was white.
But they was all equal. God didn't know no color; we all
the same. All he want from man is this heart thumping the
blood. Them what take advantage of skin like this got to
come by God. They gonna pay.

"They tell me bout ol' George Washington. He was the
first president this country ever had. First thing I heard was
he said keep us look like this down in the cornfield. He tole
em 'Dont let 'em have no guns. You ain't to let em have
no knife. Dont let 'em have nothing.' He tole em if they
wanted to have a strong nation, keep us down. He said if
ever they git guns in they hands they'll rise up and take the
land; dont let em have nothing. But he didn't says nothing
bout no pick and ax!

"They been carrying out what he said. God didn't say
nothing. That was just man's idea and here in this country
they been carrying out what old man George Washington
said. But God's time is coming.

"Today you hear all these folks got millions of dollars
talking bout God. They ain't fooling nobody, though. They
even got 'In God We Trust' on all the silver money. But it
don't mean nothing. This sun and air is God's. It don't
belong to nobody and caint no few get it all to theyself.

"People around this park can have all they want. But
you wait, God's gonna straighten it all out. Look at the dust
blowing in that wind. That's the way all the money they got
gonna be. You see folks they call white, but man aint got
no idea of how white God gon make things. Money won't
be worth no moren that dust blowing on the ground. Won't
be no men down to Washington making fifty-thousand dollars a week and folks caint hardly make eighteen dollars a
month. Everybody'll be equal, in God's time. Won't be no

old man Rockerfeller, no suh! Today you cain't even buy a
job if you had the money to do it with. Won't be nothing
like that then. He'll let loose and something'll slip down here
and them what done took advantage of everything'll be
floating down the river. You'll go over to the North River,
and over to the East River and you'll see 'em all floating
along. And the river'll be full and they won't know what
struck em. The lawd's gonna have his day.

"They'll be a war. But it won't be no more wars like the
World War. It won't bother me and you. Won't really be
no war. It'll be the wicked killing the wicked! The war like
the World War'll never be agin. They fooled now. They
building navies and buying guns. But don't you worry, it'll
be just the wicked killing out the wicked. It's coming. God's
time is coming and its coming soon!"

*June 7, 1939*

# Sweet the Monkey

## *Ralph Ellison*

**Ralph Ellison encountered Leo Gurley in the summer of
1939 on the corner of West 135 Street and Lenox Avenue.
Gurley told him this fantastic story about another invisible
man whose real name Gurley could not remember.**

I hope to God to kill me if this ain't the truth. All you got
to do is go down to Florence, South Carolina, and ask most
anybody you meet and they'll tell you it's the truth.

Florence is one of these hard towns on colored folks.
You have to stay out of the white folk's way; all but Sweet.
That the fellow I'm fixing to tell you about. His name was
Sweet-the-monkey. I done forgot his real name, I cain't remember it. But that was what everybody called him. He
wasn't no big guy. He was just bad. My mother and grand-
mother used to say he was wicked. He was bad all right. He
was one sucker who didn't give a damn bout the Crackers.
Fact is, they got so they stayed out of his way. I cain't never
remember hear tell of any them Crackers bothering that guy.
He used to give 'em trouble all over the place and all they
could do about it was to give the rest of us hell.

It was this way: Sweet could make hisself invisible. You
don't believe it?

Well here's how he done it. Sweet-the-monkey cut open
a black cat and took out its heart. Climbed up a tree back-
wards and cursed God. After that he could do anything.

The white folks would wake up in the morning and find their stuff gone. He cleaned out the stores. He cleaned up the houses. Hell, he even cleaned out the damn bank! He was the boldest black son-of-a-bitch ever been down that way. And couldn't nobody do nothing to him. Because they couldn't never see 'im [him] when he done it. He didn't need the money. Fact is, most of the time he broke into places he wouldn't take nothing. Lots a times he just did it to show em he could. Hell, he had everybody in lil' old town scared as hell: black folks and white folks.

The white folks started trying to catch Sweet. Well, they didn't have no luck. They'd catch 'im standing in front of the eating joints and put the handcuffs on 'im and take 'im down to the jail. You know what that sucker would do?

The police would come up and say: "Come on Sweet," and he'd say, "You all want me?" and they'd put the hand-cuffs on 'im and start leading 'im away. He'd go with em a little piece. Sho, just like he was going. Then all of a sudden he would turn hisself invisible and disappear. The police wouldn't have nothing but the handcuffs. They couldn't do a thing with that Sweet-the-monkey.

Just before I come up this way they was all trying to trap 'im. They didn't have much luck. Once they found a place he'd looted with footprints leading away from it and they de-cided to try and trap 'im. This was bout sun-up and they followed his footprints all that day. They followed them till sundown when he come partly visible. It was red and the sun was shining on the trees and they waited till they saw his shadow. That was the last of Sweet-the-monkey. They never did find his body and right after that I come up here. That was bout five years ago. My brother was down there last year and they said they think Sweet done come back. But they caint be sho because he wont let hisself be seen.

*June 1939*

# The Street

## *Ralph Ellison*

**The following day, Ellison interviewed an unnamed man in front of 470 West 150 Street.**

I was sitting up on the bandstand drumming, trying to make myself some beat-up change. Wasn't such a crowd in the place that night, just a bunch a them beer drinkers. I was looking down at em dancing and wishing that things would liven up. Then a man came up and give me four dollars just to sing one number. Well, I was singing for that man. I was really laying it Jack, just like Marian Anderson. What the hell you talking about; I'd sing all night after that cat done give me four bucks; thats almost a fin! But this is what brings you down. One a these bums come up to the stand and says to the banjo player, "If you monkeys don't play some music, I'm gonna throw you outta de jernt."

Man, I quit singing and looked at that sonofabitch. Then I got mad. I said, "Where the goddamn hell you come from, you gonna throw somebody outta this band? How you get so bad? Why you poor Brooklyn motherfriger, I'll wreck this goddamn place with you."

Man, he looked at me. I said, "Don't look at me goddamit; I mean what I say!"

By this time everybody is standing around listening. I said, "I oughta snatch your goddamn head off—oh I know

46

the rest'll try to gang me. But they wont get me before I get to you. You crummy bastard."

Then, man, I make a break for my pocket, like I was pulling my gun. Ha, ha, goddamn! You oughta seen em fall back from this cat. This bum had on glasses and you oughta seen him holding up his hands and gitting outa my way. Then the boss came up running and put the sonofabitch out into the street and told me to get back to work. Hell, I scared the hell out of that bastard. A poor sonofabitch! Drinking beer and coming up talking to us like that! You see he thought cause we was black he could talk like he wanted to. In a night club and drinking beer! I fixed him. I bet he won't try that no more.

Man, a poor white man is a bring-down. He ain't got nothing. He can't get nothing. And he thinks cause he's white he's got to impress you cause you black.

Then some of 'em comes up and try to be your friend. Like the other night; I'm up on the stand drumming and singing, trying to make myself some change. I was worried. I got a big old boy, damn near big as me, and every time I look up, he's got to have something. Well the other night I hadn't made a damn thing. And I was sitting there drumming when one of these bums what hangs around the place—one a these slaphappy jitterbugs, comes up to me and says, "You stink!"

Now you know that made me mad before I even knowed what he was talking about. A white cat coming up to me talking about I stink? I said, "What you talking about. What you mean I stink?" He said; "You ain't a good follow like the other cats. You won't take me up to Harlem and show me around."

I said, "Hell yes, mammy dodger, I stink! If that's what you mean I'm gon' always stink. You'll never catch me carrying a bunch of you poor sonsabitches up there. What the hell you gonna do when you get up there? You ain't got nothing. Hell, you poor as I am. I don't see you coming down to Harlem to carry me up to show me the Bronx. You damn right I stink."

Man, he just looks at me now and says, "Jack, you sho a funny cat."

Can you beat that? He oughta know I ain't got no use for him. Damn!

Another one comes up to me—another one a these beer-drinking bums—and says, "I want to go up to your house sometime."

I said, "Fo what! Now you tell me fo what!" I said, "What-in-the-world do you want to come up to my place for? You ain't got nothing and I sho ain't got nothing. What's a poor colored cat and a poor white cat gonna do together? You ain't got nothing cause you too dumb to get it. And I ain't got nothin' cause I'm black. I guess you got your little ol' skin, that's the reason? I'm supposed to feel good cause you walk in my house and sit in my chairs?

"Hell, that skin ain't no more good to you than mine is to me. You cain't marry one a Du Ponts' daughters, and I know damn well I cain't. So what the hell you gon' do up to my place?"

Aw man, I have to get these white cats told. They think you supposed to feel good cause they friendly to you. Boy I don't fool with em. They just the reason why I cain't get ahead now. They try to get all a man's money. That's just the reason why I found me a place up the street here. Got two rooms in a private house with a private bath. These other cats go down to Ludwig Baumans and give him all their money so they can meet you on the street and say: "Oh you must come up to my apartment sometimes. Oh yes, yes, I have some lovely furniture. You just must come up sometime." You know, man, they want to show off. But me I done got wise. I'm getting my stuff outta junk shops, second-hand stores, anywhere. I ain't giving these Jews my money.

Like the chicks. I used to get my check and go out with

the boys and pick up some of these fine feathered chicks. You know the light chicks with the fine hair. We'd go out making all the gin mills, buying liquor. I'd take em to a room and have a ball. Then I'd wake up in the morning with all my beat-up change gone and have to face my wife and tell her some deep lie—that she didn't believe. I don't do that no more. Now I give most of my money to my wife. And I put the rest on the numbers. And when I see the fine chicks I tell em they have to wait till the numbers jumps out.

See this bag? I got me a head a cabbage and two ears a corn. I'm going up here and get me a side a bacon. When I get home, gonna cook the cabbage and bacon, gonna make me some corn fritters and set back in my twenty-five-dollars-a-month room and eat my fritters and cabbage and tell the Jews to forgit it! Jack, I'm just sitting back waiting, cause soon things is gonna narrow down to the fine point. Hitler's gonna reach in a few months and grab and then things'll start. All the white folks'll be killing off one another. And I hope they do a good job!

Then there won't be nobody left but Sam [black people]. Then we'll be fighting it out amongst ourselves. That'll be a funky fight. Aw hell yes! When Negroes start running things I think I'll have to get off the earth before it's too late!

*June 1939*

# My People

## *Ralph Ellison and Clarence Weinstock*

**In the spring of 1939, Ellison teamed up with another WPA writer to conduct a series of interviews uptown. A heavy-set black man with a light complexion was sitting alone in the hiring room at the Harlem Labor Center on West 125 Street. In his late forties, the man was seated at a card table along a row of large windows overlooking the busy street below. On the walls nearby were posters. One showed the clasped hands of a black and white man with the slogan "Black and White Unite" on it. Another just showed a bunch of bananas with the caption, "Stay in Your Own Bunch, or You'll Get Skinned."**

My people made the trucking business. You see all these companies around here? We made em. We even built the buildings. Some of the fellows what's big shots now, used to go 'round with wheelbarrows. Now they got trucks; they're big shots. We helped em get where they are and now they don't want to look at us anymore. They don't want you. It's the same thing everywhere. Now take the World's Fair. They had us draining and fillin-in out there, working in all that filth. They got us when they wanted to get it ready and now the dirty work's done, let me see you go out there and get something. Let me see you!

Same thing, all over. Just take the truckin' business. I'm
a handler. I've been in this business since 1898. Our people
made that business; made them warehouses. Now, when
they got it made, they didn't want us. It's just like a man
makin' steps. You make the business and ask for a raise.
Well, they got to pay you. That's two steps. Then things go
long 'n you got to get a union. That's the third step. And
right there's the step they kill you on. Now they'd rather
give the work to somebody else. They don't want to pay
you that good money. Now, ain't much you can do about
it. You see that picture up there in the wall? "Black and
White Unite"? Them hands is clasped together in the picture, but here it's wide apart. Always squabbling. Cain't get
together. That's really the way it is.

I been in this business forty-one years. Sometimes I get
tired and leave it 'n get me a family. But dammit! I was
tellin' my wife the other day, the last time I did it, I believe
it changed my luck. [My wife's] folks [were] connected with
this damn Oxford movement. [It began in 1833 at Oxford
University where some members of the Church of England
sought a closer alignment with the Roman Catholic Church.]
Just a lot of damn talk. It's just like you sittin here talkin to
me; just a lot of questions.

Made me so tired, I quit the job. She was always askin'
me questions. Always wanted to know my business, made
me tired as hell. But I finally go so I could talk to em like I
wanted to 'n I told her it was just a lot of noise. The Oxford
movement, hell! She asked me all my business, just everything, trying to get in my business. Talking bout the Oxford
movement. Just trying to get in my business; that's all. So I
said "You ask me all these questions, so I'm goin to ask
you: How many times do you go with your old man a
night?" That stopped her. Hell yes I told her.

That's just what I told her. She's tellin me somethin
about [American Evangelist Frank] Buckman. Hell, what'd
he do: He couldn't get along with his parish, so he beats it

to England to do some more studyin'. Then he had some goddamn dream about Christ on the Cross 'n writes back here he's very sorry 'n everything, that he was wrong. So he starts this Oxford movement. And all the suckers, they fall for his dream. So he goes back to England and gets a big building and she tells me about this vision. Hell anybody can have a vision and then say five million dollars. 'N these suckers fall for it. Made me sick askin' all them questions. 'N they talk about [Harlem cult figure] Father Divine. Now there's a man who's doin' somethin'. Talking about the work of Christ don't cost nothin'. Hell, you get these big buildings and these coal bills 'n light bills got to comin in 'n you get all them people travelin' round with Buckman—why he had seventeen people come over with him last time—who you thinks payin' for all that? The vision? Tellin' me about visions. Hell, my luck aint been the same since I worked for them people. Ever since I worked down there, my luck's been bad; ain't had a thing to do. That's the reason I don't have no faith in man. I been around all this stuff too much. It don't mean nothin'. The unseen spirit up yonder all right. Get on your knees and get in touch with him. But man? Man ain't nothin'. That's the reason we cain't get nowhere down here with this union; man ain't no good.

Sure, there's some good. Same is all right. What did God say about em being all mixed up. He said: Let em mingle together, I'll separate the goats from the lambs. How many times you ate goat thinking you was eating spring lamb?

Yes, I believe in visions. I've had em myself. I was living downtown with a family an' seen the woman's husband who'd been dead six years. Her boy was sick 'n seen him too. He came and stood in the hall between the two rooms 'n said "I'm going to take three rooms. You can come on if you want to." The boy was a kid twenty-two years old 'n he heard 'im too. A few days later the boy was gone, dead.

Dreams come to me all the time. I get forewarnings whenever something's about to happen to me. I know just when and how. Hell, you have 'im too. All fellows do; they just forget when they wake up. I had one last night bout what this meeting was for this morning.

I had a warnin' one time when I was working. I had a piano bout to lower it out of a window on a pulley. 'N when I started downstairs to let it come, somethin said, "You better not let that down!" So I runs back upstairs 'an looks and the damn piano was hanging there by a strand. The damn rope was coming apart 'n it was just hanging there by a few strands. Now if I hadn't listened to that warning, me 'n six or seven other men would have been dead.

I have dreams all the time. I dreamed about my grandfather who had been dead thirty-three years who I'd never seen 'n I asked my mother the next mornin 'n she said, yes that was the way he looked.

*May 1, 1939*

# Pluto

## Dorothy West

On an especially cold morning in 1938, Dorothy West was interrupted from her writing when she heard a faint knock at the door of her apartment in the well-to-do-looking building where she lived on West 110 Street. The visitor at West's door that morning wasn't alone. This is West's account.

A collapsible wooden image of the long-eared, sad-eyed hound known as Pluto stands prominently on my bookcase. The cartoon version was immortalized by Mr. Walt Disney. There is no child, and almost never an adult, who does not, upon entering my house, immediately pick Pluto up, pull the strings that make him flop, and play happily for at least five minutes or at most to the end of the visit.

Today though, a child came to my house who did not run straight-away to Pluto. Maybe it was because he was a hungry child. And when is a child not a child? When he's hungry. This one had hollows under his eyes, and his body was too thin, and his clothing was not much comfort against the wind.

My apartment house has a prosperous exterior. Several times a week somebody comes to your door with a hard luck story. Generally it's a man, and so because I'm a woman, I simply say I'm sorry through a crack in the door, and shut

54

the door quickly. In New York you have to be on the look-
out for stickup men.

But today it was a woman who answered my "Who is
it?" There was something about her plaintive, "Me, lady,"
that made me open the door wider than I usually do when
the voice is unknown.

I saw them both then, the thin little black boy and the
thin black woman, both staring anxiously, and neither looking as if they had the strength or will to harm the most
helpless female.

"Yes?" I said.

The woman swallowed hard and said, "Could you give
me a quarter, missus, to buy something to eat for the boy?"

"Why aren't you on relief?" I asked suspiciously, although in my heart I was disarmed by her Southern accent.

"They said I'd get a check next week," she said helpfully.
"They was nice to me," she added.

My neighbor opened her door. She was smartly dressed.
Her little boy ran across the hall and stared up at the ill-
clad child. I was ashamed of all of us.

"Come inside," I said coldly.

The boy and his mother entered and stood awkwardly
in the center of my floor, the boy clinging to his mother's
hand as if my sunny room were a dungeon.

"Sit down," I said.

They sat down together on the couch and Pluto was
plainly visible. I saw the little boy look at it, and then he
looked at me.

For a moment I started to urge him to pick it up and
play with it. But then I remembered he had come begging
for bread and I could not offer him a toy.

The boy's grave eyes turned back to Pluto. I wanted him
to get up and go to it. It made me mad that he recognized
the place of his poverty. And then I remembered again that
he had come for a quarter and not for a plaything.

I didn't have a quarter to spare. I had only sufficient

carfare until payday. "I don't have a penny in the house." I lied. "But I'll be glad to give you something to eat. You like bacon and eggs?"

"Yes, missus," she said, and then reluctantly, "But I hates to put you to that bother."

"Not at all," I said shortly, because it was a bother. She had interrupted me in the middle of an excellent story. It was about poor people, too; a good proletarian short story.

I banged about the kitchenette, and after a while the living room was fragrant with steaming coffee and sizzling bacon. I found some cold potatoes and fried them. I sliced my last tomato. I piled some slices of bread on a plate and then I felt guilty and toasted them.

All the while I was humming to myself because I did not want that woman to tell me her story. I could have told it to her myself. It would be no different from a hundred others.

It wasn't. I could not hum at the table. I spooned a cup of coffee while they ate. Inevitably, the woman in return for the meal told me the facts that led up to it.

Widowed when the boy was a baby, knocking about with him from pillar to post, coming North so that he could go to a northern school, sleeping-in and sleeping-out for a string of slave-driving tyrants, farming the boy out to one indifferent slattern after another, never earning much, never saving anything, keeping body and soul together through sheer determination to survive. Now two weeks out of the hospital after a major operation, she was still too frail for domestic work, and her cousin by marriage, who was on relief, was letting her sleep in the living room and forage for food as best as she could. The slattern who had been keeping the boy gave him back to her yesterday. She had put him to bed without any supper.

She had brought him out this morning without any breakfast. She was on her way to the relief people now to ask them if they could hurry. As for herself, she could wait, but a boy gets hungry.

The boy had already eaten more than his share of the platter and was draining his second cup of diluted coffee. He had not said a word. He had simply looked from his mother to me during his intervals of swallowing, throughout her drab recital. It was not surprising that what she was saying evoked no response in him. He knew all about it. It was as much his life as it was hers. His life in fact was harder, for there was no way for him to know with certainty that she would come once weekly to see him, or that the slattern who beat and neglected him would be replaced by one who only neglected him.

They finished their meal, or rather the platter was clean and the coffeepot empty. Light had come into the woman's face, and the boy did not look quite so much like a wizened old man.

I got up, and the woman understood the signal. She jumped up and thanked me profusely. She prodded the boy. He did not speak, but he smiled, and suddenly he looked seven and no longer an undersized seventy.

I made a package of the odds and ends in my icebox, and after a little struggle with myself, slipped my half-dollar into the woman's hand. I could borrow carfare from a friend. Obviously she could not.

I led them to the door, but the boy broke away and ran across the room to Pluto and lovingly touched him. Pluto fell over and the boy laughed aloud. He gave him a final affectionate pat, and trotted back to his mother. He looked up at her with a face full of eager confidence. He pronounced solemnly, "I'm gonna ask Sandy for one of them dawgs."

She looked at me almost apologetically. "He believes in Sandy Claus," she said. She hurried on proudly, defensively, "He ain't failed him yet."

"That's fine," I said and shut the door. I could hear them going down the hall, and the boy was talking volubly.

I guess he was telling his mother what else he was going to ask "Sandy" for.

For a moment I wanted to believe that I had been taken in, for I am perhaps the poorest tenant in my fine apartment house. I live on the fifth floor in a tiny rear apartment, and why should she have come first to me? And then I realized that in all probability she had not.

I turned back into my room and crossed the floor to put Pluto back on his feet. It has become an automatic act when my door closes after a visitor.

The sad-eyed hound looked up at me, and his tail drooped wistfully. He did not look funny, and I did not want to laugh at him, and he is supposed to make you laugh.

I moved away and cleared the table. I was thinking that it is not right to take a child's joy away and give him hunger. I was thinking that a child's faith is too fine and precious for the dump heap of poverty. I was thinking that bread should not be bigger than a boy.

I thought about those things a lot.

*November 28, 1938*

# Rent Parties

## *Frank Byrd*

In the 1925 Harlem issue of *Survey Graphic*, Winthrop
D. Lane exposed the common scandal of widespread
rent gouging in Harlem. Quoting from a study done by
the National Urban League, then an organization of
black and white social workers, Lane reported that a
study of the rents paid by blacks and whites in the spring
of 1924 "found that Negroes paid from forty to sixty
percent higher rents than white people did for the same
class of apartments." This disparity was attributed to
the rapid growth of tenants in Harlem between 1910
and 1924. The rent party was conceived.

These social conditions were in part responsible for
the widely held belief that Harlem was also the party
capital of the world. But these legendary parties were
born out of economic necessity. Here WPA writer Frank
Byrd characterizes this cultural landmark known as the
"rent party" in a piece he wrote late in the summer
of 1938.

The history of the Harlem house-rent party dates back as
far as World War I. To understand what gave such an impe-
tus and community-wide significance to this institution, it is
necessary to get a picture of living conditions as they were
in Harlem at the time.

During the early 1920s it is estimated that more than 200,000 black people migrated to Harlem: West Indians, Africans, and American blacks from the cotton and cane fields of the Deep South. They were all segregated in a small section of Manhattan about fifty blocks long and seven or eight blocks wide; an area teeming with life and activity. Housing experts have estimated that sometimes as many as 5,000 to 7,000 people have been known to live in a single block.

Needless to say, living conditions under such circumstances were anything but wholesome and pleasant. It was a typical slum and tenement area little different from many others in New York except that in Harlem rents were higher; always have been, in fact, since the great wartime migratory influx of colored labor. Despite these exorbitant rents, apartments and furnished rooms, however dingy, were in great demand. Harlem property owners, for the most part Jews, began to live in comparative ease on the fantastic profits yielded by their antiquated dwellings. Before blacks inhabited them, they could be let for virtually a song. Afterward, however, they brought handsome incomes. The tenants, by hook or crook, barely managed to scrape together the rents. In turn they stuck their roomers for enough profit to yield themselves a meager living.

A four- or five-room apartment was (and still is) often crowded to capacity with roomers. In many instances, two entire families occupied space intended for only one family. When bedtime came, there was the feverish activity of moving furniture about, taking down cots, or preparing floor space as sleeping quarters. The same practice of overcrowding was followed by owners or lessees of private houses. Large rooms were converted into two or three small ones by the simple process of strategically placing beaver board partitions. These same cubby holes were rented at the price of full-sized rooms. In many houses, dining and living rooms were transformed into bedrooms soon after, if not before, midnight. Even "shift-sleeping" was not unknown in many places. During the night, a day worker used the room and soon after dawn a night worker moved in. Seldom did the bed have an opportunity to get cold.

In lower Harlem, sometimes referred to as the Latin Quarter and populated mostly by Cubans, Puerto Ricans, and West Indians, accommodations were worse. The Spanish have even less privacy than their American cousins. A three- or four-room apartment often housed ten or twelve people. Parents invariably had the two or three youngest children bedded down in the same room with themselves. The dining room, kitchen, and hallway were utilized as sleeping quarters by relatives or friends.

Blacks constituted the bulk of the Harlem population, however, and have since the war. At that time, there was a great demand for cheap industrial labor. Strong backed, physically capable blacks from the South were the answer to this demand. They came north in droves, beginning what turned out to be the greatest migration of blacks in the history of the United States. The good news about jobs spread like wildfire throughout the Southlands. There was money, good money, to be made in the north, especially New York. New York—the wondrous, the magical city. The name alone implied glamour and adventure. It was a picture to definitely catch the fancy of restless, overworked sharecroppers and farmhands. And so, it was on to New York, the mecca of the New Negro, the modern Promised Land.

Not only southern, but thousands of West Indian blacks heeded the call. That was the beginning of housing conditions that have been a headache to a succession of political administrations and a thorn in the side of community and civic organizations that have struggled valiantly, but vainly, to improve them.

With the sudden influx of so many blacks, who instinctively headed for Harlem, property that had been a white elephant on the hands of many landlords immediately took an upward swing. The majority of landlords were delighted but those white property owners who made their homes in Harlem were panic-stricken.

At first, there were only rumblings of protest against this unwanted dark invasion but as the tide of color continued to rise, threatening to completely envelop the Caucasian brethren, they quickly abandoned their fight and fled to more remote parts; Brooklyn, Bronx, Queens, and Westchester. As soon as one or two black families moved into a block, the whites began moving out. Then the rents were raised. In spite of this, blacks continued to pour in until there was a solid mass of color in every direction.

Harlemites soon discovered that meeting these doubled, and sometimes tripled, rents was not so easy. They began to think of new ways to meet their ever-increasing deficits. Someone evidently got the idea of having a few friends in as paying party guests a few days before the landlord's scheduled monthly visit. It was a happy timely thought. The guests had a good time and entered wholeheartedly into the spirit of the party. Besides, it cost each individual very little, probably much less than he would have spent in some public amusement place. It became a cheap way to help a friend in need. It was such a good, easy way out of one's difficulties that others decided to make use of it. The Harlem rent-party was born.

Like the Charleston and Black Bottom, popular dances of the era, rent parties became an overnight rage. Here at last was a partial solution to the problem of excessive rents and dreadfully subnormal incomes. Family after family and hundreds of apartment tenants opened wide their doors, and went the originators of the idea one better, in fact, by having a party every Saturday night instead of once a month prior to the landlord's call. The accepted admission price became twenty five cents. It was also expected that the guests would partake freely of the fried chicken, pork chops, pigs feet, and potato salad, not to mention homemade "cawn" liquor that was for sale in the kitchen or at a makeshift bar in the hallway.

Saturday night became the night for these galas in Harlem. Some parties even ran well into Sunday morning, calling a halt only after seven or eight o'clock. Parties were eventually held on other nights also. Thursday particularly became a favorite in view of the fact that "sleep in" domestic workers had a day off and were free to kick up their heels without restraint. Not that any other weekday offered Saturday any serious competition. It always retained its popularity because of its all-round convenience as a party day. To begin with, the majority of working-class blacks, maids, porters, elevator operators, and the like were paid on Saturday and, more important than that, were not required to report to work on Sunday. Saturday, therefore, became the logical night to "pitch" and "carry on."

The Saturday night party, like any other universally popular diversion, soon fell into the hands of racketeers. Many small-time pimps and madams who, up to that time, had operated under cover in buffet flats, came out into the open and staged nightly so-called Rent Parties. This, of course, was merely a blind for more illegitimate activities that catered primarily to the desire of traveling salesmen, Pullman porters, interstate truck drivers, and other transients for some place to stop and amuse themselves. Additional business could always be promoted from that large army of single or unattached males and females who prowled the streets at night in search of adventure in preference to remaining in their small, dingy rooms in some ill-ventilated flat. There were hundreds of young men and women, fresh from the hinterlands, unknown in New York and eager for the opportunity to meet people. So they would stroll the avenue until they saw some flat with a red, pink, or blue light in the window, the plunk of a tin-panny piano, and sounds of half-tipsy merrymaking fleeting out into the night air; then they would venture in, be greeted volubly by the hostess, introduced around, and eventually steered to the kitchen where refreshments were for sale.

Afterward, there was probably a night filled with continuous drinking, wild, grotesque dancing and crude lovemaking. But it was, at least, a temporary escape from humdrum loneliness and boredom.

The party givers were fully aware of the conditions under which the majority of these boys and girls lived, and decided to commercialize on it as much as possible. They began advertising their get-togethers on little business cards that were naïve attempts at poetic jingles. The following is a typical sample:

> *There'll be brown skin mammas*
> *High yallers too*
> *And if you ain't got nothin to do*
> *Come on up to ROY and SADIE'S*
> *West 126 St. Sat. Night, May 12th.*
> *There'll be plenty of pig feet*
> *An lots of gin*
> *Jus ring the bell*
> *An come on in.*

They were careful, however, to give these cards only to the "right" people. Prohibition was still in effect and the police were more diligent about raiding questionable apartments than they were about known "gin mills" that flourished on almost every corner.

Despite this fact, the number of personal Saturday night responses, in answer to the undercover advertising, was amazing. The party hostess, eager and glowing with freshly straightened hair, would roll back the living room carpets, dim the lights, seat the musicians (usually drummer, piano, and saxophone player), and, with the appearance of the first cash customer, give the signal that would officially get the "rug-cutting" under way. Soon afterward she would disappear into the kitchen in order to give a final, last-minute inspection to the refreshment counter: a table piled high with pig feet, fried chicken, fish, and potato salad.

The musicians, fortified with a drink or two of King Kong (homemade corn whiskey) would begin "beating out the rhythm" on their battered instruments while the dancers kept time with gleeful whoops, fantastic body gyrations and convulsions that appeared to be a cross between the itch and a primitive mating dance.

After some John bought a couple of rounds of drinks, things began to hum in earnest. The musicians instinctively improvised as they went along, finding it difficult, perhaps, to express the full intensity of their emotions through a mere arrangement, no matter how well written.

But the thing that makes the house-rent party (even now) so colorful and fascinating is the unequaled picture created by the dancers themselves. When the band gets hot, the dancers get hotter. They would stir, throw, or bounce themselves about with complete abandon; their wild, grotesque movements silhouetted in the semidarkness like flashes from some ancient tribal ceremony. They apparently worked themselves up into a frenzy but never lost time with the music despite their frantic acrobatics. Theirs is a coordination absolutely unexcelled. It is simple, primitive, inspired. As far as dancing is concerned, there are no conventions. You do what you like, express what you feel, take the lid off if you happen to be in the mood. In short, anything goes.

About one o'clock in the morning; hilarity reaches its peak. "The Boys," most of whom are hard-working, hard-drinking truck drivers, longshoremen, moving men, porters, or laborers, settle down to the serious business of enjoying themselves. They spin, tug, and fling their buxom, amiable partners in all directions. When the music finally stops, they are soaked and steaming with perspiration. "The girls," the majority of whom are cooks, laundresses, maids, or hair-dressers, set their hats at a jaunty angle and kick up their heels with glee. Their tantalizing grins and the uniformly wicked gleam in their eyes dare the full-blooded young bucks to do their darndest. They may have been utter strangers during the early part of the evening but before the night is over, they are all happily sweating and laughing together in the best of spirits.

Everything they do is free and easy; typical of that group of hard-working blacks [is that] most have few or no inhibitions and the fertility of imagination so necessary to the invention and unrestrained expression of new dance steps and rhythms.

The dancers organize little impromptu contests among themselves and this competition is often responsible for the birth of many new and original dance steps. The house-rent party takes credit for the innovation of the Lindy-Hop that was subsequently improved upon at the Savoy Ballroom. For years, it has been a great favorite with the regular rug-cutting crowd. Nothing has been able to supplant it, not even the Boogie-Woogie that has recently enjoyed a great wave of popularity in uptown New York.

Such unexpected delights as these made the house-rent party, during its infancy, a success with more than one social set. Once in a while a stray ofay (white person) or a small party of pseudo-artistic young blacks, the upper crust, the crème-de-la-crème of Black Manhattan society, would wander into one of these parties and gasp or titter (with cultured restraint, of course) at the primitive, untutored Negroes who apparently had so much fun wriggling their bodies about to the accompaniment of such mad, riotously abandoned music. Seldom, however, did these outsiders seem to catch the real spirit of the party, and as far as the rug-cutters were concerned, they simply did not belong.

With the advent of "Repeal," the rent-party went out, became definitely a thing of the past. Ironically, it was too dangerous to try to sell whiskey after it became legal because the laws regulating its sale were more stringent than those that forbid it to be sold at all.

So, the passing of Prohibition also killed one of the most colorful eras that Harlem, New York, and possibly America, has ever known.

*August 23, 1938*

# Buffet Flat

## *Frank Byrd*

**In an attempt to further document the rent party, Frank Byrd interviewed a woman who would identify herself only as Bernice. While she was unwilling to let Byrd use the exact address of her apartment, Bernice was candid about why she threw such parties.**

Bernice lived in a comfortable flat on West 141 Street near Lenox. While she was wary of giving her last name or allowing WPA writer Frank Byrd to record the location where this interview took place, Bernice was more than willing to talk. In fact, for someone who was at first reluctant even to admit that she opened her home to strangers every weekend, Bernice also seemed proud of her clever rent-paying scheme.

Bernice arrived in New York as a young girl of high school age from the West Indies. Two years after she married an American in 1926, he deserted her, leaving her to fend for herself as a part-time domestic worker. Reluctantly, she became a promoter of her own rent parties and later ran a "buffet flat," which is what some people called a pleasure house, uptown.

"When I first came to New York from Bermuda, I thought rent parties were disgraceful. I couldn't understand how any self-respecting person could bear them, but when my husband, who was a Pullman porter, ran off and left me with a sixty-dollar-a-month apartment on my hands and no job, I soon learned, like everyone else, to rent my rooms out an' throw these Saturday get-togethers.

"I had two roomers, a colored boy and white girl named Leroy and Hazel, who first gave me the idea. They offered to run the parties for me if we'd split fifty-fifty. I had nothing to lose, so that's how we started.

"We bought corn liquor by the gallon and sold it for fifty cents a small (cream) pitcher. Leroy also ran a poker and blackjack game in the little bedroom off the kitchen. An' on these two games alone, I've seen him take in as much as twenty-eight dollars in one night. Well, you can see why I didn't want to give it up, once we had started. Especially since I could only make six or seven dollars at the most as a weekly part-time [domestic] worker.

"The games paid us both so well, in fact, that we soon made gambling our specialty. Everybody liked it, and our profit was more that way so our place soon became the hangout of all those party goers who liked to mix a little gambling with their drinking and dancing.

"An' with all these young studs out to find a little mischief, with plenty of cash in their pockets, we soon learned not to leave things to chance. Instead, Hazel and I would go out an' get acquainted with good-looking young fellows that we'd see sitting alone in the back of gin mills looking as if they had nobody to take them out, but that they also would like a good time. We'd give them our cards and tell them to drop around to the house. Well, wherever there are pretty women you'll soon have a pack of men.

"And so we taught the girls how to wheedle free drinks and food out of the men—and if they got them to spend more than usual, we'd give them a little percentage or a nice little present like a pair of stockings or vanity case or something. Most of the time, though, we didn't have to give them a thing. They were all out looking for a little fun, and when they came to our house they could have it for nothing in-

stead of going to the gin mills where they'd have to pay for
their own drinks.

"And we rented rooms, sometimes overnight and sometimes for just a little while during the party. I have to admit
that, at first, I was a little shocked at the utter boldness of
it, but Leroy and Hazel seemed to think nothing of it, so I
let it go. Besides, it meant extra money—and extra money
was what I needed.

"I soon took another hint from Hazel and made even
more. I used to notice that Leroy would bring some of his
friends home with him and, after they'd have a few drinks,
leave them alone in the room with Hazel. I wasn't quite sure
that what I was thinking was so until Hazel told me herself.
It happened one day when an extra man came along there
was no one to take care of him. Hazel buzzed to me and
asked me if I would do it. I thought about it for a while,
then made up my mind to do it.

"Well, that was the last of days-work [domestic work]
for me. I figured that I was a fool to go out and break my
back scrubbing floors, washing, ironing, and cooking, when
I could earn three day's pay, or more, in fifteen minutes.
Then I began to understand how Hazel got all those fine
dresses and good-looking furs.

"From then on, it was strictly a business with me. I decided that if it was as easy as that, it was the life for me.

"The landlord's agent had been making sweet speeches
to me for a long time and I began to figure out how I could
get around paying the rent. Well, I got around it, but that
didn't stop me from giving rent parties. Everything I made
then was gravy; clean, clear profit for little Bernice. I even
broke off with Leroy and Hazel. She began to get jealous
and catty, and I think he was holding out on profits from
the game. Anyway, we split up and I got an "old man"
[sweetheart] of my own to help me run the house. An' when
he took things over he even stopped the girls from going
into the rooms with the men unless they were working for

us. That is, unless we were getting half of what they made. Still, the men had to pay for the rooms. And I've seen some of those girls who made enough on Saturday night to buy themselves an entirely new outfit for Sunday, including fur coat. They'd catch some sucker, like a Pullman porter or longshoreman who had been lucky in a game, and have him jim-clean [completely broke] before the night was over. Naturally, I got my cut. It was a good racket while it lasted, but it's shot to pieces now."

*October 2, 1938*

# Slick Reynolds

## *Frank Byrd*

**In the fall of 1938, Frank Byrd went to the Symphony Club on West 131 Street near Seventh Avenue where musicians, actors, and vaudeville performers often hung out. There he heard the story of Slick Reynolds, a black-jack card dealer at the club.**

**Reynolds made no secret that he had once run a buffet-flat pleasure house before it was again legal to buy booze in public saloons.**

Sure, I used to give rent parties all the time. And I made pretty good at it till repeal came along. Then I had to give it up. Too much risk. A cop on the beat could be paid off, but them A.B.C. boys (State Beverage Control Board) can't be reached even by the big shots.

There was plenty of dough in the party racket and it used to be the mainstay of a lot of the boys who needed to make a little extra dough. But the only trouble with staging rent parties as an out-an-out hustle was the lousy crowd you had to cater to. You put out your cards, hired a piano player, open your door, an' just wait for all sorts of studs and chicks to wander in. If you were lucky, you might get through the night without any major accidents—but I never seemed to have that kinda luck.

Some punch-drunk spade or dizzy broad was always

breaking up my shindigs. First they'd get loaded to the gills with King Kong, start getting rambunctious an' wanting to pick a fight at the drop of a hat. Some guy'd get accidentally shoved or just naturally get evil cause his ol' lady would dance more than once . . . [with the] same guy. The next minute, he'd be whooping like a wild Indian, waving his blade and threatening to cut anybody who came near him.

Well, that'd most likely be the end of my party. Folks would start running in every direction—out into the hallway, on the fire escape, anywhere. One Saturday night I even found a chick bracing herself inside the dumb-waiter shaft, after some Mose went haywire and shot out the lights.

It all started when his girl got stuck on a big black boy dressed in longshoreman's dungarees, who came stalking in about twelve o'clock with a pocket full of money and a mind to spend it all. He gunned this chick, liked her style, and set about making a play for her. The broad was willing and showed her teeth from then on. Her feller kept watching out of the corner of his eye, and by the time he'd been back to the kitchen five or six times for a slug of my liquid, I knew that it wouldn't be long before he'd explode.

Well, I was right. Pretty soon he walks up to the big boy an' says: "Listen, ol' son—can't you find anybody else to dance wit' 'ceptin' my ol' lady?"

"Ain't no sign on her says she's yo' ol' lady, is dere?"

"Well, sign or no sign, better not catch you dancing wid her no more."

" 'S'pose I do. What den?"

"Well, I'll either have some of you or you'll have some of me!"

"Well, don't give a damn if I do," says the big feller; an' from then on, it was on. Glasses started flying, chairs overturned, women screaming, and God knows what else. I usually ducks into a closet an' waits for 'em to finish it up before I comes out to look things over an' see how much damage is done.

Well, that's how most of my parties ended. An' then, to top it off, when the cops would come, they'd stalk through the house straight back to the kitchen and throw down a half dozen or more slugs of my likker and stuff their pockets with fried chicken.

I was lucky to make a profit at all. But what the hell, sometimes I had a good night and my books showed a pretty fair profit. Guess that's why I stayed in the racket until it finally petered out.

*September 1938*

# Laundry Workers

## *Vivian Morris*

**It's shortly after 11 A.M. in the West End Laundry on West 41 Street between Tenth and Eleventh Avenues where women from Harlem work and talk about their daily lives.**

The foreman of the ironing department of the laundry eyed me suspiciously and then curtly asked me, "What you want?" I showed him a Laundry Workers Union card (which I borrowed from an unemployed laundry worker, in order to ensure my admittance) and told him I used to work in this laundry and I thought I would drop in and take a friend of mine who worked there out to lunch.

He squinted at the clock and said, "Forty minutes before lunchtime. Too hot in here and how. Better wait outside."

"But," I remonstrated, "the heat doesn't bother me. I used to work in here."

"Say," he ignored my argument "no fishy back talk and get outside." He watched me until I was out of sight and then he left the room. I promptly darted back into the ironing room where my friend worked.

The clanging of metal as the pistons bang into the sockets, the hiss of steam, women wearily pushing twelve-pound irons, women mechanically tending machines: one, button half of the shirt done; two, top finished; three, sleeves pressed; and the shirt is ready for the finishers—that is the scene that greeted me as I stood in the laundry's ironing department.

Shirts, thousands of white shirts that produce such a dazzling glare that the women who work in this department wear dark glasses to protect their eyes. The heat is almost unbearable; there seems to be gushes of damp heat pushed at you from some invisible force in the mechanism of the machine. The smooth, shiny-faced women work in silence, occasionally dropping a word here and there, slowly wiping away dripping perspiration, then back to the machines, to the heavy irons without any outward show of emotion—no protest. The morning has been long and arduous, this is Wednesday—a heavy day but thank God half the day is nearly over.

The heavy, strong-armed woman pauses the iron, arms unflex, and she glances at the clock. She smiles. Forty-five minutes until eating time. A soft contralto voice gives vent to a hymn, a cry of protest, as only the persecuted can sing, warm, plaintive, yet with a hidden buoyancy of exultation that might escape a person who has not also felt the pathos and hopes of a downtrodden, exploited people.

She sings, a trifle louder, "Could my tears forever flow, could my zeal no languor know. Thou must save, and thou alone, these fo' sin could not atone; In my hand no price I bring. Simply to his cross I cling."

The women tend their machines to the tempo of the hymn. They all join in on the chorus, their voices blend beautifully, though untrained and unpolished they voice the same soulful sentiment, "Rock the Ages, cleft for me. Let me hide myself in thee." Stanza after stanza rings from their lips voicing oppression centuries old, but the song rings out that the inner struggle for real freedom still lights a fiery spark in the recesses of the souls of these toiling women.

The song ends as it began with soft words and humming. One squat, attractive young woman, who single-handedly handles three of the shirt machines, begins a spirited hymn in militant tempo, with a gusto that negates the earlier attitude of fatigue and the entire crew of the ironing room joins in either humming or singing.

They are entering the final hour before lunch but to judge from the speed that the song has spurred them to, you would believe they were just beginning. The perspiration drips copiously but it is forgotten. The chorus of the hymn zooms forth. "Dare to be a Daniel, Dare to stand alone. Dare to have a purpose firm and make it known— and make it known."

The woman who finishes the laces with the twelve-pound iron wields it with feathery swiftness and sings her stanza as the others hum and put in a word here and there. "Many a mighty gal is lost daring not to stand." [The words of the next line were overcome by the rise in the humming, but the last line was clear and resonant.] "By joinin' Daniel's band." The chorus was filled with many pleasing adlibs and then another took up a stanza. Finally the song dies away.

Then the squat machine handler says to the finisher who guides the big iron, "Come on, baby, sing 'at song you made up by yourself. 'The Heavy Iron Blues.' "

Without further coaxing the girl addressed as baby clears her throat and begins singing. "I lift my iron, Lawd, heavy as a ton of nails. I lif' my i'on Lawd, heavy as a ton of nails, but it pays my rent cause my man's still layin' in jail. Got the blues, blues, got the Heavy i'on Blues; but my feet's in good shoes, so doggone the heavy i'on blues."

Then she starts the second stanza, which is equally as light but carries some underlying food for thought. "I lif' my i'on, Lawd, all the live-long day. I lif' my i'on, Lawd, all the live-long day, cause dat furniture bill I know I got to pay, got the blues, blues, got the heavy i'on blues, but, I pay my union dues, so doggone the heavy i'on blues."

There is a sound of whistles from the direction of the river and the girls drop whatever they are doing and there are many sighs of relief. Lunchtime.

*March 1938*

# Negro Laundry Workers

## *Vivian Morris*

**A short time later, Morris went to see Evelyn Macon at
her home, having been given her name by the United
Laundry Workers Union, C.I.O.**

I rapped on the door at 254 West 129 Street, and a head
poked through the door and suspicious eyes greeted me.
"Well?"

The greeting was rather abrupt but I was not to be
daunted by any such trivial. "I would like to speak to Miss
Evelyn Macon, please."

"Frien' uh huhs?"

"Well—yes."

"Don't soun' like it. I'll see if she's in—to you." She
flounced heavily down the hall.

A tired-eyed, slight girl came to the door and smiled.
"Do come in. My landlady is suspicious of people who come
looking for me at night—especially after the little trouble of
a few weeks ago."

After learning my mission, she led me to a tidy little
room. It opened into a closed court, which did not allow
for much fresh ventilation but she did keep it as neat as
could be.

I sat in the one chair; she sat on the bed. Evelyn produced cigarettes. "Smoke?" We both lit up and she deliberately blew smoke through her nose and calmly began. "So

you want to know about conditions in the laundry where I work? Well—they're about one hundred times better than they were two years ago, and they're still far from ideal.

"First, let me tell you how conditions were two years ago—before our shop became almost one hundred percent Union, U.L.W.U.C.I.O. We only have one girl who is non-union in our shop now.

"Before we unionized, I worked as a press operator. Slavery is the only word that could describe the condition under which we worked. It was at least fifty-four hours a week, speed up—speed up—eating lunch on the fly, perspiration dropping from every pore, for almost ten hours per day. When I reached home sometimes I was too tired to prepare supper. I would flop across the bed and sleep two or three hours, then get up and cook and then fall back into bed immediately after eating—you know how unhealthy that was.

"The toilet at our palce wasn't fit for animals, much less people, and there was but the one for men and women. When I complained, the boss said, 'There ain't many places paying ten dollars a week now, Evie.' That ended my protests, because I didn't want to get fired.

The girls who worked in the starching department used to sing spirituals to enable them to breathe standing ten hours and sticking their hands into almost boiling starch."

"Boiling?" I interrupted.

"Almost. It's so hot that they have to put camphor ice on their hands before they can put them into the starch. Cold starch is better but hot starch is cheaper—and you know the bosses." She winked. "As I said before, the starchers used to sing, 'Go Down Moses,' 'Down by the Riverside,' and God, the feeling they put in their singing. As tired as we were, those spirituals lifted up our spirits and we joined in sometimes. That was too much pleasure to have while working for his money said the boss, and the singing was cut out.

"But, that was where the boss made his mistake. While singing we would forget our miserable lot, but after the singing was cut out, it gave us more time for thinking—thinking about our problems.

"One day a fellow applied for a job at our place as a sorter and got it. We didn't think he would be there long because he certainly did no speed up like the rest of us. The boss saw him and asked him if he was sick. He said no. The boss told him he would have to work faster. He laughed at the boss and told him that a man was a damn fool to rush during the first hour when he had seventeen more staring him in the face. I guess the boss felt like firing him but he was a giant of a man and as strong as an ox. The boss let him slide. But he caused the boss to hit the ceiling when the lunch hour came. The boss came out and yelled, 'On the fly,' which meant for us not to stop for lunch, but to eat while we worked, as there was a rush.

" 'Bruiser,' the new fellow, picked up his lunch and went out. The boss raved and cussed almost tearing his hair out because Bruiser had caused the work to slow down. In exactly one hour Bruiser was back.

"The boss charged up to him bristling with rage demanding, 'What the hell do you mean by going out to lunch during a rush?'

"Bruiser laughed at him and said he always ate his meals on time; we were sorry to see him go but the boss paid him and fired him.

"That night when I got off and reached the outside a big man came up to me smiling. The face seemed familiar but I walked faster thinking he was trying to flirt with me. Then I recognized Bruiser. He said his main objective in getting a job in our shop was to see the lousy conditions in our place. He said he was a C.I.O. organizer and he gave me a leaflet stating that he was trying to unionize our shop and that there was to be a meeting the following night.

"As disgusted as I was with my lot, I don't have to tell

you that I was the first one to reach the meeting. Almost everybody was there for the meeting. Within six months everybody had joined with the exception of one girl. She wouldn't join and when we persistently tried to recruit her she told the boss.

"The boss was frantic. First he tried to intimidate, then he offered to start his own union 'with the same stipulations in our C.I.O. contract,' but we were not to be tricked by promises. We held our ground. He fired some of us—the rest walked out and we threw a picket line round the place. We had the one 'scab' and the boss imported others, protecting them by sending them to and from work in cabs.

"They messed up so that the boss called us back to work at union hours, union wages, and better conditions. 'That's my story," she concluded.

"Why did your landlady look upon me with suspicion?" I asked.

"Oh." She smiled. "You know the bosses are diehards even though the union is in our shop they still try to intimidate me into getting the girls to join the shop union. I told him to jump in a lake. He attempted to get loud and my landlady had her hubby put him out, since then she has been leary of anyone asking for me unannounced. I tell her when I'm expecting company."

"So, it's like that, is it?" I asked.

"Yes, it's like that." She smiled.

*February 1939*

# PART 3

# Pushcarts, Thursday Girls, and Other Workers

The stories in this section are hallmark pieces showcasing the work of a shadowy Harlem figure.

The craft of this unsung Harlem writer speaks for itself and tells me the name Vivian Morris should have become part of the renaissance literary folklore. For reasons I am unable to explain here, she did not.

In fact, every attempt made over a series of years to profile Vivian Morris failed. In one instance, a librarian who was unaware of these stories, told me after an exhaustive search that Ms. Morris simply did not exist in Harlem as a writer, at least not under this name. All sorts of speculation followed.

But what remains is the solid work this woman produced in just a few years. It takes us into nooks and crannies of this community rarely seen by outsiders. It is where the nitty meets gritty. Her ability to capture these varied, rich voices alone speaks volumes about her talents as a writer and an unknown biographer of this time and place.

Using these same standards, writer Frank Byrd and the other work you will read in this section offer us unparalleled glimpses of the authentic lives and times of working black people and how they coped with the vagaries of day-to-day living.

As Toni Morrisson once said, these stories celebrate the ordinary.

# Afternoon in a Pushcart Peddlers' Colony

## Frank Byrd

It was snowing shortly after noontime, when the snow changed to sleet and beat a tattoo against the rocks and board shacks that had been carelessly thrown together on the west bank of the Harlem River early in December of 1938. The cold blasts coming from the river sent the men shivering for cover behind their shacks where some of them had built huge bonfires to ward off the icy chills that swept down from the hills above.

Some of them, unable to stand it any longer, went below into the crudely furnished cabins that were located in the holds of some old abandoned barges that lay half in, half out of the water. But the men did not seem to mind. Even the rotting barges afforded them some kind of shelter. It was certainly better than nothing, not to mention that it was their home address: the foot of West 133 Street at Park Avenue; depression residence of a little band of part-time pushcart peddlers whose cooperative colony is one of the most unique in the history of New York City.

These men earn their living by cruising the streets long before daylight, collecting old automobile parts, pasteboard, paper, rags, rubber, magazines, brass, iron, steel, old clothes, or anything they can find that is salable as junk. They wheel their little pushcarts around exploring cellars, garbage cans, and refuse heaps. When they have a load, they turn their footsteps in the direction of the American Junk Dealers, Inc., whose site of wholesale and retail operations is located directly opposite the pushcart colony at West 134 Street and Park Avenue. Of the fifty-odd colonists, many are ex-carpenters, painters, bricklayers, auto mechanics, upholsterers, plumbers, and even an artist or two.

Most of the things the men collect they sell, but once in a while they run across something useful to themselves, like auto parts, pieces of wire, or any electrical equipment, especially because there were two or three electrical engineers in the group.

Joe Elder, a tall, serious-minded black, was the founder of the group that is officially known as the National Negro Civil Association. Under his supervision, electrically inclined members of the group set up a complete power plant that supplied all the barges and shacks with electric light. It was constructed with an old automobile engine and an electrical generator bought from the City of New York.

For a long time it worked perfectly. After a while, when a city inspector came around, he condemned it and the shacks were temporarily without light. It was just as well, perhaps, since part of the colony was forced to vacate the site in order to make room for a mooring spot for a coal company that rented a section of the waterfront. A rather modern and up-to-date community hall remains on the site, however.

One section of it is known as the gymnasium and many pieces of apparatus are to be found there. There are also original oil paintings in the other sections known as the library and recreation room. Here, one is amazed (to say the least) by the comfortable divans, lounges, bookshelves and, of all things, a drinking fountain. The water is purchased from the city and pumped directly to the hall and barges by

```
*****************************************

        SENIOR SAVINGS DAYS!

        April 22-24, 2003
        Seniors age 60 and over

           SAVE 20%!

        Some restrictions apply.
        See store for details.

STORE: 0089    REG: 04/82  TRAN#: 8302
SALE           04/17/2003  EMP:  00245
*****************************************
```

a homemade, electrically powered pump. In the recreation room there are also three pianos. On cold nights when the men want companionship and relaxation, they bring women there and dance to the accompaniment of typical Harlem jazz . . . jazz that is also supplied by fellow colonists.

After being introduced to some of the boys, we went down into Oliver's barge. It was shaky, weather-beaten, and sprawling, like the other half dozen that surrounded it. Inside, he had set up an old iron range and attached a pipe to it that carried the smoke out and above the upper deck. On top of the iron grating that had been laid across the open hole on the back of the stove were some spareribs that had been generously seasoned with salt, pepper, sage, and hot sauce. Later I discovered a faint flavor of a nutmeglike spice called mace in them. The smell and pungency of it and other spices filled the low-ceilinged room with an appetizing aroma. The faces of the men were alight and hopeful with anticipation.

Oliver had more than enough for everybody. Soon he began passing out tin plates for everyone. It makes my mouth water just to think of it. When we had gobbled up everything in sight, all of us sat back in restful contemplation puffing on our freshly lighted cigarettes. Afterward there was conversation, things the men elected to talk about of their own accord.

"You know one thing," Oliver began, "ain't nothin' like a man being his own boss. Now take today, here we is wit' plenty to eat, ha'f a jug of co'n (liquor) between us and nairy a woman to fuss aroun' wantin' to wash up dishes or mess aroun' befo' duh grub gits a chance to settle good."

"Dat sho is right," Evans Drake agreed. He was Oliver's helper when there were trucks to be repaired. "A 'oman ain't good fuh nuthin' but one thing." The conversation drifted along until I was finally able to ease in a query or two.

"Boys," I ventured, "how is it that none of you ever got

on Home Relief? You can get a little grub out of it, at least, and that would take a little of the load off you, wouldn't it?"

At this they all rose up in unanimous protest.

"Lis'en," one of them said, "befo' I'd take Home Relief I'd go out in duh street an' hit some bastard over de haid an' take myse'f some'n'. I know one of duh boys who tried to git it an' one of dem uppity little college boys ovah dere talked tuh him lak he was some damn jailbird or some'n'. If it had been me, I'd a bust hell outn' him an' walked outa duh place. What duh hell do we wants wid relief anyhow? We is all able-bodied mens an' can take it. We can make our own livin's."

This, apparently, was the attitude of every man there. They seemed to take fierce pride in the fact that every member of Joe Elder's National Negro Civil Association (it used to be called the National Negro Boat Terminal) was entirely self-supporting. They even had their own unemployment insurance fund that provided an income for any member of the group who was ill and unable to work. Each week the men give a small part of their earnings toward this common fund and automatically agreed to allow a certain amount to any temporarily incapacitated member. In addition to that, they divide among themselves their ill brother's work and provide a day and night attendant near his shack if his illness is at all serious.

After chatting awhile longer with them, I decided to leave.

"Well, boys," I said, getting up, "I guess I'll have to be shoving off. Thanks a lot for the ribs. See you again sometime."

Before leaving, however, I gave them a couple of packs of cigarettes I had on me in part payment for my dinner.

"Okay," they said. "Come ovah ag'in some time. Some Sat'd'y. Maybe we'll have a few broads (women) and a little co'n."

"Thanks."

Outside the snow and sleet had turned to rain and the snow that had been feathery and white was running down the riverbank in brown rivulets of slush and mud. It was a little warmer but the damp air still had a penetrating sharpness to it. I shuddered, wrapped my muffler a little tighter and turned my coat collar up about my ears.

There was wind in the rain, and behind me lay the jagged outline of the ramshackle dwellings. I hated to think of what it would be like, living in them when there was a scarcity of wood or when the fires went out.

*December 7, 1938*

# Street Cries and Criers

## *Frank Byrd and Terry Roth*

Evans Drake, Oliver, and the other men in the pushcart colony Frank Byrd visited were among an estimated three thousand licensed pushcart peddlers and three thousand other types.

Twenty-five years earlier, even more pushcart peddlers traversed the streets of this sprawling city at will, offering their merchandise without the benefit of licenses or any other official sanctions. They often took the chance of being chased away or arrested by the police if they lingered too long in any one spot. Under one mayoral administration various streets and sections were turned over as permanent pushcart markets, and there were still about eighty of these markets in various parts of the city in the 1930s. But the old street crier has managed to survive, even though he is often persecuted by neighborhood boards of trade, who make it more difficult for him to procure a license and who have him arrested if he dares to operate without one.

The sidewalks of Harlem resound to sprightlier music than is heard downtown on the east or west sides of the city, for carefree street vendors employ amusing jingles and syncopated rhythms in offering their wares. Market songs chanted and sung by black pushcart, horse cart, and cookshack sellers of foodstuffs impart an air of bristling hilarity to the curb commerce of the section.

Cracklin's, yams, sweet potatoes, pompanos, and "greasy greens and 'buttah' beans" are inspirations for songs. The merits of the melodies on hand are extolled in songs with such lucid titles as "The Street Chef," "Ice Cream Man," "Harlem Menu," "Vegetable Song," "Chef of New Orleans," "Hot Dawg Dan," and "Yallah Yams." While many of these Harlem market songs were originated on the spot when trade dragged, others have their origin in the South and in the British and Spanish-speaking West Indies.

Here's a song that greets you from the man wheeling a white cart, laden with foodstuffs:

*Sund'y folks eats chicken;*
*Mond'y ham an' greens;*
*Tuesd'y's de day fo' pork chops;*
*Wednesd'y rice an' beans.*
*Thursd'y de day fo' 'tatoes,*
*Candied sweets or French fried leans,*
*Fish on Frid'y some foks says,*
*But Sat'd'y gimme kidney beans,*
*Yasseh! Plain kidney beans!*

Or the tune of the "Street Chef":

*Ah'm a natu'al bo'n cook*
*An' dat ain't no lie,*
*Ah can fry po'k chops*
*An bake a lowdown pie.*
*So step right up*
*An' help you'se'f*
*Fum de vittles on*
*Mah kitchen she'f.*

Many of the tunes are improvised to meet the needs of the moment. Since the migration of West Indian blacks to New York, songs typical of the Island vendors have been heard in Harlem's teeming streets. One such cry of the West Indian vendor is

> *Yo tengo guineos!*
> *Yo tengo cocoas!*
> *Yo tengo pinas, tambien!*

Several of the songs are melodic recitations of wares on hand. A notable example of this type is

> *Ah got string beans!*
> *Ah got cabbage!*
> *Ah got collard greens!*
> *Ah got um! Ah got um!*

The crier repeats all his commodities in groups of three until the list is exhausted. Then he concludes with:

> *Ah got anythin' you' need,*
> *Ah'm de Ah-got-um man!*

Only two songs mention other localities:

> *Ah come fum down in New Orleans,*
> *Whar dey cook good vittles,*
> *Speshly greens.*

Thus the clam man lifts his voice:

> *In Virginny we goes clammin'*
> *We goes clammin' ev'y night*
> *An' de water lays dere still lak,*
> *Lawd, a mighty purty night!*

*Clams an' oysters fo' de takin'.*
*Ant we gits em ev'y one;*
  *Twell de sun comes up ashinin',*
  *An' our clammin' she am done.*
  *Ho! Clahmmmmmmmmmms!*
  *Ho! Clahmmmmmmmmmms!*

Some songs die out as trade languishes and others promptly arise to take their places. So long as there are curb markets in Harlem and a spirited, joyous race to buy from them, the pushcart man and the street crier of the section undoubtedly will continue to contribute to the unique cries of the city.

Some peddlers may keep the same territory for years. His merchandise usually is honest stuff although its cleanliness may be questioned and his cargo and cries vary. But the season and the neighborhood may compel him to change his location.

In the Bronx and Staten Island areas, the fish peddler is the most colorful vendor. Early every Friday morning he pounds the pavement, pushing his cart filled with the catch of the previous day. The neighborhood is aroused by a shrill, shrieking "Wahoo! Wahoo!" followed by a list of the fish he features. During the entire operation of selling, weighing, and cleaning the fish for the customer, he continues to send out inhuman cries to attract the attention of the housewife.

Another vendor with his raucous, indistinct cry is the fruit, vegetable, and flower man. Such strange cries as "Ahps! (apples) Peeeeeches! Flowwwwhers!" herald his approach. His horse, with its unkempt hide, drooped belly, projecting bones, and spavined legs leads the way. Huge price signs, with figures large enough to be read from the top floor, entice the buyer. The peddler winds in and out of the streets of the city, bellowing, yodeling, whining purposefully indistinct cries that will attract the curiosity of the housewife and bring her to the window to discover the cause—a philosophy similar to that of the extra news hawks. She is met by the tempting display of the wares and the attractive prices. The crier has made his contact.

In the old days, the crier was a romantic figure who approached his customer with melodious madrigals, and was a respected member of the community. He was a one-man fair, who often added a jig or a touch of comedy to lend color to his little songs. Harlem particularly has managed to retain some of this gaiety, but today we have grown accustomed to look upon the street vendor as a semi-mendicant and consider our purchases almost as alms. As an institution, the street crier is obsolete, but the rapidly vanishing members of that troupe still add a touch of color to the streets of New York.

*November 3, 1938*

# Homey the Vegetable Man

## Frank Byrd

One of the most thickly populated streets in Harlem lies
between Lenox and Seventh avenues on West 133 Street.
On a late summer afternoon, a section of 133 Street presents
a squalidly picturesque sight, with housewives leaning out of
the windows watching a parade put on for their benefit almost every afternoon. A gaggle of ragged, unkempt dusty-
skinned little urchins play carelessly in the street, while vegetable men hawk their wares, and corn liquor salesmen walk
up and down the block with their kitchen-manufactured, in-
toxicating beverages weighing them down. They've got business with all-day party goers whooping it up in the upstairs
buffet flats where music machines go full blast far into the
night.

"Homey," the vegetable man, comes through the block
every afternoon about one or two o'clock. Seldom does he
vary from this schedule, and his daily visit is eagerly looked
forward to by the buxom, colorful housewives. Homey's
song is vaguely reminiscent of one known as the "I Got Um
Man." The tune is a little different, however, and even
Homey himself is not certain what theme the lyrics will follow from day to day.

But the following is typical of his long drawn-out sing-
song wail:

*Ah got green peas for duh baby,*
*Got cabbage for duh ol' lad-ee*
*Got string beans for duh ol' man-nnnnn!*

The next day his song will probably take this turn:

*Got blackberries today fo'ks!*
*Blackberries for duh baby*
*Blackberries for duh ol' lady,*
*Blackberries for duh ol' man!*

Then he'll pause and say:

*If you ain't got no ol' man, take me.*

The women, their vanity tickled by this little amorous sally, will giggle and buy an extra pound of potatoes or cabbage from Homey, a born salesman when it comes to the ladies. . . .

# Kingfish

## *Marion Charles Hatch*

One of the stars of Harlem's caravan of peddlers was a man known in the neighborhoods as "Kingfish," who pulled his cart to the curb long enough to tell an interviewer the rhymes and ditties he sang were mostly spontaneous concoctions, not lyrics he had learned.

"These songs are not written down," said Kingfish, whose real name was Clyde Smith.

"You mean that they are different?"

"Yes, I sing them different. I put the words to the tune, to fit the occasion. I usually sing songs to fit the neighborhood. If I get in a Jewish neighborhood, I sing songs like 'Bei Mir Bist Du Shon.' I pick words to git the occasion. Words that rhyme fast and they can understand them fast.

"Well, I go in a colored neighborhood and they like something swingy. I might sing the same song but I put it in a swing tune. I go into Spanish neighborhood but I speak to them in Spanish.

"When I started peddling that was in 1932, that's when I started singing them. Hey, fish man, bring down you dishpan, that's what started it. 'Fish ain't but five cent a pound.' That 'aint' is the regular dialect. I found the people liked it and it was hard times then, the depression and people can hardly believe fish is five cents a pound, so they started buying. There was quite a few peddlers and somebody had to have something extra to attract the attention. So when I came around, I started making a rhyme, it was a hit right away.

"I found that my old songs wasn't going over so good so I had to get new tunes and new words—you know, just something new to attract attention.

"Come on down and gather round, I got the best fish in the town." That was the new development.

"There was no peddlin' down in North Carolina, in that particular town where I grew up, so I did not hear such songs and rhymes when I was a boy. In Wilmington, North Carolina, there used to be a man say, 'Bring out the dishpan, here's the fish man.' I used to hear my father and them talking about it.

"One of the first things I learned about peddling was, to be any success at all, you had to have an original cry. I know several peddlers that started out and they hollered, Old Fish Man, but it doesn't work.

"I've gone blocks where several fish men have gone already and sold fish like nobody had been there. When I sing, a certain amount of people will be standing around, looking and listening, and that attracts more people and whenever people see a crowd they think it's a bargain so they want to get in on it.

"When I cry it will be so loud that the people come to the windows, look out. They come down with bedroom shoes on, with bathrobes, and some have pans or newspapers to put the fish in.

"When I first come in a block nobody pays any attention. Then I start singing, get them to laughing and looking, and soon they start buying. A lot of them just hang around to hear the song. I always try to give the best I can for the money, the best fish for the money, and that makes repeated customers. A lot of people wait for my individual cry. . . . The average day I cover about eight blocks and spend about an hour in each block, sometimes longer. Sometimes, on Friday, it takes me about nine hours to cover what I would cover in seven hours another day.

"When I have crabs the kids like to see the crabs jump and bite, so they stand around in big crowds.

"Sometimes, when I sing, the kids be dancing the Lindy Hop and Trucking. The women buy most of the fish. I find Home Relief and WPA people the best customers. They buy more. They have to budget more than the average family.

"In white and Jewish neighborhoods I feature the words, but in the colored neighborhoods I feature the tune. In the Jewish neighborhood they appreciate the rhyming and the words more, while in the colored neighborhood they appreciate the swinging and the tune as well as the words. I put in a sort of jumping rhythm for the colored folks. That swing music comes right from old colored folks' spirituals. . . . In the street anything goes. Slap a word in there. The way I was this morning I was very good. I didn't mess them up. On the street whatever comes to my mind I say it, if I think it will be good. The main idea is when I got something I want to put over I just find something to rhyme with it. And the main requirement for that is mood. You gotta be in the mood. You got to put yourself in it. You've got to feel it. It's got to be more or less an expression than a routine. Of course sometimes a drink of King Kong [liquor] helps."

What follows are the lyrics to songs by Clyde Smith. Mr. Smith offers some brief commentaries on his methods for different kinds of songs:

**Fish and Vegetables**
That was my first original fish song. I put words from this into some of the others. This was the first fish song in my own tune. So after the people begin to get too familiar with the tune then I grasped the idea

of changing my tune to git the tune of the most popular song hit of that time.

*I got the greenest greens*
*I ever seen,*
*And I sure seen*
*A whole lot of greens*
*I got cauliflower*
*And mustard greens;*
*The best cauliflower*
*I ever seen.*
*So buy some,*
*Try some,*
*Take 'em home and fry some.*

## Fish and Vegetables

A song like this I'd just look on the wagon and rhyme
up something to match with it. When I sang this
song, this morning, I was just thinking of something
to rhyme then.

*I got vegetables today,*
*So don't go away.*
*Stick around*
*And you'll hear me say,*
*Buy 'em by the pound,*
*Put 'em in a sack*
*Hurry up and get 'em*
*Cause I'm not coming back.*
*I got apples, onions, and colored greens.*
*I got the best string beans,*
*The best you ever seen.*
*I got oranges, tomatoes, nice southern sweet potatoes.*
*I got yellow yams*
*From Birmingham.*

*And if you want some,*
*Here I am.*
*And if you don't want none*
*I don't give a yam, yam, yam.*
*I got green greens*
*From New Orleans.*


**Fish Cry**
  *Yo, ho ho, fish man!*
  *Bring down your dishpan!*
  *Fish ain't but five cent a pound.*
  *So come on down,*
  *And gather around,*
  *I got the best fish*
  *That's in this town.*
  *I got porgies,*
  *Crockers too.*
  *I ain't got but a few,*
  *So you know what to do.*
  *Come on down,*
  *And gather round,*
  *Cause my fish ain't*
  *But five cent a pound.*
  *I've got 'em large*
  *And I've got 'em small;*
  *I got 'em long and I got 'em tall;*
  *I've got 'em fried,*
  *I got 'em broiled;*
  *And I can't go home till I sell 'em all!*
  *So yo, ho, ho, fish man!*
  *Bring down your dishpan!*
  *Cause fish ain't but five cent a pound!*

**Fish Cry in Spanish**

*Pesco fresco senquo contivo libera!*
*Fish, fresh, five cent a pound!*

**Crab Song**

*I've got crabs.*
*They bite and nab.*
*I got crabs,*
*That punch and jab.*
*I got crabs,*
*That sing like Cab [Calloway].*
*So be like my cousin,*
*And buy a couple of dozen*
*Of my crabs today.*
*Buy 'em by the dozen.*
*I'll put 'em in a sack,*
*Hurry up and get 'em*
*Cause I ain't coming back.*
*Come on, folks,*
*I got crabs today.*
*Better get some,*
*Before I go away.*
*Cause all my crabs*
*Are nice and live,*
*You can take my word*
*That that's no jive.*

**Shad Song**

I made that tune up myself.
*I got shad,*
*Ain't you glad?*
*I got shad,*
*So don't be mad.*
*I got shad,*
*Go tell your dad.*
*It's the best old shad he ever had.*

*I got shad,*
*Caught 'em in the sun.*
*I got shad.*
*I caught just for fun.*
*So if you ain't got no money*
*You can't have none.*
*I got shad,*
*Ain't you glad?*
*I got shad,*
*Tell your great-granddad.*
*It's the best old shad he ever had.*

## Tisket-a-Tasket

A couple of years ago, when this song was popular,
they liked it then. When a song is popular and I
work up my time to that, I work out words to fit the
tune. When a song is in its height of popularity
people will ask you to sing that fish song at that time.
When the popularity of the song dies away that
song ceases to be a hit even with the fish customers.
So each of my songs represents a certain era of
music.

*A tisket, a tasket,*
*I sell fish by the basket.*
*And if you folks don't buy some fish,*
*I'm gonna put you in a casket.*
*I'll carry you on down the avenue,*
*And not a thing you'll do.*
*I'll dig, dig, dig, all around,*
*Then I'll put you in the ground.*
*A tisket, a tasket,*
*I sell 'em by the basket.*

## Stormy Weather

I wouldn't sing this one in a Jewish neighborhood.
They don't know the tune and they couldn't appreciate that song. Only in a colored neighborhood.

*I can't go home till all my fish is gone.*
*Stormy weather,*
*I can't keep my fish together,*
*Sellin' 'em all the time.*
*If you don't buy 'em*
*Old rag man will get me.*
*If you do buy 'em*
*Your folks'll kinda let me*
*Walk in the sun once more.*
*I don't see why*
*You folks don't come and buy,*
*Stormy weather,*
*Come on,*
*Let's get together,*
*Sellin' 'em all the time.*

## Bei Mir Bist Du Shon

This goes over good in either Jewish or colored neighborhoods, but I have to swing it up a bit in the
colored neighborhoods.

*Bei mir bist du shon,*
*I got big break on fish again.*
*Bei mir bust du shon,*
*I think they're grand.*
*I could say bello bello,*
*And even voom de van.*
*That would only tell you,*
*How grand they are.*
*Bei mir bust du shon,*

*I got flounders again.*
*Bei mir bist du shon,*
*I know they're grand.*


## Jumpin' Jive

In these jump joints, that means where they dance and
drink and smoke marijuana weeds. The marijuana
weed is a jumping jive. The expression is 'Knock me in
a jive there, Gates.' That means 'Give me a marijuana
cigarette.' The jumping jive is suppose to make you do
all these things. When you have the jumping jive on,
you're supposed to do all these things and buy the fish.

*Jim, jam, jump, jumpin' jive*
*Make you buy yo fish on the east side.*
*Oh, boy,*
*What you gonna say there, Gates?*
*Jim, jam, jump, jumpin' jive.*
*When you eat my fish,*
*You'll eat four or five.*
*Pal of mine, pal of mine, Swanee shore.*
*Come on, buy my fish once more.*
*Oh boy, oh boy,*
*Jim, jam, jump, jumpin' jive.*
*Make you dig your fish on the mellow side.*
*Oh boy, what you gonna say there, Gates?*
*Don't you hear them [hep cats call]?*

[That means the music is in you and you're all livened
up. You want to dance and swing it.]

*Come on, boys, and let's buy 'em all.*
*Oh boy, what you gonna say there, Gates?*

["Boy" is a variation for Gates.]

**Hi in Ho Fish Song?**
[Tune of "Minnie the Moocher."]

*I'm the hi di hi di ho fish man;*
*And I can really sell fish, I can;*
*Some time I sell 'em high.*
*Hi de hi de hi de hi.*
*Some time I sell 'em mighty low.*
*Low, ho, ho, ho, ho, ho.*
*I sell 'em up,*
*I sell 'em down,*
*I sell 'em all around this town.*
*So hi de hi de hi.*
*And hi de ho de ho,*
*Hi de hi de hi.*
*Hi de ho, ho, ho, ho.*

**Don't You Feel My Leg**
*Don't you feel my hand*
*Cause I'm that old fish man.*
*And if you feel my hand,*
*I'll fill up your pan.*
*So don't you feel my hand.*
*No, don't you feel my thigh,*
*I'll tell you why,*
*And if you feel my thigh,*
*You'll come down and buy.*
*You'll come down and buy.*
*You'll go home and fry.*
*So don't you feel my thigh.*

**Song to Kid the Ice Man**
*Say, ice man,*
*I want some ice today,*

*So hurry up and bring it,*
*Before I go away,*
*Bring fifty pound,*
*And hurry right down,*
*Cause you got*
*The best ice in this town.*
*You can chop it up*
*And make it small,*
*Better bring it quick*
*Or not at all.*
*I want to put it on my fish*
*Because it's nice and hot.*

## Coal Cry

[A phonetic approximation.]
*I got coal,*
*So get your gold!*
*I got coal,*
*And I'm gettin old*
*So get your gold,*
*And buy my coal.*
*Better buy my coal*
*Doggone your coal.*
*I got coal.*

## Once Upon a Time

*Once upon a time I fell in love,*
*With an angel from up above.*
*Yes, I fell in love,*
*With a heavenly dove,*
*Once upon a time.*

## Let's Go Fishing

The zazu part came out of a song but the rest of the
tune I made up myself.

Let's go fishing,
Down by the hole.
You get the bait
I get the pole.
Let's go for a ride,
Let's don't go far.
I'll furnish the gas,
You furnish the car.
Let's have a fish fry,
Let's begin.
I got the fish,
You get the gin.
Za au, whoo, za zu, zee.
Zazu, zazu, zazu, zoo.


## Song about the [WPA] Recording

Now I sing all these songs,
For Mr. Halpert and Hatch.
I bin singin' an hour,
I guess I've sang a batch.
They seem quite appreciative
And I enjoyed it, too.
If nobody else don't like 'em
They know what they can do.
Mr. Hatch asked me to sing 'em
For the WPA.
So when you hear them
Just swing and sway.
Don't fuss,
And don't fight,
Cause the jive is right.


*November 29, 1939*

# Life in the Harlem Markets

## Frank Byrd

Mae Berkeley is probably the most unique merchant in the Park Avenue Market. She is not a licensed peddler and, unlike many of those who are, she does not work at her stand every day. On the contrary, she puts in her appearance only on those days when she feels particularly good or when the weather is bright and inviting. She is a vendor of native African curios done in clay, brass, wood, straw, ivory, and other materials available to the tribes of Africa.

How Mae, who lives at 222 West 121 Street, began selling these pieces of native handiwork in the marketplace is a story all by itself. Mae is not African. She is from Trinidad in the British West Indies. She has always been interested, however, in black folklore and art, and as a consequence, she has sought in almost every direction for additional information concerning every branch of black art. Feeling that she could attain a wider and more authentic knowledge by studying the most authentic forms, she naturally turned to the African.

Her first step was to widen her acquaintance among Africans in New York. Her search led to the discovery of the Native African Union at 254 West 135 Street. Here she met all, or practically all, of those who make their homes in Harlem. She also learned that a troupe of native African ballet dancers was staging periodic dance recitals at Town Hall, Roerich Hall, and occasionally, in Harlem. Through some of her newly found friends, she was able to study and dance with this group, having already achieved a fair reputation as a dancer in Harlem and Greenwich Village nightclubs. Her dancing led to more friendly relations, and she soon began to inquire about the possibility of importing native handicrafts from the various tribes represented by the group. The idea met with approval and it was not long before she was receiving regular shipments of curios, war implements, etc., from both the South and West Coasts of Africa.

When Mae received her first shipment of goods, she was dancing in a little nightclub in the Village called the Rubyait. She received permission from the management to sell her things there. Her sales were far more numerous than she expected. It was not long before she had placed parts of her shipment in curio shops in West 4 and 8 streets. They attracted much attention. Mae decided to branch out to Harlem. She began with free exhibits in the public library and in the homes of various club women. This gave her the necessary publicity. She let it become known that she could be found either in the Eighth or Park Avenue markets or at the Native African Union.

Mae's sales have increased greatly in the past two years. If it were not for her dancing, which takes so much of her time, she would probably make a regular, paying business of this hobby. Instead, she devotes only a comparatively small part of her spare time to it. She does, however, exhibit her own private collection at all dance recitals of the group.

When asked why she does not open a regular shop or place a helper on each of her stands in both Harlem markets, she replies: "Some day, perhaps, I will. Now, I am much too busy with my dancing. Besides, I don't just want to sell them. I want my people to learn of the value of their native art."

*January 19, 1939*

# The Harlem Market

## Frank Byrd

The Harlem Market at three o'clock in the morning is a kaleidoscopic canvas of bright lights, scurrying figures, and the dim outlined silhouettes of trucks, baskets of fruit, and many-sized crates of fresh vegetables. It is a part of New York little known and seldom seen by any persons other than those who make their living there; yet it is vitally important to the daily welfare of more than half the population in all the surrounding community.

Walking through the dark streets in the early morning, one notices that the main roadway is filled on both sides with trucks, wagons, and merchandise piled harem-scarem on the sidewalk, awaiting delivery to the many retail stores and pushcart markets of Harlem. Around these trucks and in the warehouses surrounding them, a veritable army of workers sort and load the produce that must be delivered not later than nine o'clock in the morning.

All of this activity is the result of the commission-merchant business. This business came into existence when the peddlers found it increasingly difficult to put in their daily appearances at the markets and carry on the bargaining with farmers who came there to dispose of their wares. Besides that, many of their stands were located so far away from the wholesale market that it was quite impossible for them to deliver their own merchandise. They were forced to hire independent truckmen who charged them exorbitant rates and made it virtually impossible for them to make a decent profit from the sale of their goods. The commission merchants who owned their own trucks were able to offer them a reduced rate, providing the peddlers bought their produce from the "middlemen." They were also able to save the peddler two or three hours each day by relieving him of the responsibility of coming to the market, shopping around for his merchandise, and usually going back to his stand so tired that he was unable to work. The peddlers, realizing this, eventually gave up going to the markets themselves or sending their truckmen. They found it very convenient to let the commission merchants do their shopping for them. When this became customary, the commission merchants immediately increased their prices to a rate that yielded them more net profits than the farmer who originally produced the foodstuffs or the peddler who sold it to the customer.

Being the middlemen, they discovered, was far more profitable than being either the producer or retailer. Sometimes they are able to make especially good bargains with the farmers by purchasing huge lots outright and selling them at the regular price to the retailers.

On these days, they make what is colloquially known as a "killing." To a great extent, they corner the market on certain rare fruits or vegetables that are then in demand and sell them at such high rates that it is almost impossible for the peddler to buy them. Yet he cannot refuse to buy them because customers demand the article. Therefore he is forced to carry it as a part of his stock.

Many peddlers have corroborated this fact, including Louis Feldstein, a pushcart peddler of the Eighth Avenue Market who has been in business for thirteen years. He explained that when he is able to go to the market (where the farmers congregate) he is very often able to buy merchandise at almost one-half the price he ordinarily pays for it. This is especially true when the farmer has been in the market all night and is anxious to go home. He might be willing to let a large lot of produce go for only a small part of what the wholesale price for that day would be.

The commission merchants are also alert for these bargains. It is then that they are able to make their best profits for, even though they are able to buy cheaply, they always sell at the current market price. For instance, they might buy five or ten thousand carrots at a half-cent each and sell them for one- and one-half cents a piece. The peddler, in turn, will sell these same carrots at the rate of ten cents a bunch (five in a bunch), or two cents each, which means that he makes only a one-half-cent profit on them while the commission merchant realizes a clear profit of one cent on each carrot. These figures, of course, are only comparative, but they are accurate enough to give the reader a fair idea of how these transactions are carried out.

The farmers and the pushcart peddlers spend long hours of hard work producing and passing this merchandise on to the consumers, but the middlemen are really the ones in the tri-cornered deal who benefit most by the transaction. There are times, of course, when the peddler is ambitious enough to save the middleman's fee on his purchases. At such times, he rises early (about three o'clock in the morning), goes to the market, bargains with the farmers, and hires an independent truckman to deliver his goods. The tariff on trucking, incidentally, is greatly reduced in comparison to what it used to be. For this reason, it is to the peddler's advantage to do his own buying and later hire an independent truckman to make deliveries for him. The current price on deliveries runs from eight to ten cents per crate or basket.

The commission merchants, in order to meet the competition of these new, low prices, have (in the cases of many old customers) resorted to free or half-price delivery. Only the larger firms are able to afford this, however, because of the high cost of gasoline and oil, not to mention the wear and tear on their trucks. The independent truckmen seem to feel, however, that this is only a temporary measure and are confident that the commission merchants, if they continue this policy, will only increase the price of the merchandise.

At East 102 Street near the East River, the farmers congregate in a separate market of their own where the buyers from the wholesale houses as well as the itinerant pushcart peddlers come to bargain with them. Many of the farmers come there (in summer) as early as eight or nine o'clock at night and remain there as late as seven or eight o'clock the next morning. It is at this time that the individual peddlers have an opportunity to shop for themselves. In winter, it is different. The farmers come at about three or four o'clock in the morning, dispose of their produce and leave immediately. At this season of the year, the peddlers make less profit than usual because they are forced to buy at standard market prices. The only thing that keeps prices down is that practically all of the commission merchants, with the possible exception of a very few, are individual dealers.

## Eighth Avenue Market: Pickle Peddler

Patsy Randolph is undoubtedly one of the most unusual pushcart peddlers in the Eighth Avenue Market. Unlike the average peddler there, she has no specialty, such as fruits and vegetables, but sells any and every kind of product that she feels is seasonally the most valuable and desirable. There are times when she peddles cooking utensils, cosmetic products, odd and damaged lots of men's and women's furnishings, or thoroughly blackened canned goods bought wholesale or at fire sales. Her current product, however, is the most unusual of all. She is selling pickles, pepper sauces, spices, and relishes exclusively. The pickles she makes and packs herself.

The biggest seller of this entire lot, incidentally, happens to be pickled watermelon rind. Her profits on this Southern delicacy amount to something well over ninety-five percent because the rinds cost her absolutely nothing. She has obtained the permission of store owners who sell individual five- and ten-cent slices at their street stands to collect all the rinds she wants from their baskets. At the height of the summer season, she takes these rinds home, prepares and packs them in fruit jars, and sells them to a highly appreciative buying public that has long since been accustomed to this fine "down-home" dish that adds a tasty flavor to meats, especially roast pork or the more widely favored pork chops.

The secret of her sales success for this particular product, she says, depends entirely upon the way it is prepared, and as further proof of her versatility, she offers the following recipe as permanent proof of her claim to the title: "Best-maker-of-pickled-watermelon-rinds-in-Harlem."

"This pickle is very easy to prepare," she declared. "First you scoop out all the remaining red meat from the inside of the rind. Now peel the thin green rind from the outside. Cut the white rind into small cubes and cover with water that has been salted, two teaspoons of salt to the pint. Leave the rind in the water for an hour or two, while you prepare this syrup: Add a quart of cider vinegar to two pounds of brown sugar. Add two tablespoons of whole cloves and a few small sticks of cinnamon. You can also add a few raisins as an additional flavoring and dressing. You don't have to, of course, but they help to round out the flavor. Bring this liquid to a slow boil. Afterwards, drain the brine from the melon rind and rinse the pieces with fresh, cold water. Add the melon rind to the syrup and let it cook until tender. Guard against letting it get too soft, though. You can find this out by sticking it with a fork.

"When the rind is tender, put it in fruit jars and pack them tightly. Now reheat the syrup and pour it boiling into the jars over the rind. Add a few cloves to each jar. Be sure and seal the jars tightly. This keeps them from spoiling and protects the good, homemade flavor."

## *Popular Southern Foods*

Located at frequent intervals in the heart of the Eighth Avenue Market, there are more than a dozen stoves on wheels that indicate to the neighborhood shopper another stand dedicated to the preparation of good old Southern yams. The number of these street stoves is also sufficient proof that yams (baked, candied, or fried) rate exceptionally high with housewives of the neighborhood who, because of long hours on their jobs, find it difficult to do their own baking of this ever-popular delicacy of the old South.

A recent interview with operators of these stands revealed that baked yams are purchased in great numbers not only by the potato-loving Negroes from Dixie, but also by the many buxom black women hailing from one of the several West Indian Islands. Even in those remote corners of the globe the popularity of the lowly sweet potato has achieved a new market high. The vendors were almost unanimous in their explanation of the reason why so many people buy their yams in the market in preference to preparing them at home: in order to keep their gas bills down to normal, many of these women who might enjoy cooking their own yams refrain from doing so for reasons of economy.

Beside that, it is usually late in the afternoon when the majority of these housewives leave their service jobs in various sections of the city. When they arrive at home, it is too late to do much cooking, even if they would like to.

"That's the way we keep in business. We sell our yams so cheap that it don't pay for the people to cook them at home. The extra trouble is worth the few extra cents they'd have to pay for enough for a good meal."

Inquiries about the production of the potato crops

yielded the following information: that North Carolina, South Carolina, and Georgia are the biggest producers of the more or less famous yellow yams. Virginia, however, has championship claims on the production of the giant white yams that are so popular in that section of the country prior to and during the Christmas holiday season. The holiday season brings to mind "potato-pone" (pronounced, "p'teter peon" in Georgia). This unique dish is a holiday delicacy that is enjoyed in the home of the poorest person at Christmastime. This does not mean, however, that it is monopolized entirely by the poor. In the homes of the old gentry, it is served and eaten with gusto. The final product is somewhat similar in taste to well-seasoned potato-custard pie but it contains so much nutmeg and other spices that it emerges from the oven with a dark, muddy color faintly reminiscent of overdone bread pudding. This unappetizing color in no way detracts from the fine flavor and palatability of this down-home concoction, however. Within the past few years the dish has achieved surprising popularity in Harlem. It was first introduced locally by natives of Georgia who came to New York during the sudden postwar migration of Negroes from all parts of the South to various cities in the East and Midwest. New Yorkers ate it first with much misgiving but ended up pleasantly surprising their hostesses by asking for second helpings.

The recipe was passed around from one person to another until today this dish alone is second in Harlem to hogshead or pigtails-peas-and-rice as a Christmas holiday dish. In the markets, the yam vendors who are enterprising enough to make their own potato-pone at home bring it to their stands, keep it warm on top of their ovens, and find a ready sale. In fact, the demand is far greater than the available supply.

The popularity of the sweet potato is further attested to by the composition of a popular market song exclusive to Harlem. The name of it is "Th' Sweet Pertater Man." The lyric, composed by heaven knows whom, extols the hugeness and the delicious flavor of the potatoes sold on his, John Peddler's, stand. It is typically expressive of the merits and popularity of this vegetable that, in Uptown New York, it is not just another dish for the table but a glorified delicacy of the first order.

*December 28, 1938*

# Fatso the Slickster, Pullman Porters', and Dining Car Folklore

## Frank Byrd

Shortly after the Civil War, a cadre of uniformed, clean shaven, black men made their appearance in towns and cities across America wherever rail lines crossed. For the next one hundred years, these ail servants—known as Pullman porters—were a fixture on long-distance trains that crisscrossed the nation. The name was derived from the company these men worked for, the Pullman Company, the Chicago company that manufactured sleeping cars. Later they organized into a union called the Brotherhood of Sleeping Car Porters.

"It is regrettable . . . that the name of the first Pullman porter isn't known," according to Stewart H. Holbrook, author of *Life of the Pullman Porter*. The great Chicago fire of 1871 destroyed all of the early records of the Pullman Company. Holbrook speculates that the first Pullman porter was probably a "well trained ex-slave."

In black communities, employment as a Pullman porter was considered an honorable profession, and in some respects, an elite one usually populated by sophisticated men with college degrees who were unable to find better jobs in their chosen professions.

"The Pullman porter is selected with discrimination and is also carefully trained," Holbrook said in his 1947 book. "Many families now have their third generation of porters on the road, for [the] occupation tends to become hereditary and Pullman employees stand high in any Negro community." Wages for these men, members of the Brotherhood of Sleeping Car Porters, ranged from a minimum of $89.50 a month to $112.50 for a porter who doubled as a conductor of his car. By comparison, the WPA writers qualified for welfare and were paid about $80 a month.

One of the places where these soldiers of service on the nation's rail lines were commonly seen was the streets of Harlem. The following story is lore that Frank Byrd acquired about one of these porters, known as Fatso the Slickster.

Some guys are too smart for their own good. But you couldn't tell Fatso that. He believed that a sucker was not only born every minute, but that he was born to be taken by Fatso, himself, in person. He also figured the world owed him a living . . . a soft living. No other kind would do. And so, with only these simple rules to go by, Fatso constantly kept his eyes peeled for a "square," a soft touch on the loose.

The porters in our crew were running between New York and Chicago before Repeal [of alcohol prohibition. The sale of alcoholic beverages was outlawed in 1920 and did not become legal again until Repeal came in 1933]. One weekend we laid over in Chi, the next we spent in New York. Fatso let no grass grow under his feet in either place. He got himself a beat-up apartment in both towns and opened up a corn joint; one of those places where porters, taxicab drivers, occasional strays, and local lushes hang out during their spare time. In short, a clip joint.

He did a good business in both places, too. What with corn selling at fifty cents a pint and him being able to make five or six gallons in one of his homemade stills for less than a buck a batch. He also carted a good supply along with him on the trains and was able to clean up when we ran into a bunch of traveling salesmen or good-time-Charlies who used to need a quick one to wake up with. Once in a while he would make a pretty good sale to a group of chorus girls, jittery from a long trek on the road and in need of a little something to celebrate their homecoming. Yes sir, it was Fatso's theory to catch every living human.

"I misses nobody!" he was fond of saying. "When dem quartahs start jingling in mah jeans, I don' know duh diff'ence. Dey all makes de same kinda sof', sweet music tuh mah yeahs."

But what I started to tell you about was Fatso's joint up in Harlem. He had a cute little coffee-colored chick in there who had his chops to the right turn and waiting for him on the back of the stove whenever he hit town, and who had the week's receipts totaled down to the last nickel. She was hip too. Whenever any of the plainclothes boys came gum-shoeing around, the kid knew what to do. She could look as innocent as a MGM starlet an' they never got to first base with her. No sir, nary a drink could they get from that baby.

One Sunday night some of us went up to Fatso's, got to fooling around playing tonk and pinochle, and it was seven o'clock in the morning before we knew it. Well, we were due at the yards by ten, so we decided to make a night of it. Some guy dressed in overalls and looking pretty down in the mouth came in. He was a stranger to us but he wanted to take a hand in the game, so we let him. Especially since Emma, Fatso's old lady, didn't seem to mind. We decided he must be one of the boys from the block.

Not long afterwards, Big Tom, the collector for the music company (you know, those nickel machines they have in the back of gin mills) came in. He fumbled around for a while taking the back off the box and collecting his change. Then he played us a few free records.

Pretty soon, the guy in overalls said: "Hows about a drink, boys?"

"Don't care if I do." Blue-Jay answers him.

"Okay with me too," I says. "We may as well go in right this morning."

So the guy calls Emma.

"Knock us a little drink of King Kong, babe," he tells her. Emma don't make a move. She just stands there looking at him with a queer sort of expression on her face. Then I figures something must be wrong. Maybe the guy's a flatfoot.

"I'm sorry, Mister," Emma opines. "I ain't got no King Kong." "Sure you have, girlie," the guy insists. "I'm all right. Don't you remember me? I was up here th' other night with Steve an' Eddie an' some uh th' boys."

"Naw suh," Emma says, backing away. "You all mus' be thinkin' bout some otha place. 'Twont hyeah."

Fatso is laying in bed in the other room with the door open and hears the conversation. He raises up on one elbow and we hears the bed groan under the weight of his 265 pounds.

"Emma!" he calls out, "What you mean sayin' we ain't got nuthin' tuh drink? Hyeah 'tis Monday mo'nin' an' I ain' broke duh ice yet, an' you sayin' we ain' got nuthin'? Gi'e dat man a drink!"

Emma always did what Fatso told her without question but this was once when she stood her ground.

"Ef'n you all wants him tuh have one, Fatso, you be'er come an' gi'e it to 'im yo'se'f."

The next minute Fatso came paddling out of the bedroom with his pajama shirt flapping over his big belly, and looking for all the world like a flannel horse blanket, shuffled over to the icebox and pulled out a jug of corn. He set it on the table, gave each of us a glass, and said: "Go fo yo' se'f, boys."

To the man in overalls he said: "Ten cents a drink, brother."

The guy filled all our glasses, tasted the stuff, spat it out on the floor and stood up.

"All right, big boy," he drawled, "Git your pants on. We're gonna take a little walk."

"Well, you should a seen Fatso's face. I'll never forget it. It was a sight to remember."

*March 9, 1939*

# Fatso's Mistake

## *Frank Byrd*

Small's Paradise on West 135 Street is a well-known joint uptown where you can usually find Pullman porters killing time during layovers. Officially, they belong to the Brotherhood of Sleeping Car Porters. Leroy Spriggs was one of them. Listen in on a conversation Spriggs has about the legendary Fatso one afternoon at Small's.

"Set up another one, Mike, then I've got to go," Leroy said. "I'm late."

Mike came down from the other end of the bar, refilled the two glasses and went on with his crossword puzzle. Leroy began where he left off.

"I walked into this guy Fatso's place to collect the nickels from the machine. That was while I was working for the Gabel Music people, the year before I got this porter's job. There sat Fatso playing Tonk with Pretty Boy Matthews. You know Matthews, the plainclothes cop who works out of the Thirty-second Precinct?

"Well, I been knowing him long before he ever thought of being a cop; we were kids together back in the old days in Thirty-fourth Street. Matthews had done me a lot of favors too. So, in a way, it ain't up to me to tell Fatso that he's playing Tonk with a cop who's dressed up like one of the truck drivers or longshoremen who hang out in his place.

Cause if I hip him, Matthews will know I'm responsible and it won't help me none in my racket, see? Still, Fatso is a good customer of mine and I often take twenty-five or thirty dollars out of his machine in a week. So, I'm in the middle. Course I hates to see this guy Fatso go to jail, seeing as how he's just getting started in his new joint; I figures it would be a shame to see him fold up without giving the place a chance.

"Well, I fumble around with the machine for a while, count my change, and start over to Fatso with the receipt. Then I get the idea of writing a note on the back of the receipt which Fatso has to sign. So I quickly scribbles: 'I think the guy you're Tonking with is a cop. Don't sell him no drink.' Then I hands it to Fatso to sign. He sees my note and says kinda saltylike: 'Don't you think I know how to run my business, ol' man?'

"That's all I need to hear. I grabs up the receipt, hustles back to the machine, and gets ready to get outa there as fast as I can when Matthews says: 'Well, Big Boy, I'm broke. Gue'ss I'll be going.'

" 'Aw don't go man,' Fatso pleads. 'Stick around and get even. I'll give you a deuce on that fine watch you're wearing. We can play one hand for that an' if you wins, that'll put you even.'

" 'Okay,' Matthews agrees, taking off his watch. Then he plays the hand and Fatso beats him again.

" 'Looks like I can't have any luck,' Matthews observes. 'Give me a drink and I'll go get a new bankroll. How much is it, a quarter?'

" 'Yeah, if you want a double,' Fatso tells him.

" 'All right, lemme have it. I got just a quarter left.'

"Fatso brings out the drink but it's easy to see that he don't believe Matthews's story about having more dough.

" 'Well, pal,' he says, 'I always collects in front. You don't mind, do you?'

" 'No, I don't mind.' Matthews says, reaching into his pocket. 'Will it be all right if I pay you with this?'

"He pulls out his police badge and throws it on the table. Fatso takes one look at it, measures the distance from where he stands to the window, but just as he's about to try for it, Matthews reaches over and slaps the cuffs on him. Not until then does Fatso realize his mistake."

*March 22, 1939*

# Chef Watkins's Alibi

## Frank Byrd

New York Sleeping Car porters on the Pennsylvania Railroad fondly just called it "the Pennsy." Old Chef Watkins, a short, fat, squatty little black man was one of them. He also had the meanest disposition of any cook I've ever known, and I've known some mean ones in my time. He had a jet black skin, full pork-chop lips, and a belly on him that shook like tapioca when he was working the lunch-hour rush. He could cuss like a top sergeant and seemed to take a fiendish delight in giving the boys hell.

When we had taken about as much of his crap as we could stand, the boys got together and hatched up a plot to get rid of him. The trouble was, he stood in too well with the big bosses. He was one of those kowtowing, old-fashioned, handkerchief-headed darkies who would grin and yes a white man to death and give his Negro subordinates hell from morning till night.

We all knew that Chef Watkins was killing the company for everything he could steal. He had bought a huge, rambling old country house down in Maryland and a large breeding farm for jumping horses and prize stock . . . and you can't do that on what the Pullman Company pays you even if you have worked for them twenty years and have full seniority rating.

Nothing was too big or too small for him to steal. He had worked out a system with the commissary steward, and between them they did an awful lot of bill padding. In addition to that, he used to throw hams, chickens, legs of lamb, and anything else off to his wife or children whenever he passed his place near Bowie. You know, that junction where the Pennsy crosses the Seaboard?

Well, the boys got together and decided that Old Chef had to go. So what we did was to drop a little hint here and there to Mr. Palmer, our chief steward, that if he'd just happen around the kitchen when we were nearing that Seaboard crossing, he might find out what was happening to all our missing supplies that he was catching hell about back in the New York commissary.

To make it short and sweet, when we neared the junction this day, Chef Watkins was busy, as usual, getting his hams and chickens together to toss out the window to his wife who was armed, as was customary, with her old potato sack in which she carried home the bacon; not to mention the eggs (well-packed, of course).

Just as the train slowed down and the chef leaned back, ham poised like a football about to take flight, Old Man Palmer drawled in that deep Southern accent, as only Old Man Palmer could: "What in hell do you think you're doin' there, Watkins?"

Well, you could have knocked the chef over with a feather. He stumbled, coughed, and did everything but turn pale. It's the only time I've ever seen him stuck for words.

"Know one thing, Mr. Palmer?" he finally sputtered. "Dere's a ol' black, nappy-headed woman who stands out dere by duh crossin' and cusses me an' calls me all sorta names ever time I pass hyeah, an' it makes me so mad I jus' grabs up duh fus thing I gits mah han's on an th'ows it at 'er."

# Chef Sampson's Icebox

## *Frank Byrd*

When we were running on the Pennsy, there was an old chef on our run who was the most ornery old cuss you ever heard of. His name was Sampson and he could out-cuss a blue streak. He was a dictator in his kitchen and there was hell to pay any time the dining car waiters and cook's assistants did not hew the line as far as chef's kitchen rules were concerned.

There was one thing he was particularly mean about. He didn't allow anybody, not even the steward or second cook, to go into his icebox. The steward had the right to, of course, but even he used to humor the old man because he was so efficient in his work. And any time the second or third cooks wanted anything, they had to say:

"Going in, Chef!"

Meaning, of course, the icebox. Well, if he felt in the mood, he'd say: "Go 'head in!"

If he didn't, the answer would be: "Wait a minute. I'll git it for you. I got my box 'ranged jus' lak I want it an' I don't want it mixed up."

We also had an inspector named Mr. Trout. He was a tall, rangy, mean-looking cracker from down in Georgia. He used to pop up unexpectedly in all sorts of little out-of-the-way stations, board the train, and start gumshoeing around, seeing what he sees. Well, this day he climbs aboard at Altoona and just when we're speeding through the mountains to Pittsburgh, Old Man Trout eases back into the kitchen and starts rummaging through Chef's icebox. Chef had his back turned and was busy chopping some onions on a board near the window. He heard the commotion, however, and, without turning around said: "Git the hell outa dat icebox."

Old Man Trout said nothing, but continued his inspection.

"Git outa dat icebox, I say!" Chef repeated, still without turning around.

Old Man Trout straightened up to his full six, rawbony feet, took one contemptuous look at Chef Sampson and said: "Who in hell do you think you're talkin' to? My name is TROUT!"

Chef Sampson stared back as cool as you please. Finally he drawled: "I wouldn't give a damn if it's CATFISH. You git duh hell outa my icebox!"

*March 28, 1939*

# West Indies

## *Ellis Williams*

This first-person account by Ellis Williams is a departure
in style from the other pieces in this collection. However, similiar accounts were quite common in WPA regions throughout America. The archives contain many
similiar narratives where WPA writers offer personal
glimpses of various places, events, or experiences they
encountered. Williams's piece follows this style.

Down in the West Indies, I am a law clerk and stenographer.
I was largely dependent on my parents for existence, and
because of that I am discontented with my lot. I am Aquar-
ius, born to travel they say. The nomadic urge engulfs me.
I want to leave home and the dependency of my folk. I hear
and read a lot of America. People say it is a "bed of roses."
A fortune easy to acquire and a profession easier still. I want
to go! I want to go!

I am only in my teens and my parents try to discourage
me. I listen to their good counsel but cannot be dissuaded.
I feel that I have been a parasite on them too long. I am
going even if I suffer, and there is one thing certain, if I do,
they will never learn it from me.

I saved my pence the lawyer paid me and booked a passage. Dad came to the rescue and furnishing me with a good
cabin and placed me in the care of the captain who knows

something of the family because of shipments of produce to America by the same line.

The trip is uneventful. America is beautiful, but I am anxious to get adjusted and find employment. I am assured it is only a question of time and perseverance. Encouraged, I go into the tall office buildings on lower Fifth Avenue. I try them all. Not a firm is missed. . . . I walk in and offer my services. . . . I am black, foreign looking. My name is taken and I will be sent for in a short time. "Thank you." "Good day." "Oh don't mention it." I am smiled out. I never hear from them again. . . .

Eventually I am told that this is not the way it is done in America. What typewriter do I use? Oh! . . . Well go to the firm that manufactures them. It maintains an employment bureau for the benefit of users of their machines. There is no discrimination there, go and see them. Ere I go, I write stating my experience, etc., etc., etc., etc. In reply I get a flattering letter asking me to call. I do so.

The place is crowded. A sea of feminine faces disarms me. But I am no longer sensitive. I have gotten over that . . . long since. I grit my teeth and confidently take my seat with the crowd. At the desks the clerks are busy with the telephones, filling out cards and application blanks. I am sure I am not seen. I am just one of the crowd. One by one the girls, and men too, are sent out after jobs. It has been raining. The air is foul. The girls are sweating in their war paint. They are of the type that paints their lips, pencil their brows, rouge their cheeks and up to themselves: "Clothes, I am going downtown; if you want to follow . . . hang on." At last they get around to me. It is my turn.

I am in front position. In order to get to me the lady is obliged to do a lot of detouring. At first I thought she was about to go out, to go past me. But I am mistaken. She takes a seat right in front of me, a smile on her wrinkled old-maidish face. I am sure she is head of the department. It is a position that must be handled with tact and diplomacy. She does not send one of her assistants. She comes herself. She is from the Buckeye state. She tries to make me feel at home by smiling broadly in my face.

"Are you Mr. . . . ?"

"Yes, I am."

"That's nice. How much experience you say you have had?" She is about to write.

"I have stated that in the letter, I think. I have had . . . I worked for . . ."

"Oh yes, I have it right here. Used to be secretary for a lawyer. . . . And you took honors in your class at school. That is interesting, isn't it?"

I murmur unintelligibly.

"Well," continues the lady, "we haven't anything at present. . . ."

"But I thought you said in your letter you had a position for me. I have it here with me. I hope I have not left it at home. . . ."

"That position wouldn't suit you," stammering. "It, t, t, t, t, t, it is a position that requires banking experience. It is one of the largest banks in the country. Secretary to the vice-president. Ah, by the way, come to think of it, you know Mr. . . . of Harlem?

"You do! I think his number is . . . Seventh Avenue. Here is one of his cards. Well if I were you I would go to see him. . . . Good day."

Dusk is on the horizon. I am once more on Fifth Avenue. I am not going to see the gentleman. The man she is sending me to was my father's groom.

*January 11, 1939*

# Worker's Alliance

## *Vivian Morris*

"Let's git set, brothers n' sisters; we's got plenty a business t'have done. Time's gittin' late. If om chairman om callin' the meetin' t'order. Take you seats now, please. 'At's it. Brother Finance, you got yo' records awready, I hope? An you too, Brother Membership—?Let's git settled—'at's it."

The speaker was the leader of Local 30 of the Worker's Alliance Union at 306 Lenox Avenue.

"Okay, brothers an' sisters. I calls this meetin' in full session. First I suggests we stan' up. Stan' up, please. Let's give a prayer on nis importan' occasion, for on nis occasion we needs a bit a prayer t'help us along.

"O'Lawd, we is here gathered to say a prayer unto you fo' help an' inspiration. We ast you to listen t' us an' help us what we gonna do. We needs yo' help, Lawd, an' 'at's why we startin' this meetin' with yo' name, an' offerin' to you our hearts an our hopes. We is gathered here, all aus, black an' white folks, in nis here organization because we is gonna do sump'n to git ourselves an' our chil'ren food an' cloes an' decent lodgin'.

"We's all poor folks, Lawd; we ain' neva had much an' now this here relief welfare don' give us much. We all wants t'live like human men an' women, an' wants our chil'ren t'be fed an clothed. We been askin' an'askin' at the relief station' t'git some of us onta relief but it's hard t'git on. Some a us 'at's on is bein' thrown off an' 'at works hardships on us an' on our chil'ren. We's goin' t'decide at this meetin' whut's gonna be done an' whuteva we decides, we know we's in the right fo' we fightin' hard fo' our rights. Some a us is black an' some a us is white. An' why are we here t'gether? Because we's all folks in a same boat. We's got wives an' kids an' we unastan' 'at hunger ain' yet showed no favorites between the white an' black skins. We knows you hol' yo' chil'ren in a same regard, O'Lawd, no matter whut culla they be. We ain' used t'be gathered here like this before, fer we wuz separated before—the whites fum the blacks an' we didn't have no respeck fo' each other. It's diff'rent now. This here's a united front because we's all sufferin' alike. I knows you makes no distinction, fo' it ain' right an' it ain' human. An' we in nis organization knows that if we black people wuz t'go alone they won't be much use, same as with the whites. They ain' no discrimination in yo' eyes, Lawd, an' they ain' none in nis here organization. We's askin you fer yo' blessin's, Lawd, an' t'keep us t'gether an' t'help us win in nis fight agens discrimination an' agens our misery. We thanks you, Lawd, an we gives you our hearts an our hopes, Amen.

"All right, brothers an' sisters, let's git started."

*June 19, 1938*

# Laundry Worker's Choir

## *Vivian Morris*

It was just about noon, early in March, at the West End
Laundry downtown where black women work in the ironing
department. The foreman there eyed me suspiciously and
then curtly asked me, "What you want?" I showed him a
Laundry Workers Union card (which I borrowed from an
unemployed laundry worker, in order to ensure my admittance) and told him that I used to work in this laundry and
I thought I would drop in and take a friend of mine who
worked there out to lunch.

He squinted at the clock and said, "Forty minutes before
lunchtime. Too hot in here and how. Better wait outside."

"But," I remonstrated, "the heat doesn't bother me. I
used to work in here."

"Say," he ignored my argument, "no fishy back talk and
get outside." He watched me until I was out of sight and
then he left the room. I promptly darted back into the ironing room where my friend worked.

The clanging of metal as the pistons banged into the
sockets, the hiss of steam, women wearily pushing twelve-
pound irons, women mechanically tending machines—one,
button half of the shirt done; two, top finished; three, sleeves
pressed and the shirt is ready for the finishers—that was the

scene that greeted me as I stood in the laundry's ironing department.

Shirts, thousands of white shirts that produced such a dazzling glare that the women who work in this department wore dark glasses to protect their eyes. The heat was almost unbearable; there seemed to be gushes of damp heat pushed at you from some invisible force in the mechanism of the machine. The smooth shiny-faced women worked in silence, occasionally dropping a word here and there, slowly wiping away dripping perspiration, then back to the machines, to the heavy irons without any outward show of emotion—no protest. The morning had been long and arduous, this was Wednesday—a heavy day, but thank God half the day was nearly over.

The heavy, strong-armed woman paused the iron, arms unflexed, and glanced at the clock. She smiled. Forty-five minutes until eating time. A soft contralto voice gave vent to a hymn, a cry of protest, as only the persecuted can sing, warm, plaintive, yet with a hidden buoyancy of exultation that might escape a person who has not also felt the pathos and hopes of a downtrodden, exploited people.

She sang, a trifle louder, "Could my tears forever flow, could my zeal no languor know. Thou must save, and thou alone, these fo' sin could not atone; In my hand no price I bring. Simply to his cross I cling."

The women tended their machines to the tempo of the hymn. They all joined in on the chorus, their voices blending beautifully, though untrained and unpolished they voiced the same soulful sentiment, "Rock of Ages, cleft for me. Let me hide myself in thee." Stanza after stanza rang from their lips, voicing oppression centuries old, but the song rang out that the inner struggle for real freedom still lit a fiery spark in the recesses of the souls of these toiling women.

The song ended as it began with soft words and hum-

ming. One squat, attractive young woman, who single-
handedly handled three of the shirt machines, began a
spirited hymn in militant tempo, with a gusto that negated
the earlier attitude of fatigue the entire crew of the ironing
room joined in either humming or singing. They were entering the final hour before lunch but to judge from the
speed that the song had spurred them to, you would believe they were just beginning. The perspiration dripped
copiously but it was forgotten. The chorus of the hymn
zoomed forth.

"Dare to be a Daniel. Dare to stand alone. Dare to
have a purpose firm and make it known—and make it
known."

The woman who finishes the laces with the twelve-
pound iron wielded it with feathery swiftness and sang
her stanza as the others hummed and put in a word here
and there.

"Many a mighty gal is lost darin' not to stand . . .
"The words of the next line were overcome by the rise in
the humming, but the last line was clear and resonant . . .
"By joinin' Daniel's band." The chorus was filled with
many pleasing ad-libs and then another took up a stanza.
Finally the song died away.

Then the squat machine handler said to the finisher
who guided the big iron, "Come on, baby, sing 'at song
you made up by yourself. The Heavy Iron Blues." Without further coaxing the girl addressed as "baby" cleared
her throat and began singing. "I lift my iron, Lawd, heavy
as a ton of nails. I lift my i'on, Lawd, heavy as a ton of
nails, but it pays my rent cause my man's still layin' in
jail. Got the blues, blues, got the heavy i'on blues; but my
feet's in good shoes, so doggone the heavy i'on blues."
Then she started the second stanza which is equally as
light but carried some underlying food for thought. "I lif'
my i'on, Lawd, all the livelong day. I lif' my i'on, Lawd,
all the livelong day, cause dat furniture bill I know I got

to pay, Got the blues, blues, got the heavy i'on blues, but, I pay my union dues, so doggone the heavy i'on blues."

There was a sound of whistles from the direction of the river and the girls dropped whatever they were doing and there were many sighs of relief. Lunchtime.

*March 9, 1939*

# Thursday Girls

## *Vivian Morris*

In the fall of 1938, WPA writer Vivian Morris began
a series of stories covering a seldom recognized work-
force who toiled at the same kinds of jobs as slave
women—house cleaning and the general domestic
chores of daily servants.

In pieces called "Slave Markets in the Bronx,"
"A.B.C. Employment Agency," "Wage War in the
Bronx Slave Markets," and "Domestic Workers
Union," she chronicled the stories of these women
who were commonly known in Harlem and in other
black communities as "Thursday girls" because
Thursday was generally their day off and it was usually
when they could be seen shopping, dancing or resting
on the stoops of the rooming houses where they lived.
Morris wrote these stories between November 1938
and February 1939.

On December 2, 1938, at 9:45 A.M., Vivian Morris
conducted at interview in room 212B at 200 West
135 Street. ABC Employment is situated on the third
floor and is owned by a man identified only as Mr.
Creque. The room where the interview took place was
a small, stuffy room with eight or ten benches, six of
which were reserved for women, the remainder for
men. A wooden partition with a small glass window
separated Mr. Creque from his clients.

Mr. Creque was a short red-skinned black man, with large bland eyes that did not belie the guile that lay in his alert scheming brain. He knew the tricks, all right.

The phone rang.

Mr. Creque picked it up and placed it between his shoulder and his ear, holding it this way so that he could write more freely. "ABC Employment Agency," he said.

The people out front who were seeking jobs suddenly halted their conversations so they could better hear the telephone conversation going on in the office back of the glass partition.

"You want a girl for eight hours? That will be three dollars and twenty cents, Mrs. Fink; No, you pay carfare both ways. I'll send her right out. Goodbye Mrs. Fink."

Creque got up and walked over to the opening that stood for a door. His eyes roamed over the group as if he were searching for someone to send to Mrs. Fink, but he knew that Mrs. Banks would be the person elected to be sent out. Hadn't she been the first to be sent out every morning when there was a call for day's work? In fact the massive Mrs. Banks was so certain, that she had already risen from her seat.

"Mrs. Banks," Creque beckoned to her.

"Who me? Ah'm sho lucky!" beamed the beefy Mrs. Banks as she flounced out of the room to the office.

"Here, Mrs. Banks," said Creque, handing her a card, "Mrs. Fink is expecting you in half an hour."

"Fink?" asked Mrs. Banks dubiously. "Ain't she Joosh? You know Ah don't work fo' no Joosh folks, cause dey sets de clock back an' . . ."

"Mrs. Banks, you know I wouldn't send you out on a Jewish job. I have never done it, have I? Of course not. Forty cents, please. That's ten percent of three dollars and twenty cents."

"You sho' calc'late fas'!" said Mrs. Banks handing him

the money. That job being settled, the hubbub burst out again among the hopefuls in the receiving line.

A smart, young girl in a green hat was talking confidentially to a girl in a yellow coat:

"You know, chile, ah'm goin' tell you something dat he'ps you git on roun' heah. Yo' know ole Crick, whatever his name is, he likes me. Bet ah gits the fust part-time job dat comes heah. Nevah tek nothing' but part-time, honey; you' makes more money dat way. As ah was goin' to say, the way to git roun' ole Crick, in dere is to say in a whiny voice, 'Mr. Crick, why don't ya gi' me a break on these part-time jobs. Ah'm a hard-working girl trying t' git along. Dat ole fool will fall all over hisself trying' to git fresh, but you'll git jobs long as you don't let him date you up. Ah know chile—Oh! an' you can kind o' show y'o figger!" Dere's the phone now. Part time. Watch 'im call me."

She started to powder her nose.

"Miss Lane," said Creque, talking to her. The lady in the green hat got up and went to Mr. Creque's office. A lady with white, high laced-up shoes dropped her lower lip and began grumbling:

"Lawd sho' don' know why dat li'l fas' gal gits all de part-time jobs fus'. Mr. Crick mus' be lakin' huh!"

There was subdued laughter from the other members of the unemployed audience.

Creque rapped, sternly, on his desk and the merriment ceased. As he was talking to Miss Lane, a spry, wiry young woman quickly came in.

Her entrance startled Creque so much he seemed confounded by her presence. Indignantly, he started to speak to her, saying "Mrs. Gray, why don't—? "Don't Mrs. Gray me," flamed that little lady. "What do you mean sending me and six other women after one job?"

"Mrs. Gray—"

"Shut up! Give me my four dollars! she commanded.

"After four days—"

"I want my money, now!"

Creque got up and gingerly touched the arm of the irate woman, saying: "Please sit down and lower your voice. P-l-e-a-s-e."

"Lower nothin'," fumed the lady condescending to sit down.

"Now the law says after three days, you can collect your money if I don't get you another job."

The lady stood up swelling with anger, a vitriolic outburst was on the way.

"Please sit down," said Creque, softly, "I'll give you your money." Creque handed her the money under the desk, saying: "Please keep quiet. Now, Mrs. Gray, come in Friday, and I'll return your money if I've found no other job for you. Good-day."

Mrs. Gray tucked the money in her stocking, looking at Creque as if he were insane. What was he talking about? With an apprehensive glance, she scurried from the room.

A tall, raw-boned bumpkin walked in and made his way to Mr. Creque's office. He stood twisting his cap and shifting his feet.

"Well, what is it?" asked Mr. Creque, confidently.

"Well," fluttered the gawky youth, "dat job you sent me on at dat dere bowlin'-alley—"

"Well"?

"Dat woman down dere toll me dat y'o worked twelve hours stead of eight. Y'o does the janitor's work, an' you only gits paid every mont'."

"What?" asked Creque, in mock surprise.

"Yassuh. An' 'stead of gittin' thirty-six dollars a mont' ya only gits thutty-five."

"I'll call them up," fumed Creque, as he picked up the phone. "Misrepresenting the facts to me."

He dialed a number quickly. He waited, then said, "Hello. I sent a boy down dere and I want to know who talked to him. Miss Cohen? Wait a minute."

He turned to the boy asking: "Who talked to you? Miss Cohen?" Then he turned back to the phone and said: "Okay. I have it straight now. Good-bye."

"Is it straight now?" asked the gawk.

"Yes—er. You went to the wrong woman. You were to see Mrs. Foley—Mrs. Foley—yes—Mrs. Foley."

"Den Ah mus' go back?"

"No, no," said the flustered Creque, quickly. "I'll send you out on a better job. Let me see—tomorrow—yes, tomorrow."

"My money—?"

"Oh you won't need dat money after you get your job tomorrow. . . . Good day."

"Yassah." The gawky fellow shuffled out.

"What a hell of a trying day an employment manager has," I thought. But the people who came to ABC faced worse—the bitter disappointments that come from waiting all day for that one case in twenty that turns into a good job.

At least they could revel in the fact that their disappointment came in warm, dry surroundings. Many others fared much worse in these times.

# Slave Market

## Vivian Morris

**In this piece, compiled from three separate stories written in the fall of 1938 and the winter of 1939, Morris set out to cover the ways in which domestic servants hustled to find work. To do this, she interviewed union organizers downtown and freelance workers from Harlem who traveled to the north Bronx to find "days work." There she finds the story she has been looking for among scores of black women domestics.**

**In November, Morris confirms the rumors that were common in beauty shops all over Harlem about the deplorable conditions under which these women worked.**

**On a corner in the Bronx just north of Harlem, she encounters Minnie Marshall, who lives on West 132 Street in Harlem. Several stores surround this neighborhood, generally referred to by the women who frequent it as the "slave market." The name refers mainly to the south side of the street near a five-and-dime store, where the Madams shop for domestic necessities, including girls and women like Minnie who hire themselves out for low wages paid to them daily.**

There were always rumors of a "slave market" somewhere in the Bronx where black women were hired out like their ancestors for just pennies a day. According to hearsay, this market was operated by white "Madams" who arranged for these black women to work in white homes and stores.

Early one November morning, I decided to confirm these reports by making a personal tour of the neighborhood where the condition was supposed to exist. While walking down West 167 Street as I reached Girard Avenue, I found the object of my search. I was confronted by sights and tales of woe that I shall always remember.

There, seated on crates and boxes, were a dejected gathering of black women of various ages and descriptions ranging from youths of seventeen to elderly women of maybe seventy. These women were scantily attired—some still wearing summer clothing. The cold November wind swept and whistled through them and they ducked their heads. They tried to huddle together for warmth, pushing themselves as close to the wall as they could.

I joined the group as though I too were looking for a job. Although properly clothed, I too suffered from the bitter cold which made me shift from foot to foot. Immediately my thoughts strayed to these twenty or more unfortunate women who were partly clothed, some with tennis shoes, cut-out men's shoes, warped women's shoes bearing the Wanamaker's department store seal—the cast-offs of some forgotten past "Madam."

A woman with a gold tooth smiled and invited me to share the wooden box she used as a seat. Her face bore cuts over both eyes and the corner of her mouth. She appeared to be as broad as she was tall, but, despite all this, her flat face sported a kindly expression. I allowed her to assume that I too was in her category, and she became sympathetic and . . . began to relate her futile struggle, which she said began thirty years earlier in the South.

Minnie was born in 1908 in the tidewater section of Virginia not far from the port city of Norfolk. She looked substantially older than her story indicated. Her father was a black sailor "brawny of arm and smooth of tongue." This was her mother's description of a man Minnie had apparently never known. To confirm my suspicions, I interrupted her to ask.

"He had gone down with his ship, so Ma said. "I had been yanked out of school in the third grade at the age of fourteen, in order to take my ailing mother's job at Miss Sarah's—mother died in a few days."

As I listened, attentively, I gathered that Minnie had been repeatedly fired from various positions owing to lack of experience and youth—not having enough endurance and muscle for fifteen to eighteen hours of strenuous laundry and housework. She decided to take a fling at marriage at the age of sixteen. She married a hard-drinking sailor thrice her age who gave her fifty dollars for a wedding present, and told her, "Get some puddy clo's fo' you' se'f." Minnie, unaccustomed to having such a large amount of money, decided to save it, having first had the satisfaction of touching, feeling, and counting it.

The next night, her husband returned home roaring drunk and demanding money—"five dollars." When Minnie timidly took the roll from under the pillow and peeled off the requested amount, he attacked her, cutting both her eyes and mouth and knocking out her front teeth. He took all of the money, stumbled out, and disappeared into the night. She never saw him again!

During the next twelve years, Minnie worked steadier, became adjusted to conditions, and was now a squat, muscular woman whose endurance was surely beyond the average. Now she could work unlimited hours without audible protest.

By the time I came across her, she had replaced her front teeth with gold ones. "But the scars will be with me till my dying day," she told me that cold morning.

She had arrived in New York just a month ago, using twenty dollars she had saved to migrate to New York. She arrived here with about six dollars and paid four for a room.

Though she was hungry, she was afraid to spend money for food that first night. Early the next morning, Minnie went to an employment agency.

Yes, they told her, they had jobs that paid forty dollars a week that were sleep-ins or out. She almost shouted for joy—that was more money than she could make in Norfolk in two months! But this was New York. The employment agent signed Minnie up as a good cook–houseworker, etc., then he proffered her a card, saying: "Four dollars, please."

Minnie said her shoulders sagged!

"Fo' dollars fo' whut?"

"For the job; ya don't think I run this agency for my health, do you?"

"No, suh, no suh, Ah only got two dollars 'tween me an de Lawd. Ah clare, mistuh, ah'll give you de res' fus' week ah woks, hon-es', Mistuh."

He tore up the slip, saying: "Ya'll pay me when you get paid? That's a hot one. Keep your two dollars, lady!"

Minnie said she tried agency after agency but the results were the same. They wanted their money first. She couldn't get day's work or part-time work because the agents had special cliques to whom these choice jobs went. It was rank folly for any outsider to think of getting one of these jobs. After many days of trying, her rent was due, her money gone, a sympathetic girl in one of the agencies told Minnie that when she was out of money, she stood on one of the corners in the Bronx, where women came and hired you.

"Next mo'nin' Ah gut up prayin' that de lan lady woudn' heah me and walked de fifty-some blocks to dis place, an' I saw othah gals standin' heah, so Ah stood wid dem. Soon a fine cah driv up. Dere was a lady hol'in' some o'dem eyeglasses yo' hol' in yo' han' an' peepin' at us. Dem di'-mons on huh finguhs mos' blin' you an' de mo'nin' too!" She pointed our way an' de big black buck chauffeur got out an' 'proached us sayin', 'Come heah.' Ah sed, 'Who me?'

"He sez, 'Yes. Yu wanna wuk, don'cha?'

"I walked to the cah an' he says, 'get in.' Ah staht to get in the back but de madam was dere—he in de front—wheah could Ah set? "Git in the front. Doan tank ya'll set in de madam's lap, does ya?' De gals laughed.

" 'Vill you get in, goil?' sed de madam. 'Hi got no time for dot foolishness.' The gals laffed.

" 'Hi pay twenty-five sants an hour—is dat all right wit you?' "Ah said: 'Yas'm.' After all, I was bout to be put out doe's.

"De drivuh drive down Walton Avenue a ways an' stop 'fo' a fine 'partment house. De madam tuck me up to huh 'partment an' ah 'clare, dese seben rooms she point out to me ain' fittin' fo' hawgs to live in. Dey was sum dirty!

"She say: 'Listen, goilly, hi vant you to do a gutt job. H'im having company tomorrow. Hi vill tip you fine. Your time begins now. You vill be pait by dot clock. See—nine-forty-five?"

"Dat dam' clock sed de same time dat she said, so Ah tho't mah clock was wrong. All the gals carry clocks. Ah sta't wukkin' an' wo'n mo'n fifteen minutes begin, when dot ol' heiffer was givin' orders, do dis an' do dat. She 'zasperate me so dat ah cud choke huh tongue out'n huh but ah beared huh. Bout six o'clock, Ah tol' huh ah's thru."

"She sehs, 'Bout time,' Den she sta'ts reachin' in con'-ahs fo' dust—feelin' huh husban's shoit colla's to see ef 'nough sta'ch in dem—lookin at de flo,' almos touchin' nit wit' huh big nose, nea' sighted se'f. Den she smile and seh, 'Vas de lunch gut?' (Dat ole slop-fish, two days ole!)

"Ah said: 'Reck'n so!"

"Den she gi' me mah money—dollar, eighty-seben cent. "Ah sehs: 'Miss Gol' blatt, ain' you' miscalc'late? Ah wukked eight hours—tu'k fifteen minutes fo' lunch?'

" 'Listen' dear goil, Hi neffer cheat hany body. You voiked seven hours—fifteen minutes, vich giffs you vun dollar, heighty-two sants, hand hi took hout fife sants for bringink you here, vich makes hi should giff you van eighty-seven, bud hi giff you, per agreement, a nize fat tip of tan sants—van eighty-sefen. Good-bye!'

"Ah was mad den, but when Ah got out an' foun' dat it wus eight o'clock and dat ole heifer done cheat me out of two hours, ah cou'd a kilt huh. Well, ah at leas' had sumf'n fo' my lan'lady."

Here, Minnie paused awhile and squinted her tired eyes, and said, "Ah hates the people ah wukks for. Dey's mean, 'ceitful, an' ain' hones' but whut ah'm gonna do? Ah got to live—got to hab a place to steh. My lan'lady seys ah gotta bring huh sumf'n or ah can' stay dere tonight."

Suddenly, her demeanor changed. She became alert, telling me quietly, "Wait!"

A little woman, with aquiline nose, thick glasses, and three big diamonds that seemed to laugh at the prominent-veined hands they were on passed down the line of women, critically looking at the girls. When she reached Minnie, she stopped peering: "Can you do woik-hart voik? Can you vash windows from de houtside?"

"Ah c'n do anything—wash windows, anywhere." Time was passing, she had to get a job or be put out.

"Twenty-fife sants an hour?"

"No ma'am; thirty-five."

"I can get the youngk goils for fifteen sants, and the old vimmen for tan sants." She motioned toward the others who were eagerly crowding around.

"Yas'm; ah' ll go," said a frog-eyed, speckle-faced, yellow gal, smiling idiotically.

"Me, too," chimed a toothless old hag with gnarled hands—a memento of some days in Dixie.

"See!" said the woman.

"But dey caint do de wokk Ah kin do," rebutted Minnie defiantly.

"Thirty-sants," said the bargain-hunter, with an air of finality.

"Le's go," said Minnie flashing me a gold-toothed smile.

"See you latuh, honey. Ta'k to some o' de othah gals 'bout dere troubles. Sho' he'p yo' wile yo' time 'way."

"So long, Minnie," I said.

"Hope yo' don' meet no heifer lak' ah did on mah fus' job," she added. I waved goodbye to this days work "slave" as she plodded away.

# Domestic Workers Union

## *Vivian Morris*

In February 1939, Morris wrote a rare follow-up story
to the previous one. It came after she headed downtown
to interview the Executive Secretary for the Domestic
Workers Union at 241 West 84 Street.

The Domestic Workers Union is located in the heart of
Yorkville section of Manhattan. It was just past the noon
hour when Rose Reed conducted me to this temple of fidel-
ity, which housed a group of unceasing workers who dedi-
cate their lives to providing ways and means of lifting the
level of the shamefully neglected domestic workers.

As we entered, Rose inquired of a sharp-eyed nimble
white worker, who was deftly cutting stencils for a batch of
petitions, about the approximate hour that Miss Jones (the
executive secretary) would be in. She continued working but
answered in a polite affable tone that Miss Jones was expected momentarily and asked us to inspect the headquarters
pending any tardiness on the part of Miss Jones.

I noted that there was a group of women seated around
a large table drinking coffee and eating sandwiches, which
were prepared by a pleasant-looking woman who stood over
a gas stove snugly situated in a corner, making it imperceptible from the big front office where official business was carried on. When I looked at Rose with a noncomprehending
expression on my face, she promptly enlightened my befud-

dled brain by telling me that this was a daily procedure. The women who had come for days' work and had not succeeded in finding it, or the part-time job seekers, were allowed free use of the gas stove and cooking utensils.

I marveled at the varied tasks that the women pursued between bits of sandwiches and sips of coffee. Some chatted in sincere animated tones about the frankly exposing article appearing in a local tabloid, written by Damon Runyon. It scathingly denounced the housewives who work their maids lengthy, inhumane hours at a starvation wage. Every scalding word was caught by straining ears, as the smooth-toned young girl, whose sole ambition was to emulate Marion Anderson, read them off for the older women some of whom had "left their glasses at home." Others admitted that they could not read.

A few of the group haltingly tried to remedy their defective reading; another, having finished her meal, had pushed her chair back from the table and was poring over a booklet on elementary arithmetic.

After the Runyon article had been duly discussed it was decided that it was to be clipped from the paper and pinned to the bulletin board. While the young lady was pinning the article on, I ventured to look at the very informative bulletin board. There were numerous clippings from papers, pamphlets, and periodicals pertaining to the domestic situation throughout the country. There were notices of bills to be presented, bills that had been presented, and petitions to be signed by the members of the union. Directly in front of the bulletin board was a well-stocked bookcase with many trade union books, pamphlets, union activities periodicals, and a few popular magazines.

The young lady having finished her petitions surveyed them with pride and beckoned to me saying, "What do you think of the petition?"

I read the heading of the petition, the gist of which was a plea to the members of the state assembly to limit the domestic workers to a ten-hour day, a sixty-hour week, a fifteen dollar minimum wage, day's work at $3.50 a day, an hour for lunch, and agitation for the inclusion of domestic workers in the Social Security Act, in view of the fact that eighty percent of all black women workers were employed as domestic servants.

At about this time, Dora Jones came in. She was a plump, energetic, round-faced black woman with all-engulfing eyes. The worker who had been running off the petitions (the educational director), introduced me to Miss Jones. Impatient to learn about the origin of the union, I immediately inquired about its beginning. With pleasant alacrity Miss Jones complied with my hasty request.

"Our union is eight years old. It was started by a group of Finns and a few blacks in Harlem, who saw the necessity for a fight against exploitation of domestics. Until 1935 the office was located in the Finnish neighborhood, but the hunger riots of Harlem on March 19, 1935, marked the demolishing of the office by the rioters. In 1936, we set up the Domestic Workers Union Local 149 A.F. of L. in this building. We have grown not spectacularly, but at a steady clip. The members we get, we hold."

She waved her hand toward the group, which was collectively folding a bundle of letters that were to be sent out to the various members. "One big happy family." She smiled.

"Now, Miss Jones," I hesitantly interposed, "I want to know your stand on the various slave marts—?"

"I'm glad you brought that up," she interrupted. "That problem has been a thorn in our side for many a day, but I think we have a solution for this dilemma. We have sent out a suggestion to the rabbis in the various synagogues and white clergymen that they should stress to their congregations that they should stop hiring the girls from the slave marts at starvation wages, and have an organization set up and supervised by the members of the church, or some community house in the neighborhood, and let the girls come there and wait for jobs. We don't stop here, but we suggest that a minimum wage law be agreed upon by arbitration and this will help do away with the slave mart," she said.

"But, this will not entirely erase domestic slavery; so," she added, "so we sent out letters to the ministers of black churches where these habitués of the slave mart attend, and urged them to impress upon these women the direct harm they do to themselves and others by going to these slave marts and accepting the low wages that these heartless employers offer them. We want the pastors to insist that they go to these places that I am confident will be set up by the rabbis and white clergymen. In this fashion, having experienced a taste of fair wages and conditions, they'll want better conditions—and that's where we, the union come in."

# Domestic Price Wars

## *Vivian Morris*

**Two months earlier, however, Morris had seen for herself how successful this attempt at fairness had been. She went to the Walton Avenue neighborhood Minnie Marshall had talked about near West 170 Street, which was one of the swanky addresses in this part of New York at the time.**

I wended my way to this location in the December cold that morning. It was a nasty, hazy morning and a cold, sticky rain padded the gritty New York sidewalks. As I made my way to my destination it was with a firm suspicion that the corners would be deserted on such a morning.

When I reached my destination, I found that I was very, very wrong because "the sisters of the market" were standing in the corner store doorway and also blocked the door of the next building. They carried their working paraphernalia in their shopping bags, little grips, brown paper bags, and newspapers.

Some of them peered out of the doorways, shifting from foot to foot and humming as they watched and waited. As a whole, these women were better dressed and warmer clad than the ladies at West 167 Street and Gerard Avenue. I moved in, trying to force conversation with the women, and got exactly nowhere, because these women were tight-lipped and viewed me with distrust, answering in monosyllabic yesses and no's.

I tried a new method of opening the conversation by saying, "I don't see as many young girls around here as I did on the other corner."

"What co'ner?" asked a balloonlike lady in a tight brown coat.

"One hundred sixty-seventh and Gerard," I answered.

"You come from dere?" she asked belligerently.

"Yes at least I was there last week."

"Well ain' no use you cheapies comin' fum 'roun' dere an' tryin' to mek' business bad 'roun' heah fo' us," she grumbled, evilly rolling her eyes at me. "We run many a one' way fum heah."

The mumbling undertone her fellow watchers gave vent to "seconded the motion" on her none-too-veiled threat.

"Oh, I wouldn't do a thing like that," I assured them firmly.

"Doan' know, you may be lak dem Father Divine people," she jerked a thumb in the direction of some women who were in a doorway across the street.

"What did they do?" I asked, feigning nonchalance.

"Dey do everything 'rong," answered the large brown-coated one. "Comin' 'roun' heah shoutin' 'peace sister,' an wukkin' fo' nuthin'. Dere was a time w'en we got good prices on dis co'ner; but den dey come. Dey take fifteen, twen'y, an even as low as ten cent a hour. Until dey come, nobody never tu'k less dan twen'y-five cent an hour fo' days wu'k."

"But they aren't on your corner, now," I coaxed, seeking still more information.

"Oh, me an anudder girl beat two of dem up so, one day, till dey 'uz nigh senseless. So now dey doan' come on dis pa'tiek'ler co'er no mo'!"

"What did they do?" I asked. She was thawing out by the minute.

"Me an' de girl wuz bein' interviewed by two fine madams who looked high class and high toned. Dey had 'greed to pay us fifty cents an hour fo' ten hours wu'k and we were on de way to de job, w'en up come two of dem wenches talk'in bout 'peace, madam, does ya'll want someone tuh wu'k? We'll wu'k fo' thutty cent an hour.' De madams stopped and dey both got red in de face an' looked at each udder an' den say to us, 'Sorry girls but we'll tek de two udder girls.'

"We wuz fit to be tied w'en de girl wid me say, 'Ah'll wu'k fo' thutty cent' an' not to be outdone Ah say me too. W'en dem 'madams' warn't lookin', we both shuck our fist at dem ol' women an 'dey den went away. De nex' day, we come to de co'er an' dere dey were. Widout sayin' nuthin; we jist' lit into dem an' beat dem up bad. Dey didn' lif' a han' to proteck dey se'fs. Dey jis' let us beat dem an' dey jis' pray an' pray, takin' bout 'Peace, Father is wid us.'

"Some uh de udder girl pried us loose f'um dem an' dey went 'bout dey bus'ness. But now mo' of dem come den evah. Look at dat co'ner." She points to the old women on the other corner, who are dressed in plain old-fashioned clothes. "But dey bes' not light heah."

"Do they get much work?" I asked.

"Yeah de cheapies go over dere an hire dem. Dey wu'ks fo' nuthin; I get long pretty good do'. Ah 'got two reg'lar days an' mah madam be long any minute now. W'en dey want classy wu'kkers dey come to dis co'ner. Nobody heah wu'ks fo' less dan thutty cents an' hour; if dey do, we run dem off dis con'er, understan?" she looked meaningfully at me.

"I see," said I.

A long, low black car pulled up and the only person in it was the chauffeur. He beckoned to the girl who had been talking to me. Her face spread wider and she beamed, saying to me, "Deres my madam's chauffeur now, honey. Ain't he a sweet thing?"

As the brown-coated one minced through the rain to the car, one of the women from the opposite corner started across the street. The brown-coated one stopped and stood with arms akimbo, ignoring the rain. "Doan you dar' cross dat street an' think you c'n steal dis job f'um me, you low-down thing. Git on back cross de street," she commanded. The woman stopped for a few seconds, then turned and retraced her steps.

# Private Life of Big Bess

## Frank Byrd

In the fall of 1938, I took to the streets with a mission of great humanitarian merit.

Sidney Bowman, night deskman at the *Amsterdam* where I work the society beat, called me a crazy hack. Well, what he said was worse but that's the gist of it.

But I had a mission. I called it my Social-Ethnic Study of Harlem. When I came to New York from Fisk, I put my undergraduate days behind me. In all the years I've been a reporter at the *Amsterdam News,* I had never felt a greater need to use my education and the understanding it gave me of the underclass that lived shadowy lives uptown. Sidney, the old slick-headed night desk editor teased me, saying I was just trying to get myself a piece a free uptown pussy.

I picked last night to start what Sid called my Hooker project, cause there'd be women everywhere that would be more than willing to give up a little trim, making it impossible for a hooker to find a date.

To most people, Harlem and wild orgies and prostitution are synonymous. There is some actual foundation for this [impression]. Many of the newspaper stories about so-called goings-on in Harlem, however, are greatly exaggerated. It is true that Harlem probably has the greatest percentage of prostitution of all the five boroughs, but the community of

Harlem itself is essentially a quiet, peace-loving, law-abiding place. Prostitution, to a great extent, is segregated to lower Lenox Avenue and that section of Harlem sometimes referred to as the Latin Quarter that extends from West 110 Street and Central Park North to West 116 Street, and from Fifth Avenue on the East Side to Morningside Avenue on the West.

Evidence of the "oldest profession" crops up in the most unexpected places, however, and almost every uptown street has known it at one time or another.

I have long suspected that women who are hookers are exploited; forced into prostitution to have a place to sleep.

"Street walkers are just weak bitches that can't find a man like normal," Sid scolds whenever I've tried to get him to run this largely unreported item. I've been pitching hooker stories to him for years. Not one has ever run.

"What's the lead, Mr. High Pockets," he told me the last time I tried the pitch.

"The lead, Mr. Low Life, is the mere fact that these women are no different from the house cleaners who give it up for Mr. Man in Scarsdale while Miss Minnie is out shopping," I told him.

"You can't write that story either cause you wouldn't be caught dead with a Thursday girl waving a fist full of Lincolns, Mr. High Pockets. I'll tell you what you're trying to do. You think you going to sneak your way into the heart of some Lenox Avenue hooker and get to try her on for size. That's what I think, Mr. High Pockets," he said, pulling the green eye shade he always wore down tighter on his shiny bald head.

"Hookers are made not born," I countered.

"How would you know, son?"

"I want to write a series on the true predicament of this underclass," I told Sid.

"Ya want a piece of ass and think you can use a press card to pay for it, boy."

"I have undertaken the recording and reporting of some of the impartial facts regarding the activity in the profession in Harlem today," I countered.

"Name one hustler I know and I'll turn you loose on this one," Sidney bellowed, spitting that disgusting brown juice that is always smeared on the corners of his mouth out into the wastebasket nearest his desk.

"Big Bess," I spat back at him. "Lenox Avenue Bess." I grabbed my Chesterfield coat and left the newsroom. As I waited for the elevator, Sid stuck his head out into the hallway. "You running with girls in the rackets?" he asked seriously.

"Just to do my job," I said.

"Your job is to tell me when Joe Louis gets some, and if the Brown Bomber liked it, not listening to hookers cry in the beers I am paying for."

"I'm getting real stuff," I countered.

"Yeah, you damn betcha, it's real. Can I print it, that's what I am wondering?

It was as cold as the tip of an ice pick in January when I walked the few blocks from the paper for the second night in a row to see her. It was nine o'clock on a Wednesday night. The streets were crawling with Thursday girls, house cleaners, nannies, washerwomen, and black cooks who kept the white world that surrounded Harlem working like a wristwatch. They'd come in packs from their sleep-in jobs in Scarsdale, Irvington, or Greenwich. We called them Thursday girls because that was their night off and they always came with cash money they were more than willing to part with. Even pimps understood this competition and gave their girls the same night off. This two-day party usually began at six o'clock on Wednesday night and stretched deep into midday on Thursday. By six o'clock Thursday night, they'd leave town and the whores, who rested up while they were in town, could pick up the prowl again until next week.

Out on the street, I strode east down West 145 Street, the wind from the west side pushing me down the steep hill toward Lenox. I had a date with Lenox Avenue Bess. I was already beginning to understand this needy side of Harlem. The interview I was about to have was set up for me by a beat cop—an Irish rookie in the 38th Precinct, who had rescued Bess one night after she got beat up bad by Slick Reynolds, a smoothie suspected of being her pimp. She denied it, with half of her face hanging off her skull when O'Rouke found her bleeding not far from one of her usual haunts.

What Slick Reynolds did know was Bess wasn't just any girl, and she certainly wasn't typical when it came to defending herself in an ass-whipping contest. But that's what I was tying to get Sid to see. Women like Bess are complicated, more complex than they're ever given credit for. That's the story I wanted to write. Sidney said an *Amsterdam* reader could care less whether Lenox Avenue Bess really had a heart; they've read about her if Joe Louis said so but not if Chancey Paige, society writer for the *News* slipped her on for size.

Lenox Avenue Bess came from St. Louis with real blues all her own, that's my lead. I've been following her story ever since she hit this town a year ago. Tonight is my second real interview with her, although I've wanted her to go on the record about her life the whole time I've known her. "You wanna date Bess?" was always her response before she sauntered off down the block in search of the fame and fortune I believed all hookers sought.

Bess just appeared out of nowhere, and her life, when she leaves the Avenue at dawn, has always been a puzzle to everyone. That is, it was until last night. What happened to make her break that long silence is more than I can understand. She was drunk, it's true, but that's nothing new to Bess. She's always drunk, more or less. Drinking, with her, is like eating or sleeping. It's the most natural thing in the world. At any rate, it never seemed to make any difference before. Usually, when she's out looking for a date, she sits at the corner table in the back of Red's place and stares mournfully off into space.

Last night, however, she broke a precedent of long standing. She invited me to sit down and have a drink with her. It was a peculiar thing. For a minute, I couldn't believe that it had actually happened. It seemed more like a dream than a reality, yet there was no getting around the fact that the place was Red's Joint and that it was Bess, the hard-boiled, who walks her beat rain or shine inviting me, a man, to share her table and, what's more, have a drink at her expense.

Now Bess has never been known to give away anything in her life. At least, that part of her life that has been spent in uptown New York. She's especially tight on men. They are, it appears, her pet hate. Yet, she makes her living by being nice to them. In fact, hardly a day passes when she doesn't sleep with at least a dozen.

But that's getting ahead of my story. This baby that's supposed to have a heart that could make Hard Hearted Hannah look like an angel of mercy, breaks down and confesses to me that she's lonely. Lonely! Can you beat it? Well, you could have floored me with a feather. I sat there too dumbfounded to utter a word: hanging on the ropes, you might say, waiting to see what would happen next. Then she began to talk—about herself, and if you think you've been through the mill boy, just get a load of this baby's MOs. Here's some of it straight, just as she told it to me:

"You know, kid," she said after the first couple of drinks, "I'm lonely tonight. Damn lonely! This business of mine makes you like that sooner or later. It's a tough racket and it's got so a girl can hardly make a decent living anymore. Too many girls. There ain't enough business to go around. In fact, it's lousy. There was a time when a girl could go out there and pick up a couple hundred a week. But that was a long time ago. You gotta do some tall hustling to even get by nowadays. In the first place, the cops are getting so they want almost half what you make for protection. Well, I don't mind kicking in with a few dollars now and then but this business of hustling for somebody else is a different story. Of course, there are a lot of cops who will let you off easy if you are willing to do them a little favor when they're off duty, but most of them can't be trusted. I know a kid who was run in by a cop only last week and he's one of the very guys she's been paying off to for the past coupla years. Anyhow, the last time she went out with him, he turned around and pinched her for soliciting. Now she's cooling her hips in jail. The trouble with that guy was that he was sore because he thought she was giving too much money to her pimp instead of him.

"Speaking of pimps, they're just as bad as the cops. I've never seen a lousier lot of bums in my life. I never got an even break from one since the first day I went into the racket. They're all alike. They put you in some cheap, two-dollar joint or send you out to pound the pavements, then take every dime of your money and think you oughta like it. Once in a while, they go out and buy up a lot of hot clothes and act like they're doing you a favor by buying you some beat-up stuff with your own money.

"I'll never forget the first pimp I had. His name was Charlie and I met him one night at the restaurant where my aunt had got me a job. That was in St. Louis. I was eighteen then and I lived with my aunt. My old man and old lady had died when I was just a kid. Anyhow, this guy Charlie looked like a good guy. He was a big black boy with a wide smile and a lot of gold teeth that flashed at you every time he opened his mouth. He was a swell dresser too, and free with his money. He gave me fifty-cent tip the first night he came in there. After that, he used to come by every night for about two weeks. One night he asked me to go out with him. I went, and it wasn't long before I found out what a swell lover he could be. After that, I was a setup for him.

So when it finally dawned on me what his game was, I had reached the place where it didn't make any difference to me. I was willing to do anything he said. So I left home and went to live with him.

"Not long afterwards, he put me in a two-dollar joint. I didn't like it there and told him so, but he always kissed me or petted me and said that after a while I wouldn't mind it at all. When he was nice and made love to me like that, I forgot all about everything else and the only word I knew was 'yes'! He could have made me do anything.

"I worked there for about seven months and one day one of the girls got drunk and told me to wake up and get wise to myself: that I was only being a sucker for Charlie and that he had four girls working for him in different houses about town. When I asked him about it, he told me to go to hell and mind my own business. Then, when I tried to leave him, he beat me up and gave me a couple of black eyes. After that when I came in at night, he took all my money and told me he'd cut my throat if I tried to hold out on him. He even used to come to see the woman that ran the house so he could find out how much I was making. This way, he was able to check up on me. Sometimes, though, I got a good customer who slipped me an extra five or ten. I kept this money and hid it until I had enough to go away. Then one day while Charlie was at the club gambling, I got on the train and went to Chicago.

"I had never been there before and, at first, it was tough learning the ropes. But one night I went down to one of those black-and-tan joints on the South Side and got to talking with a girl who was one of the entertainers there and who, finally, broke me in right. She offered to introduce me to some of the boys but I told her I was through with pimps and wanted to be on my own. This good resolution didn't last long though and after three or four months, I wanted someone of my own in the worst way. It's awfully tough going home to an empty room night after night like that. If

Charlie had come along then, I think I would have even gone back to him.

"That's when I started drinking. It was the only way I had of passing the time. Night after night, I wandered from one cabaret to another, just drinking or sitting and watching the dancers. It was while I was out on one of these bats that I met Johnny. He was an awfully nice feller but it didn't take me long to find out that he was in the racket, too. He wore a lot of flashy clothes and spent money like it was water. I was too wise to fall for that gag, though. They all do that at first. Making a flash, they call it. That's just a bait to make a girl fall for them. So, when Johnny pulled this stuff on me, I told him to nix out. I wasn't interested. I liked my new freedom too well. But he must have seen something in my eyes that told him how lonely I was.

"Every day, after that, he used to send me flowers, candy, and presents. He treated me like I was a lady. Once he sent me a ring and when I had it appraised, the man told me that it was worth two hundred dollars.

"The next time he came to see me, it happened. I just couldn't hold out on him any longer. He was so nice to me. He was that way for a long time—but I knew it couldn't last. His way of doing things was just a little different, that's all. So, when he began hinting that he needed money, I told him he could have every cent I made. There wasn't any need for him to kid me. I knew what he wanted and was willing to give it to him. It didn't matter to me any longer, anyhow. Having money didn't matter, I mean. All I wanted was him, but I soon found out that that wasn't as easy as it sounded. There was too much competition for him. Everywhere we went, the girls I knew, and some I didn't know, were making a play for him, right and left: especially some of those who made more money than I did.

"Johnny was a good-looking brown-skinned boy with dark, wavy hair and eyes that did something to you. He was a nice boy, too. He had been to college and knew how to talk in that smooth easy way, so different from the rest of those roughnecks around Chicago.

"It wasn't long before I knew he had another girl. Johnny was like that—ambitious—always wanting more than anybody else, and the best of everything at that. I was jealous and started playing around with some of his friends just to make him sore. One day he came home and found one of them there with me. That night, he left. There wasn't any quarrel and he didn't beat me. Johnny was like that—always the gentleman. He was the only man I ever had who didn't beat me. He didn't believe in leaving enemies behind him. It was always his policy, he said, to part friends. When he left he gave me a beautiful ring: a lovely diamond. I've still got it. It's the only thing I've got that's never been in the pawn shop.

Bess held up a finger and Red came out from behind the bar and filled them up again. It was about the tenth time he had done that. When she sipped a little of her drink, she went on in the same low, confidential voice.

"Being without Johnny was worse than I thought it could be. It finally got so bad that I went to him and begged him to come back to me but it wasn't any use. He had moved in with a little Spanish chick by the name of Consuelo. She worked in a ritzy joint and made a lot of money. If it had been anybody else, maybe I wouldn't have felt so bad about it but I never did like that little dame, even before I knew she was after him. She used to hang around the cabarets once in a while, acting snooty and showing off her clothes.

"When I thought of her with Johnny, I was almost crazy with jealousy. Once I went on a wild spree and didn't go to work for more than a week. When I finally showed up, another girl had taken my job. After that, I didn't try to find work. Instead, I just lay around drinking with a lot of bum friends who came around and sponged on me. When I got broke, none of them would lend me a dime;.

"One night when I couldn't stand it any longer, I went

to the club where Johnny gambled and asked him to give me some money. He told me that taking money was his business, not giving it. I was so mad I went crazy I guess. That same night I got lousy drunk and waited in Lulu-Mae's place where I was sure he would meet Consuelo after she got off from work. When he showed up, I asked him once more if he would come back to me. He only laughed at me and I was so mad that I went half crazy. I opened my pocketbook and pulled out a little gun that I had been carrying around with me. When Johnny saw it, he dived after me and I pulled the trigger. The next minute, he grabbed his stomach and fell forward on his face. That's all I remember except that the cops came and took me away with them. I didn't care. If I couldn't have Johnny, I wanted to die, anyhow. I told them that I didn't want a lawyer but they gave me one just the same, and he told me a lot of things to say but I wouldn't say anything. He was smart, though, and got the charge reduced from murder to manslaughter. When it was all over, they sent me up for ten years. But after doing five of them, I was paroled. Not long afterwards, I came to New York. That was eight years ago.

"Well, New York's just about the same as Chicago as far as the racket's concerned, only it's harder to fix the cops here and especially the Health Department M.D.'s who examine you when you're picked up on the streets. I've spent a lot of time on Welfare Island 'taking the cure.' Even when I'm able to beat a soliciting rap, these doctors slap a positive-label opposite my name and the Health Department won't let me go until I'm O.K. Sometimes, it takes three, four, or even six months. In Chicago, it was different. All you had to do was get a smart lawyer who knew the ropes or a fixer who could put a few dollars in the right places for you. That way, you could get a negative label whenever you needed it.

"I'm getting sick and tired of this life, but what can I do? I don't know any other kind of work and even if I did, where would I find it? Besides, once you get accustomed to seventy-five or a hundred dollars a week, it's pretty hard trying to get by on fifteen or eighteen. Christ! I never did anything to deserve a life like this. God knows, all I did was to fall in love with a man! There is a God, ain't there? I'm not sure that there's anything anymore except cheap women and cheating men and hell on earth. Or maybe there's a heaven and I'll go there someday. God! I'd give anything to know what'll become of me!"

Bess didn't have to wait long.

*November 11, 1938*

# Betty

## Frank Byrd

Luigi's speakeasy did an all-night business but you had to know what to say before they'd let you in. Whenever the bell rang, Jimmy got up and peeped through a little hole in the door. Well, he did the same thing the night Betty walked in. It was the first time I had seen her; I won't forget it. She was the kind of girl men fight for . . . and like it; but on a Harlem police blotter, they had "prostitute" scribbled opposite her name. Not that she looked like one. Her eyes were a pale, lovely blue, her hair soft and brown, and she had the sauciest two lips in the world. Another odd thing about her was that she never carried a watch. I suppose it was because time meant nothing to her. She was in love. The boy's name was Bill.

When Jimmy opened the door, Betty, eyes sad, pocketbook under her arm, and looking tired, hesitated in the doorway before walking to the far end of the room. No one looked up apparently, but several pairs of eyes followed every movement of her graceful body, movements emphasizing primitive appeal and simple loveliness.

"Ofay [white person] in a Harlem hot spot peddling her youth away for a nigger man," a party of white and colored people whispered.

"How's things, Joe?" Betty greets the bartender.

"Hi ya, Betty," Joe said without looking up. "Note for you."

She lit a cigarette and casually unfolded the piece of paper. Her features lit up. Business . . . more money for Bill who understood her and needed her.

Drawing her coat a little more closely near the waistline, Betty walked briskly toward the door. Her walk now was alive with rhythm and vitality. Sam, the taxi driver, followed. He had that something closely akin to a sixth sense. It told him whenever Betty wanted him to drive her places and, if necessary, collect for her. Both of them disappeared into the dark street. Jimmy closes the door behind them.

Girls like Betty, they say, are all alike. Perhaps they are. I don't know. But I do know she was a Wellesley graduate . . . and all girls are not Wellesley graduates.

Betty came to Greenwich Village to write. They brought her to Harlem to get "local color." Well, she got it.

Bill was working in a nightclub, one of those dingy, smoky little basement places. You remember them. Betty liked him and he saw in her all the things he had missed in other women. He sang for her. Afterward she went home to the Village with her friends. The next time she came to Harlem, she came alone. The place had "got" her, as they say. There was something about it she liked.

Cigarette smoke, fast living, and basement gin put an end to Bill's love songs. He left for Arizona. Betty hoped he might get over it but she knew that wasted lungs are not cured overnight.

It cost her $200 a month to keep him in a sanitarium there. For a long time she was able to sell enough stories and piece out her income with a little ghostwriting here and there, but when she finally had to look for a job, she found they were scarce.

That, of course, was before she began coming to Luigi's. After that, she didn't have to worry about bills and money. She always had more than enough.

Men loved Betty. When she smiled at them, they did anything she wanted. Many of them wanted to marry her but she only looked at them with a little amused smile playing about the corners of her mouth.

A hijacker once gave her two truckloads for a kiss. A boy from Park Avenue lost a $1,000 bet on her. He thought she'd say yes when he asked her to marry him . . . and she knew his family was one of the oldest in the social register. On a weekend party once, she fought a man. He insulted her. He thought she'd be flattered instead.

Betty had to have money . . . for Bill. So she got it. Nothing else mattered to her. Men brought it to her and were happy because it made her smile. Even though it was a long time ago, I can still see her smile.

But the reason I tell you this is because she came to Luigi's new place on the Avenue last night and it was the first time I had seen her since the old days. She was certainly not the same carefree Betty I once knew.

Bill, of course, did not come back. He was too far gone, the doctors said.

The kid is still very good to look at and while she was perched on the stool at the bar, one of the men who used to know her walked over and said something. She shook her head. Then he pulled a wad of bills out of his pocket and showed them to her.

I could see her reflection in the mirror and what her lips said was "I don't need it." The man went away puzzled. He couldn't understand such a complete change. He couldn't, of course. He never knew about Bill.

# Commercial Enterprise

## *Vivian Morris*

The girl stood near the curb leaning heavily against the hydrant at the corner of West 111 Street and Seventh Avenue. She was in earnest conversation with a man who shook his head violently from time to time and then edged away. She stood glaring at him as he walked down the street. When the man turned the corner, I walked over to her.

"Whut you want?" she said, with evident annoyance and suspicion.

"Y'aint gotta git sore at me." I tried to be as hard as she, assuming an attitude of one who's in on it. To come as an inquiring reporter would have evinced either suspicion of a policewoman, or a healthy stream of invectives and risk being told to mind my goddamn business.

"How come I ain't gotta git sore at you? Who you? I ain't seen you before. Watcha want, huh?"

"Sure y'aint seen me before. I just got into town. I been workin' this in Philly an' business is so hell lousy I just couldn' do much. The cops gettin' strict. Wuz run in last week an' got warned to stay hell outa Philly or be sent away. So I come here. I don't know nothin' about New York. I gotta get acquainted. I gotta talk to somebody. I don' know one square from the other. So I come over t'you. Nothin' wrong in that, is there?"

"Naw, I s'pose there ain' nothin' wrong. Whatcha wanta talk about? That ole John got me sore. They're gittin' cheaper alla time. I gotta make a livin'. What the hella they care. They ain' gotta heart. Offerin' me a buck. Imagine! A buck ! Just the kinda guys that want more outa yuh fur their lousy buck than whut they use to git fur five.

"Well, c'mon, sister; let's go ova t'my bung hole an' I'll show yuh th' ropes. But don't cha go pickin' up on nis block. We' strict on territory, an' th' boss ain' got no sympathy with outside chisilers. Maybe he'll take ya in an' maybe not. Let's git." The girl pulled herself off the hydrant, shuffled her clothing, and took me to her room. The room was the filthiest affair imaginable—not like those in the wealthier districts that cater to the monied population. The whole getup consisted of a bed with soiled linen and no pillow, an old bureau, and a single chair. The walls were de-plastered in numerous places. No windows.

"Some dump," she stated factually.

"There's worse. Whut else d'ya need?"

"Whut else? Oney ina las' year I been pullin' in cheap customers. Had a joint ten times bettern nis. Them days is gone. Let's git t' talkin'."

"How'dya git inta this business. Y'r pretty young yet. Been in it long?"

"Naw, oney four years. T'ain't long; some a us has worked fur the boss ten n' fifteen years. Been doin' swell some a em till the depression. Things kinda fell out. Some em customers lost jobs an' asked fur cuts. We hadda accommodate or else lose em."

"How come ya got inta this stuff? It's kinda lousy business. Y'ain't so bad lookin'."

"Hey, you askin' me questions or whut? Awright, ain' no harm askin'. Yeh, it ain' hot. Yur right, sister. I hates it like all hell. I hates myself too fur doin' it. But whut the hell are yuh gonna do? Whut? I ain' got no folks. I'm twenty-two now, oney twenty-two. Figger it out. Been at it four

goddamn years. Means I wuz only eighteen when I git
started. Why? Cuz I didn't have nobody here an' didn' have
no job an' no money. I gotta eat, I gotta live, hey? I need
clothes. Livin' in a stinkin' hole ain' no joke. Nuthin' wuz
in sight so I hadda ump. I hadda. I wuz oney eighteen, see,
eighteen. Imagine."

The girl burst into tears that left tracks down her heavily
rouged and powdered face.

"All right, I don' hafta cry. It's a long time ago. A whole
lifetime fur me. Oney four years an' 'at means a whole lifetime, see? Whut wuz I t'do? I gits acquainted with somebody
an' gits introduced to this here boss, an' the bastard makes
more outa it than I do. I supplies myself an' he takes the
cash an' gives me a goddamn handout. I can't even do business ona side. He'd kill me. He'd break my neck. I tried it
once an' he beat me up. I ain' done it since. Jail? Been in
jail more'n hair on yo' head. They gits tired jailin' me. All
they say is 'Again?' Take a tip, sister: if yuh works fur somebody git holda white customers. They pays better. Yeh, I
wanta git outa this like all hell.

"When? An' how? No jobs forced me in an' no jobs is
keepin' me in. They says this is a rich country. I ain' seen
it, nevva. I don' expects t'see it nevva. I almos' give up hope
fur anythin' except this here so-n'-so business. Whut else is
there, huh? Nothing. Well, if ya wanta see th' boss, let's git.
Y'ain' goin' now, awright—I'll be seein' yuh!"

*June 1, 1939*

# Dancing Girls

## *Vivian Morris*

Lilly Lindo, one of the Apollo Theatre dancing girls, isn't
as happy as she looks when she trips out on the stage four
times each day, seven days a week. In between shows and
after the last show at night, she rehearses for the next week's
bill. "I been doin' this for goin' on two years now, hopin'
an' wishin' that someday I'll get a break an' be somebody.
I want t'see mah name in 'lectric lights an' in alla newspapers. Knows I'm black, an' I knows black folks has gotta go
a long ways befo' they arrive. But I got one thing in th' back
a this head a mine, an' that is 'Color Can't Conquer Courage.' I'm gonna be a [famous singer] like a Florence Mills.
Does you remember her, Miss?

"Y'knows when she started dancin' she was oney five
years old? At an entertainment her Sunday school was put-
tin' on it was, an' she kep' on from there to the nickelodeons
on 135th Street an' on, an' on, till she became the sensation
of two continents. She danced an' sung for kings, princes,
an' all the rest a royalty. Lawd, am I wishin' an' hopin' that
one a these nights some a them white folks who come to
Harlem lookin' for talent will see sumthin' in me an' give
me a chance where I wouldn't have t'do four shows a day
for seven days a week.

"Florence Mills knocked 'em dead ev'vy time she came
on the stage. The Duke a Win'sor saw her 'strut her stuff'
thirteen times. They even call her the black ambassador to
the world, but things like that never went to her head. Her

spirit was typical of the black, and did she have pride in her own people! Whenever she was playin' in a show on Broadway she always seed to it that it came to Harlem even for a week so that her own people who didn't have money enough to go down on Broadway would not be denied the privilege of seein' her. Lawd, I can see an' hear her now, singin': 'I'm a little blackbird lookin' for a bluebird,' in her small warblin' voice, her figgitin' feet dancin' as though she was walkin' on fine wires an' had 'lectric sparks goin' through her body. Jesus! she shore did her stuff with enjoyment. I'm gonna be that someday, shore enough. I'm twenty-three now. Keep watchin' the newspapers—you gonna read about me. Florence Mills was one a God's chosen chill-ren. She make as much as three thousan' five hun'red dollars a week an' she didn't leave 133rd Street either, until God saw fit t'take her offa this wicked earth, an' she was moved outa there. Sometime I think God ain' fair as He should be. Florence Mills die when she reached the top. She didn' enjoy the money she made. She was in demand. They had big plans for her an' all of a sudden God came on the scene. She was one of His chill'ren; he step right in an' clip her wings. Her shufflin' feet danced her way t'Glory. She was a God-given genius. People like Florence Mills make this world a better place t'live in. She did a helluva lot t'wipe out race prejudice. If all they say about the Hereafter is true, then the Heavenly Gates must a swung ajar for Florence Mills t'enter an' shine in Heaven, cause she sure did shine down here.

"That was some year an' month a disappointments in Harlem, November 1927. The Republicans swep' Harlem, Marcus Garvey was bein' deported, an' our Queen a Happiness died."

*July 14, 1939*

# Finger Waves and
# Nu Life Pomades

*Vivian Morris*

The largest and most profitable profession indulged in by
black women in Harlem is the beauty shop. Beauty culture
takes care of over fifty percent of the black professional
women as well as supplying jobs for a goodly portion of the
male populace in the role of salesmen, advertisers, and
beauticians.

The most widely known of the persons who took advantage of the knowledge that black women desire beautiful hair
and soft attractive skin was Mme. C. J. Walker who cleared
over a million dollars through the sale of her skin bleaches,
hair pomades, etc. The better known systems that are used
by the several hundred beauty shops that are sprinkled
through Harlem are the Apex, Poro, Nu Life, and Hawaiian
systems, and the money made by the owners of the schools
teaching by these systems contributes greatly to the economic life of Harlem; were they stopped it would leave a
big vacuum in the community's budget.

There are four general headings under which the shops
of Harlem may be listed according to clientele. From West
135 Street down to 110 Street on Eighth, Seventh, and
Lenox Avenues, known as lower Harlem, are the shops

where the "average Harlemite" gets her work done. From West 135 to 138 Streets on Seventh Avenue is the section where the theatrical group gets its hair done. From West 138 Street north on Seventh and Lenox Avenues to Sugar Hill, which is above West 145 Street, is the location of the shops that cater to the Black elites who dwell in the fashionable Sugar Hill section. The numbered streets contain beauty shops that draw the bulk of their patrons from the particular locality from which the operators come; if the operator is from Columbia, South Carolina, then the persons who are the clients in that particular shop are from that section as nearly as possible. Hence there are four classifications of shops, "average Harlemite," "theatrical," "elite," and "hometown."

I happened to be in a shop in the "average Harlemite" area on a Thursday, just before the afternoon rush of the women who do domestic work and get a half Thursday off. I heard a grumbling conversation going on between two apprehensive operators. "Well it's Thursday again," said the tall one. "Soon the place will be so crowded with kitchen mechanics you can't move."

"Yeh, it wouldn't be so bad," sighs the stocky one looking at her feet reflectively, "if you didn't have to work so long. We won't be able to leave this shop until two o'clock tomorrow morning."

"The Union did do a little bit of good by saying that we had to close the doors at ten P.M., because we used to get out at five and six in the morning before," said the first speaker.

"One of these days," said the stocky speaker, "when this place is full of people who come in just before closing time, without an appointment, I'm gonna jump salty [fly off the handle], and throw up both hands and holler."

"It's sure no bed of roses," agreed the tall operator. "We learned beauty culture to get away from sweating and scrubbing other people's floors and ran into something just as bad—scrubbing peoples scalps, straightening, and curling their hair with a hot iron all day and smelling frying hair."

"Yeh," answers the short woman, "and you sweat just as much or a damn sight more and most of em are in a hurry. But I think it's a little better than housework—it's cleaner and you don't have no white folks goin' around behind you trying to find a speck of dirt."

"Oh, here comes one of my calkeener broads (a woman who cooks in a private family). If she mentions her madam I'll choke her. You'd think on their day off they'd forget their madams.

"Hello, Miss Adams. You're on time," said the tall operator.

"Yeh," says Miss Adams, popping chewing gum and all in a dither. "Got to make time. Me and my boyfriend got a little matter to straighten out this afternoon. He's got to tell me one thing or another. Then, we're gonna dig that new jive [see the new show] down the Apollo; then we'll cut out to the Savoy and beat out a few hoof rifts [dance] till the wee hours then I'll fall on back to the righteous mansion [job] dead beat for shut-eye [sleepy] but willing to carry on [work].

"You sure are making the most of your day off," avers the operator, covering the woman's head with a bubbling shampoo and dousing her head in the sink, scrubbing vigorously with a stiff brush.

"I didn't tell you what my madam said—hey take it easy on the top piece [head]," yells Miss Adams as the operator scrubs vigorously and looks at the other operator meaningfully as Miss Adams mentions her madam.

"My madam," resumes Miss Adams, "asked me what I had done to my hair last Friday when she saw it all curly and pretty. I told her I'd been to the hair dresser. She asked me how much it cost and when I told her she just looked funny and started to ask me how I could afford it. She needn't worry cause I'm dead sure I'm gonna ask her for a raise cause this little money she pays me ain't a drop in the bucket."

I dropped in one of the "hometown" shops and saw a breezy, well-groomed man enter and make his way to the back of the shop saying, "They're at the post. Don't get left."

The operators excused themselves and handed the man a piece of paper, which he copied. "Hey Ann," he asks. "Is this five-one-seven or five-eleven? Your figures are so hard to figure out."

"Five-one-seven," retorts Ann, "You can't read. Better get them numbers right, cause they're hot."

"Is that the number man?" asks a customer, "Give me three-seventy, for a dime. I dreamed about my dead uncle and every time I dream about him three-seventy comes out."

The mentioning of the number as a "dream number" causes most of the customers and the operators to play it because they all believe in dreams. When the writer leaves his book is loaded with the 370, which thereby becomes a "hot number."

In another "hometown" shop, I found operators selling tickets to a Beauticians Ball, while the customers sold them tickets to a supper for the church or their own house rent parties.

When I entered a shop in the "theatrical" area a male operator was washing a person's hair whom you would assume to be a woman in slacks. When the person turned around, it was a man. Yes, the theatrical men and a few nontheatrical men get their hair straightened and waved.

The conversation was about a currently popular star. The fellow who was getting his hair washed says, "Chick Webb sure pulled some 'hep jive' when he signed Ella Fitzgerald up. I hear from good sources that Benny Goodman offered gangs of money for her contract. Chick said no can do.

"Yeh," answers a dreamy-eyed girl getting wavy ringlets

pressed over her entire head. "I remember Ella when—ain't changed a bit towards little Fifi."

"The *Swing Mikado*'s been sold I hear," says one girl as a hot comb is pulled through her hair.

"The actors think that's weird jive" says another. "They ain't comin' up to that tab." [Don't want to work for a private owner.]

"I know what the jive is. WPA says the sale is left up to the cast. They want to put us back on relief. Too many of us on Broadway at the same time. A hundred and ten of us in *Hot Mikado* and seventy-five of us in *Swing Mikado*. They'll either take us out on the road or fire us here. If Equity takes us in then we have some protection, but they'll ditch us before Equity gets around to us. What the hell is the difference anyway? They got the money and they'll keep you right where they want to, unless we have a goddamn riot, and how much good would that do? A hell of a lot, don't fool yourself. Didn't we get jobs on a hundred and twenty-fifth Street after the March nineteenth riot?"

In the Sugar Hill area I found well dressed women pulling up in big cars. Their topics are the grave international situation, and the latest plays, and the teachers discuss schools. "I see where *Address Unknown* was a best-seller for last month. The copies were sold almost as soon as they reached the bookstores," says one.

"Oh yes," remarked another woman (wearing two diamonds and an imported wristwatch) from under her application of bleach cream. "The author was very fortunate. At another time it would just have been another book—interesting reading, of course, but the story—then the book was published at the precise, psychological time when the Madman of Europe was shedding blood all over Germany. Result? A best-seller."

Suddenly a man darted in the swanky shop with a bag and made his way to the rear, with significant nods to the others. The operators went to the rear singly. He was peddling "hot stuff." The operators made their purchases and hurried back to their customers. A nosy customer asks, "What is he selling? Last time I was here I got some lovely perfume very cheap."

"Lingerie," says the operator.

"Reasonable?" asks the inquisitive one. "They have ten dollar tags. He sells them for three," answers the operator.

"Please tell him I want to see them," says the customer jumping out of the chair, with her beauty treatment half finished. With the apron around her neck she goes to the rear of the shop followed by more interested customers.

*April 19, 1939*

# PART 4

# Uptown Gods, Kings, and Other Spiritual Entities

If you were to count landmarks on the streets uptown, one of the things that would not go unnoticed are the number of churches, temples, and the wide variety of places where spiritual people meet with their gods.

Whether its people are worshiping in traditional places or fall willingly at the feet of idols who promised to deliver them from evil, Harlemites had no trouble filling up places that offered them hope and salvation.

In the following section, we meet Mother Horn, a storefront preacher whose huge flock of the faithful not only worship God in the presence of this charismatic leader, they seem to worship God's messenger.

In pieces called Peace in the Kingdom by Frank Byrd, a similar one by Dorothy West called Temple of Grace, and Divine Comes to Harlem, we meet some of the most influential spiritual leaders ever to travel north of West 96 Street. Together, these stories cover what safely could be called the spiritual history of this part of Manhattan.

As is often the case with religion and spiritual entities, it is sometimes difficult to separate the gods from their messengers.

# God Was Happy

## *Vivian Morris*

Mother Horn was as much of a Harlem landmark during the Depression years as Sugar Hill, Striver's Row, or the Apollo Theatre are icons of this community.

The Pentecostal church she headed was one flight up over a hardware store with seating for eight hundred people. As you entered the door you were greeted by portly black women garbed in white who poked out a collection plate to lift the silver offering.

To the extreme right were uninterrupted rows of chairs arranged from the back all the way up to within three yards of the pulpit. The pulpit faced the front seats and rostrum with about eight chairs on each side; they were occupied by the angels.

In a little cranny, which jutted from the left, were about six rows of seats, enough to seat thirty-six people.

To the left of, and above, the pulpit were eight crutches, purported to have been left by Mother Horn's followers who had walked away healed.

It was a cold Sunday night in November, just four days before Thanksgiving, and the house was filled to capacity, with many worshippers standing in the aisles and doorways.

Mother Horn stretched forth her firm brown hands in a silent command for quiet; a hushed awe struck the group that comprises the disciples of her Pentecostal church on Lenox Avenue in the heart of Harlem.

The sixteen hundred eyes of this congregation were glued to this strong-featured, commanding black woman, who was dressed in white from head to foot. A shimmering silk gown differentiated Mother Horn (affectionately dubbed by some of her followers as God's right arm) from her "angels," who were dressed entirely in white cotton raiments.

The angels who were seated in the pulpit and in the front rows of the church formed a white phalanx of avid worshippers. They sucked in their breath with spellbound ecstasy as the drops of wisdom began to flow indirectly from the holy lips of God through Mother Horn.

"God . . . is . . . unhappy," she slowly intoned with a slight, deliberate pause between words.

"Oh. Mother Ho'n whut we done done?" agonized a big frog-eyed black angel, as she slowly clasped and unclasped her hamlike hands that had become so from years of toil and back-breaking labor in an Alabama cotton field. Her body was broken, but her spirit lived.

A low wail swelled from the entire group of angels and they slowly waved their arms, warding off sin.

"Please, dear Angels, "t'aint whut you done done. Hi'ts de worl dats displeasin Him—dese debbil-infested fo'ks." She slowly stretched out her arms, her magnetic fingers swaying the wills of her disciples. They followed her every move with their bodies.

"Wicked, wicked, people," chanted the angels, swaying from side to side then rocking to and fro in hypnotic unison.

Then suddenly, Mother Horn was transformed into a dynamo of action. Her eye flashed, her tensed body seethed, swirling religious fervor out into this huge room like sprinkles of magical, unseen dust. God's right arm stormed the pulpit transmitting her fiery words out into the room where they were absorbed by her disciples and all who were in earshot of them.

For the next three hours Mother Horn was throttling the problem at hand, wiping out sin by rubbing and preaching with words and action.

God must be appeased, pacified, and made happy.

"God is in me," flamed Mother Horn. She stamped her foot to the off beat of the hand-clapping tempo, kept by the members. "Dese sins mus go."

With an imperceptible motion of her hand Mother Horn signaled the drummer, piano player, and tambourine beater to swing out, slowly, softly, ever increasing in crescendo and time.

"Mus Go," screeched the disciples. They waved their arms, jerked their heads, twisted squirmed.

"Got to git fiah" screamed Mother Horn, bucking her head and rollin her eyes up toward the ceiling.

"Fiah! Fiah! Fiah! Burn out de sin!" chanted the disciples. Her face was distorted with paroxysm after paroxysm of fervor.

A thin dark-skinned woman, clad in a close-fitting red dress, suddenly jumped up trembling, swaying, then she thrust out her stiffened arms. This was a victory dance. She must please the gods. She swayed from side to side in sinuous rhythm to the hand clapping and maddening thumps of the drum. Wild primitive jungle music was leaping from the piano, from the tambourine.

"God, oh, Laud God Almighty mus be pleased," she shouted.

The music became faster, faster, faster. She gave a frenzied unbounded exhibition of trucking the Susie Q, Shag, a popular dance, but there was not one vestige of sacrilege in her prancing.

"Have Mercy Laud. Have Mercy Laud, Mercy, Mercy," she said. The disciples were rolling, reeling, and stamping wildly. The lady in red was running around the church mumbling a weird chant. She was joined by a woman in black, another, then another, until the whole church joined in.

Everybody was rolling, crawling, running, or babbling—old women, young girls. The angels had their hands full trying to control the other disciples.

The lady in red was reaching a climax. She stopped and was instantly surrounded by five angels waving away and quieting her down. She stuttered, saying only short phrases like "Sh, Sh, Sh, Mother Horn, Sh, Sh Mother Horn." She groaned as she stiffened then collapsed into the waiting arms of the angels who quickly dragged her to a corner and covered her with an old, dirty blanket. They left her lying in a state of coma from whence she would awake as a disciple of Mother Horn.

The lady in black fainted. Here and there a holy roller twitched in religious ecstasy, then was silent. The angels worked like fury, using blankets and coats to cover their fallen sisters and brothers. Blankets and people were dropping like hail.

At a signal from God's right arm, the three musicians slowed their tune, decreased their crescendo, then dwindled away. The disciples slumped limply in their seats; the floor was littered with disheveled inert forms dotted here and there with the sweat-stained garments of a Holy Ghost–ridden angel. Here and there a tired angel could be seen still rubbing a convert—her back, her breast, rubbing out sin.

Happy sighs and short yelpings of relief pierced the church, punctured by a few "Mother Horn's," added by the people who were gradually coming out of their stupor. Mother Horn, ever forceful, beamed with a calm triumph as angels swarmed, one gently wiping perspiration from her face, another adjusting her raiment, and a third holding a glass of water for her to drink.

Having completed their task, they were calmly waved to their seats with heavenly words.

Mother Horn raised her hand for silence. She said solemnly, "We will now witness de fo' mal ceptin' into God's Kingdom of de new disciples."

"Amen"

"Ah will 'noint dey hands wid de holy watah, cod'n to de Bible."

"Amen"

She poured water from a glass and the new saved sisters half dragged by the hefty angels were passed under the holy hand, and with many holy gestures and an unintelligible prayer they passed into the kingdom of the saved. As the last sister passed under her hand, Mother Horn, "God's Right Arm" raised both hands, palms facing the audience and said, "God is happy."

A month later . . . these worshipers returned on Christmas night. The air was charged with religious zeal, brought on by the holiday season, which seemed to exude from the fanaticlike faces of Mother's followers.

The services began in an unprecedented fashion. A collection was taken up while the different saints of this church and its members got up and testified.

A big fine-looking sister gave the salutatory preface. She raised her arms, saying, "Saints and brothers, we's goin' tuh take the collection firs' cause we wants tuh tak' up as much money wile Mother Ho'ns away as we do wen she's heah. De on'y way we kin do dis is to tek up three collections. One at the beginning, one in de middle, an' one at the en. We'll begin by my testifying den y'all can testify as de spirit moves yo."

She waved her arms as a signal for sisters in the strategic points of the church to begin their job of collecting the offerings.

"Now, I'll tell y'all bout a wonderful thang that happened to me las' week. I wanted wuk, in de wus way. So I got down on mah knees an' start praying. Next day jobs came tumblin in, evah which-away. One came from White Plains an I tol' de lady I wouldn' tek' less dan five dollars a day, cause I didn' want de job anyhow. Den, praise de Lawd, de 'oman say she give me five dollars an!—praise Gawd—car-fare. Amen . . . Amen.''

Several of the steady sisters wagged their heads from side to side then nodded a vociferous approval.

A young girl, of an easily-moved temperament, jumped up and began testifying in a shrill voice. Her story did not ring true, but she carried the crowd with her tearful rendi-tion. "Day before Christmas I tol' my mother I wanted shoes for Christmas an' she said I couldn't have them because the rent was due and had to be paid," she said tearfully.

The members listened silently.

"Then, I opened the door and started to go out, I saw a lady outside of our door an' the Lord said for me to follow her. I followed her to a Hundred and twenty-fifth Street an she opened her pocketbook an' took out five dollars an' gave it to me an' tol' me to get myself a pair of shoes!"

The church was pierced with short, "Huhs," "Praise Gawds," and "By de will uh de Lord." Then a sister started to softly hum a tune. The others joined in and soon the church was rocking to the hand clapping of the sisters and the rhythm of the hymn.

The young girl who had testified became filled with the "spirits" and, after a few preliminary yelps, took a running dive and landed in the laps of the white-clad saints sitting in the first row. She stretched out rigidly and the sisters gently put her on the floor and covered her with a filthy blanket.

The two white men sitting on the left of the pulpit, one of whom was the guest preacher for a week, slapped their thighs, exchanged remarks, and laughed loudly. [Maybe that was the way the spirit moved them.] Their mode of religious expression merits only a disapproving glance from the three gargantuan sisters seated in front of the pulpit. They became silent.

At the conclusion of the hymn, a muddy yellow man, who was seated on the right of the pulpit, jumped up and lifted both hands sayin' in a booming voice, "Evah-body say Amen."

"Amen!"

"This sho is good meat, roun' heah tonight." He stood, smiling, with his thumbs hooked in the arm holes of his vest. He looked like a retired gambler who had dropped into preaching in his old age because it was a soft racket.

"Evahbody say Amen, again," he repeated.

"Amen!"

"All right," he said, "now sing one uh dam good ol' sweet hymns 'Walk in Jerusalem Jus' Like John'!"

The piano played a chorus, other voices blended in. There were varied interpretations of the words but the music was sweet, touching something deep, intangible. Maybe the Holy Ghost really was here.

One of the younger brothers was seized with the spirit and he charged down the aisle and leaped straight up, twisted, and landed on his head with a sickening thud. No faking there—he was out like a light. A blanket was thrown over the inert, crumpled form.

A young girl, attired in a swanky fur coat, began to walk up and down the aisle warming up for the "rolling" exhibition that she was to put on in a few minutes.

The singing increased and the girl in the fur coat walked faster. Up the aisle—down. Up—down—up—down—she was running. She threw her arms out wildly shouting, "Glory, glory!" Some women in white grabbed her. They took her watch off and rubbed her spine, her breasts, frenziedly. She passed out.

Two little boys, about four or five years old, began swaying their arms in hypnotic cadence. They fixed their eyes vacantly on the ceiling. It was a well-rehearsed act.

After a long time, the big brother who looked like a gambler, raised his hands for silence. "We'll now introduce the speaker of de evening! He's gonna make a fire-and-brimstone talk on backsliders. Dis is Reb'n Crum."

Reverend Crum was a shabbily dressed, red-faced individual with stringy light hair. He walked to the center of the pulpit with a bouncing stride and began in a cackling, fishmongerlike voice, "We're going' to talk about, on this glorious Christmas night, backsliders and these penny-pinching women. Praise God."

"Amen."

He spread his stumpy legs apart and shook his pudgy fingers at the congregation, saying snappily, "You know, brothers an' sisters, there's some of us sisters (puts hands on hips and mimics a woman) who pinch a penny here and pinch a penny there, an' hide it in the piano. You know." He winks.

"Amen!" chorused the brothers in the room.

"Gawd don't like that—Praise his name!" said Crum. "But that ain't the worst of it, oh no. When they git a few dollars saved, they sneak out to the gin joints and drink gin and smoke cigarettes and come in at one or two o'clock and say to their husbands, "Sleep on, dear, I've been to church.""

"Preach," the brothers yelled.

He looks at the audience in a mock startled fashion. "What are you brothers talkin bout? Your turn is next. Oh yes, Praise Gawd."

"Aha! chortled the sisters gleefully.

"Some of you men leave your wives and put the blame on them, oh yes. You say they are no good—don't you?" Crum looked around dramatically.

"Yeh!" say the sisters (some of them evidently having been ousted by their spouses).

"When the real reason is," he paused, "you want to move in with some other no 'count jezebel!"

The women screamed in approval and stamped their feet

in a steady acclaim. But Crum didn't know how to clinch
his point. He rambled off on some other muck that did not
interest the members and they began leaving. First, they left
singly, then they left in droves.

"I see some of the brothers and sisters can't take these
stones I'm throwin'," Crum smirked.

The faithful saints in white supported him with weak,
mechanical, "Amen, Amen."

But the people continued to leave.

The sister who was in charge of lifting the collection
looked at the people who were leaving, with a frantic, anxious expression.

Reverned Crum took a hint and cut his sermon down.

He had barely finished speaking when the sister jumped
up with the collection plate, saying to the few remaining
people, "Y'all haf to sacrifice more, 'cause so many left an'
I wants one dolla' from everybody heah. If you can't give,
jes' set still an' pray dat dose who can give, give enough to
make' up yo' share. Amen. Pass de plate, sisters."

The sisters passed the plates and lifted a goodly unannounced amount.

The big, gamblerlike brother motioned for everybody to
bow. He prayed.

*November 23, 1938*

# Peace in the Kingdom

## *Frank Byrd*

A story that is often overlooked when discussing Harlem folklore, is the lofty tale of a man who lured Harlemites into his confidence and converted them into faithful followers of what became known as the cult of Father Divine.

Father Divine gradually became known in the mid-1930s to the police in Sayville, Long Island. He became an almost legendary figure in lower Long Island where he first set up his cult headquarters. Many stories about his peculiar religious doings and subsequent tiffs with the law are told by local inhabitants.

When they first came to town nobody paid much attention to them. They were just another group of blacks who had come to Long Island. But it soon became apparent that this group was different in any number of ways that had initially gone unnoticed.

Like most of the blacks who came to the island, they worked hard in the white folks' kitchens all day. But after work, they seemed to finish up with their pots and pans and make a bee-line for Father Divine's little meeting house in the back of Joe Korsak's grocery store.

Major T. Divine, a squat, woolly-headed, middle-aged little black man with a sly, roguish gleam in his eye, was their leader. In the daytime he ran the Sayville employment agency for "colored domestics" but at night, he was a man of God.

In fact, many of his followers insisted that he was "God Hisself—in person" and nobody could dispute them. Their bodies belonged to the white folks during the day but their souls, both day and night, were the exclusive property of their foxy, pint-sized leader. They even slept with him in a big old house planted among a grove of elm trees at the end of Plum Hill Road. They called themselves his disciples, his children. And they called him "Father— Father Divine."

Well, the townspeople didn't mind this so much, but that business of nightly worship in the back of Korsak's store began to get them down. When the sisters and brothers began to feel the spirit in earnest, they whooped and hollered something awful. And their shouts, in a suburban place like Sayville where everyone went to bed early, could be heard for miles around.

The townsfolk rose up in arms and got together to see what could be done about it. They finally decided that Divine had to go. A committee waited on him at his place of business bright and early one morning and did what they could to persuade the good reverend to move on to greener pastures.

"Nothing doing!" or words to that effect, answered the right reverend. He was doing all right in Sayville and the idea of giving it up was the last thing that ever occurred to him. His disciples were all employed as cooks, maids, gardeners and chauffeurs, in the homes of the country-side's wealthiest people and they brought all their earnings home to him. Why should he move? The very idea was preposterous.

The natives retreated for another war council and Father Divine's disciples continued happily, almost ecstatically, about their work. Whether they were in the midst of shopping for their employers, or baking a deep-dish apple pie, they unexpectedly used to burst with little exclamations of delight like "Peace." "It's truly wonderful!" "Thank you, Father!" and so on. Even when they stumbled and fell or accidentally upset a glass of water in their masters' or mistresses' laps, they said: "Thank you, Father. I'm sorry."

Well, even then, the employers couldn't find it in themselves to be mad.

"They're just great big children," they'd say, and smile indulgently.

The fact is, the religious satellites, who called themselves by such funny names as "Happy Boy Job," "Patience Delight," "Eternal Faith," etc. were honest people and were excellent servants, according to their employers.

And so, Father Divine remained. And when the white housewives greeted their cooks and maids with an amused, "Good morning, Charity Light. How are you today?"

Charity Light would answer in all earnestness: "Peace, ain't it wonderful? Father Divine is god! Do y'all want bacon 'n' eggs fo' breakfast dis mo'nin!"

Even on Main Street it was not unusual to hear one of Father Divine's angels, in a none-too-melodious voice, sing "Father Divine is the Light of the World."

The Divinites, as they were called, soon saved enough to buy the two houses adjoining their property on Plum Hill Road. One of the houses was converted into a sort of temple where the nightly meetings were held and Sunday dinners served. Free dinners, they were, and sumptuous. Feasts to rival those of Biblical times. Not only the angels participated. Everyone was invited. Not many outsiders came at first. They were still a little wary. A few of the bolder townspeople ventured in, however, and came away with wild stories of the huge banquet tables and savory cooked meals.

More and more people appeared as the Sundays passed.

Some came all the way from the city or the end of the island. And they were not disappointed. The banquets were as colorful and extravagant as they had been pictured. But most amazing of all was that, of all the hundreds of people who ate their fill, nobody paid. Everything was free. The treat was on Father Divine.

"God provides everything for his people," some of the angels were heard to say, as the free chicken, pork chops, roast brown duck and suckling pig, smothered spare ribs, and an assortment of vegetables, fruits, and nuts were passed around in abundance.

Eventually, hundreds of black people from the city were attracted to the quiet community and they arrived in rusty, broken-down cars every Sunday afternoon. Neighbors complained that they drove over their carefully tended lawns and trampled the municipal shrubbery, until the ire of the townspeople was aroused once more. They trooped down in a body to demand that the police do something about it.

"Police Chief Tucker," the spokesman for the group began, "you've got to do something about those people. They're a nuisance and are running property values down to nothing. They've got most of us crazy, whooping and hollering until all hours of the night."

It was an election year, so Tucker got busy. He posted No Parking signs everywhere in the vicinity of the Kingdom, as Father Divine began calling the enclave where he worshiped with his angels. No one in town could remember ever seeing a No Parking sign before this time. Many of the poor whites saw the town's problem as an opportunity for them. They let visitors to the Kingdom park their cars in their yards for twenty-five cents.

Chief Tucker, not to be outdone, began stopping all cars, looking at registration certificates, and being generally annoying to all black people seen driving a car in the neighborhood. This did not stop the crowds. In fact, they got bigger. Chief Tucker cussed over it. He pulled his hair out. But no matter what he did or how much he raved and ranted, the influx could not be stopped.

"Boys," he said to the citizens' committee, "I've tried everything I could think of but they keep comin'. I'm sorry. There's nothing else I can do."

The town fathers, more alarmed than ever, got together and petitioned for Divine's arrest for being a public nuisance. The petition specifically cited the nightly goings-on at the Kingdom for causing the populace to endure many sleepless nights, thus becoming increasingly jittery, and Father Divine was hauled unceremoniously into court. The atmosphere there was so hostile, however, that the defense moved for a change of venue, and the proceedings were resumed in a little neighboring town.

Judge Smith, who presided at the hearing, was known to dislike black people. He found Father Divine guilty, sentenced him to spend a year in jail, and fined him five hundred dollars.

Four days later, much to the surprise of everyone, Judge Smith dropped dead. The doctor said, "Heart trouble."

Father Divine looked and acted like the cat that swallowed the canary and took credit for the judge's demise, saying, "The force of nature work with me."

The townspeople back in Sayville began to wonder if there wasn't something to the story of old Divine having magical powers.

The "angels" went hop-skipping through the streets shouting: "We told you so! Father Divine is God! Peace! Ain't it wonderful?"

Meanwhile, Father Divine had hired lawyers from Harlem who appealed the case against him, and the judge's decision was immediately reversed. Then things escalated. The night Father Divine was exonerated, the angels celebrated. They danced wildly around the grounds, holding their hands skyward, and babbled in unknown tongues and sang, more lustily than ever: "Father Divine's the prince of world!" And there was peace in the kingdom.

*June 1936*

# Father Divine Comes to Harlem

## *Levi Hurbert*

**Divinites set up shop in Harlem, taking advantage of the unemployment that soared beyond fifty percent in uptown neighborhoods in 1938. Hungry people—black and white—came to Father Divine's missions and stores throughout Harlem and found cheap food. It cost them only a few pennies and the time it took to hear the many impromptu sermons delivered freely by the angels who served them.**

It takes forever to be served at the Eighth Avenue cafe where Brother All Peace Little John is manager. But the place is entertaining in an odd sort of way and is always filled up with a wide variety of hungry, ill-clad customers who seem willing to wait their turn for the plentiful bounty served here.

This eating place is the business of the Peace Movement, whose members act as cooks, waiters, and the pantry help. But the customers who seem to wait patiently for the meals are here because the prices are lower than probably any cafe in the city serving similar meals. Even smokers crowd into this nonsmoking restaurant and wait their turn, even though the workers are liable to break out into songs with a distinct religious message at any time.

Brother Little John is a fifty-eight-year-old disciple of the Father Divine Movement. Easily mistaken for one of the many cults that operate in these uncertain economic times, this home-grown religious order operates restaurants, a grocery store, and a rooming house. Like all followers of Father Divine's teaching, Little John does not smoke, drink, or even chew gum or have sex—period. While the order advocates unity, this practice of total abstinence has been cited as a leading cause of divorce among converts. These guiding principles can be easily found in *The Spoken Word,* the order's weekly newspaper written for all Divinites. It is here that converts can read for themselves every word ever uttered by Father Divine, faithfully recorded by John Lamb, his personal secretary.

It's Saturday at 2539 Eighth Avenue, where the Brother Little John balks when asked his age, saying he was only truly born when he became a Divinite eight years ago. "I am a part of the immortality of Father Divine now," he says. "Peace."

This, the universal slogan of the Father Divine Movement, was spoken quietly by this brother, whose real last name, or should I say previous name, was Singleton.

Like the many other followers, Brother Little John is always willing to fill in the details about this religion he has followed so earnestly. In his view, Divinites participate in a vital movement, whose religious leader was ordained to take over the United States.

This is the story, as Brother Little John tells it.

"As far back as 1931, when father Divine had established a Heaven in Sayville, Long Island, the people of the world told and retold stories that were founded on first-hand evidence as well as on hearsay," he said.

"Every Sunday in 1931 it was the custom of the Father to invite Harlemites out to the Heaven and sit them around the festive board and allow them the use of the many automobiles in the Father's garage.

"One of the visitors, a young girl of about twenty, had begged a ride out to Sayville. She sat down at the table and ate a large meal, good wholesome food, which she admitted had become rather hard to get in Harlem, what with the Depression and being unemployed. The Father noticed this young girl and spoke to her.

" 'My child, would you like to stay here for a few weeks and enjoy the blessings of Heaven?'

" 'Father, I would be delighted.' "

Father had one of the archangels escort the young girl upstairs after dinner and when she reached the room set aside for her, she found shoes, stockings, a dress, and underthings, all new and exactly her size, laid out on the bed.

"The archangel smiled and said, 'Ain't it wonderful?'

"The girl asked, 'Are these clothes for me?'

" 'Yes. The Father, who knows everything, is aware of the sorry time you are having and it was he who put it in your mind to come out here. Now that you are here, he will see that you want for nothing as long as you believe. Ain't it wonderful?'

" 'It is truly wonderful,' said the amazed girl.

"The Evil One got into the folks of Sayville about this time and the police of Sayville arrested the entire household one Saturday night; most of us were held on a charge of disorderly conduct but the Father was charged with maintaining a disorderly house and held for the action of the court.

"When the judge asked us whether we had made loud noises and created a disturbance, we sang hymns in the courtroom and said that it was true that we were rejoicing in the favor of the Father and being glad would only disturb unbelievers.

"The judge charged us ten dollars and cost, each one, except the Father. The judge said that he would have to have a trial and stay in jail until that time. The Father paid our fines and when the police made us leave the courthouse, the Father said, 'My children. I will watch over the faithful. It is part of my will that I stay in jail, but I'll only stay here as long as I will it. So, go home, and everything will be all right, Peace.'

"We all shouted, 'Peace, Peace,' and went our way.

"Father was put in a cell and remained quiet all night, but when the keeper came in the morning with the coarse prison food, the Father wouldn't touch it. He had the keeper take the tray away.

" 'But, remember,' the keeper said, 'you get nothing else to eat.' Father said, 'Peace,' and immediately a beautiful breakfast appeared.

"The keeper passed the cell and was amazed to see the Father eating fresh eggs and ham with coffee. We were in the Heaven gathered around our breakfast table and Father's place was set as usual. Father came to the table and blessed the food for us to eat. The Father can be any and all places at one and the same time.

"When the Father was convicted, the judge didn't sentence him right away because he knew what had happened to two other judges who did that and died suddenly. So sure 'nough, the Sunday before the judge handed down a writ of doubt, and since then the case has never been brought to trial. The power of the Father is too well known to chance anyone fooling with it.

"The Father does not allow gum to be chewed by his followers, no smoking, and the hair must not be straightened, but must be as natural as it was ordained.

"Anyone who violates the teachings of the Father is bound to feel the anger of the Father, but those who believe in him are sure to have his blessings fall down upon them.

"I remember the woman who was helped by believing in the Father. She was without work, had no money, and the landlord was about to dispossess her. Her so-called friends had abandoned her, and in her hour of need there was no one to turn to; no one, that is, but the Father. She had heard of his doings and now that her sorrow was great, she prayed to the Father for help.

"She was in her almost empty apartment, down on her knees, asking for the Father to bring her strength and safety.

"It has been told me, and I have no reason to doubt it, that out of a hole in the wall a rat brought two fifty-dollar bills, which he laid at the poor woman's feet. Her troubles were over and I feel certain that the Father was the one responsible for the money sent her.

"I know because a few years ago I was unable to get work, and today, with the help of the Father, I have a restaurant where the people can get good food at a reasonable price. No one is turned away if he doesn't have the money. I also have a grocery store where the everyday necessities of life can be purchased much cheaper than elsewhere.

"All the money I make goes to keep up the good work of Father Divine. I sell *The Spoken Word,* in which is recorded every word spoken by the Father to his children. In this way I do my share and show my gratitude to the Father for his many blessings.

"Do you remember last summer? Those hot days were a warning to the people of the world that he was still watching and taking into account all the many things said against him.

"Father doesn't allow any of his children to go on relief and if any of them have ever been on relief Father makes them pay back all the money they ever got.

"Sure, some people have died in the Heaven. But they have been without faith. Perhaps they had faith for a while but Father would not have allowed them to die if they still believed in him.

"Faithful Mary was sick and living in sin when Father took pity in the goodness of his heart and made her well and let her live in Heaven with him. She tired of the happy way and went off with money which she had been keeping for the children. But she didn't really hurt Father because he is above such things.

"Roosevelt will be the last president. After him will come

the Divine Executive who will rule the world properly and all Father's children will once more live in Heaven. There will be peace in all the world."

*November 12, 1938*

# Emancipation

## Frank Byrd

The brother John Lamb speaks for the divine one himself at Father Divine's Extension Kingdom on West 123 Street and Lenox Avenue.

Lamb is part of something called the Jewish Conciliation Court of America, most likely a recruiting arm of the Divine empire.

Father Divine once said: "Emancipation is now open to those called Jews, by their accepting my message with the spirit of sincerity, forgetting their Adamic lineage, and recognizing the Christ consciousness as the Redeemer and Savior. The persecuted and downtrodden Jews in this, as in the old era, are crying out in anguish for their Savior. I am the answer to that cry and prayer, offering them complete emancipation, if they will but hear my voice and obey."

Not long after this public invitation, many persons of Jewish faith joined the Divine Movement. "Truly Wonderful," the following treatise, is a story of one of these religious converts.

No one would have objected, apparently, had she only attended one of Father Divine's meetings or even used her "highest intuition," as the squat, diminutive little black evangelist and spiritual cult leader advised her to do. Publicly forsaking and denying the Jewish faith, however, was a horse of another color; at least, that was the opinion of certain leaders of the Hebrew Benevolent Society, of which plump, redheaded Mrs. Sadie Bergenfeld [afterward known as Thankful Purity] was a full-fledged member. The society, in fact, felt so strongly about this matter that they called a meeting before the Jewish Conciliation Court of America for the sole purpose of giving the good lady the legal boot. In other words, they wanted to dispel her from their strictly orthodox society and deprive her of her rightful financial benefits that were due her after twenty years of monthly dues paying. But Thankful Purity was not the type to give up without a fight, so she took the witness stand to testify vehemently in her own behalf, her amber-green eyes flashing an indignant fire.

"Peace!" she began, with a decided Bronx accent. "It's wonderful!"

The three presiding judges were a little nonplussed by this strange procedure but bravely tried to carry on.

"Is it true that you belong to Father Divine's Heaven?" one of them asked.

"Belong?" Thankful Purity asked, puzzled. "What means belong?"

"Are you one of Father Divine's followers?" the judge amended.

"I follow the best" was the answer he got. "Father Divine is wonderful. I like him. Peace!"

"How did you become an 'angel'?" another judge wanted to know.

"It happened two years ago," the witness explained eagerly. "I was feeling very, very bad. I saw hundreds of doctors and they all told me I must have an operation, but they refused to guarantee that I would get well. So one day I was sick in bed when a colored girl came in to clean my house. I told her I was sick and she said I should go to see Father Divine.

"I got up and went right away to one of his meeting

rooms, and then I heard him speak. He was wonderful. He spoke of things I never heard of before; things I couldn't understand. I asked one of the women how I could speak to Father Divine and she told me to walk right up to him and say 'Peace!'

"When the meeting was over, I rushed up to the platform, grabbed Father Divine's hand, and cried: 'Peace!' I asked him what I must do to cure myself."

"What did he say?"

"He said: 'Use your highest intuition!' "

"Did you?"

"I don't know. All I remember is that I went home and fell asleep. When I awoke in the morning, I was feeling fine. Since that day I have never been sick. Now I am sure Father Divine is God."

"But," one of the judges protested, "this organization has a legal right to expel you. Their constitution says they can expel any member who leaves the Jewish faith. That is what you have done."

"I have not left the Jewish faith!"

Thankful Purity was very indignant in her denial.

"I am now more of a Jew than the rest of you. I can shake hands with the whole world. I am not prejudiced. I love everyone. That is peace . . . heaven on earth. Don't you believe in peace?"

"Don't you think it would cause peace," judge number two inquired, "if you resigned from the society?"

"I want peace. The lodge doesn't want peace. Why should they take away all my benefits for which my husband paid?"

"But you have violated the constitution by worshipping a different God."

"I am not worshipping a different God!" Thankful Purity shouted. "There is only one God, Father Divine. You don't know who God is. You don't know Father Divine."

"Well, what do you suggest that we do?" the court finally asked.

After thinking it over for a while, Thankful Purity said: "I want peace. I'll give up everything. I don't want anything they were supposed to give me. They can have it. I don't need anything. I've got heaven right here."

Without handing down any formal decision, the court assured the society that Thankful Purity [that is, Mrs. Bergenfeld] would resign from the organization. Thankful Purity, rising and walking from the room with aloof spiritual dignity and wearing an expression of glowing beatitude, stopped at the door and shouted a last-minute invitation in the direction of the judge's bench.

"Gentlemen," she said, "I wish you would come to our meetings. You would learn something. Peace! It's truly wonderful!"

*May 25, 1939*

# Divine Is Gawd

## *Herman Spector*

The little brown man is seated at the center of a long table
that forms the lower bar of a festive U in the rather dilapidated [place called] Heaven. (It's a religious sanctuary, a
banquet hall, and social icon at West 123 Street and Lenox
Avenue.) Electric bulbs sparkle; posters proclaim the message, inculcate the proper attitude:

NO NEGATIVE DISCUSSIONS OR GOSSIPING . . .
BUT MORE PRAISE FOR FATHER.

An endless succession of dishes, heaped with the bounty
of the Presence, are handed along the flanking tables, where
colored and white believers ingest a fifteen-cent banquet that
is beyond understanding. Flimsy balconies on both sides of
the hall are packed to the handrails with swaying, shouting,
singing, stamping women:

*O, Father is a victory,*
*Father is a victory,*
*Father is a victory*
*That overcomes the world . . .*
*We know that Father is a Victory.*

People standing inside and outside the U do not venture to approach too closely, but watch intently every movement and gesture made by this man, known throughout this city and others with large black populations as Father Divine. He looks downward, beneficent and unaware of the glaring red slogans: FATHER DIVINE IS GOD, unaware of the chair covered with baize upon which has been lovingly embroidered in white letters: GOD.

He is not eating; he toys with an array of glistening silver utensils, spread out like a fan on the tablecloth before him. He waits until the hullabaloo, the enthusiasm, and the chanting has died down. . . . Then he rises abruptly, deliberately speaks:

"Peace, everyone!" There are echoes of these words that spread throughout the hall. "Thank you, Father, let us be glad and rejoice in the living splendor of the Lord! So glad, Father! I am here to materialize all spiritual things by the recognition and the consciousness of Gawd among men! Yeah, Father! My personal presence is immaterial, I am not bound personally, I am impersonal, as the unifying presence of all things. This is the mystery and the parable in the unity of the Spirit. Gawd is so effectively present, even when He is absent, which proves all material things is spiritual, and all spiritual things is material. Just the same, it is true Cain did slay his brother Abel. Nevertheless he was and still is his brother's keeper. As a keeper of the sheep, as a shepherd, you shall cooperate together and look for the welfare of your fellow brother."

"Hear, hear! Yeah man!" someone shouts. "So sweet, how sweet!"

"So why should they fight together? Why not come together in the unity of the spirit an' unite together as one in one reality? The diverse systems of the universe should unify together! With all comfort an' security! For you an' your body shall be unified together! Like capital an' Labor, in one reality! I came here as one man in Jesus; as they were in the beginning all of one language an' of one speech. But this present generation has brought about a division, an' a language of diverse tongues was instituted! But I came here to bring them together on this earth, in the U.S.A., that they might come together as one man, E PLURIBUS UNUM!" he mumbles, saying words that resemble Latin phrases.

"An' I have been preordained as the kingdom of Gawd legalized, in the Constitution, by expressing that Gawd is a livin factor among us! Yes, it's a glorious privilege to live in the actual presence of Gawd, where it is rarest, it's a sweet feeling in the land o the Free! So glad, Father! So it was essential to me as I came, to prepare myself a tabernacle, an' I am not any special anybody, any special nationality, any race, but am Hu-man-ity itself!

"Yeah, man. We know you're Gawd!," someone shouts.

"I am not more than I am the other, for this is the living reality of the establishment of the Kingdom of Gawd, E PLURIBUS UNUM! Which shall be purged of all its un-righteousness, which shall create its own righteousness, in its own image, as exemplified by this which is in the Father-hood of Gawd, therefore you shall believe in Gawd, an' trust in Gawd as He trusts in Him, even as I will bring about Happiness, Prosperity, Peace, Pleasure, and Destiny of all my subjects!"

The Father, concluding abruptly sits down. Cheers, whoops, and hysterical shrieks fill the hall. After a slight pause, a middle-aged mulatto woman, attendant of the Lord now seated before her, rises, dances around a bit, and begins:

"Father Divine is Gawd, we knows that! There wouldn't be no person speakin in all power, dominion, and authority if he wasn't Gawd. He is the Eternal King, Yeah man! He is riding over every opposition, he' steppin' over everything, and thasa why I'm so happy, thass why I'm so glad! It was misery before but now Gawd's here, an he's gonna bind de Devil an' cast him down into the dungeon! What I'm talkin about, it's not thinkin', it's not believing, it's knowin'! Not a soul on earth can stop Gawd Father Divine; he just can't be stopped! Haw, haw, can't stop 'im nohow! He been crucified he been hindered but now he's ri-i-isin', triumphin', an' no man in all the universe can hinder him. They's gotta stand still, they's gotta git underneath. How kin ya hender Him who made all things? There is no other propituation, man only stands for a little while, then he's gotta be brought into submission! O, I'm tellin' ya, He gits sweeter an' sweeter evvy day! He's the unseen guest but he's there an' he knows it; if it's not righteousness he's like a moth, he eats it up! It's time ta git into subjection, it's time to stop, think, and consider, an' take up the cross an follow on! Father Divine is the living presence of the lawd, in all power, dominion, an' authority," she shouts.

*February 20, 1939*

# Temple of Grace

## Dorothy West

The New York stamping ground for Daddy Grace, the self-styled rival of Father Divine, is 20 West 115 Street. It was to this building that Daddy Grace came roaring when he left Washington, with the as-yet-unfulfilled promise of dethroning the Father. Divine's lease on this property had expired, and at renewal time it was discovered that Daddy Grace had signed ahead of him. Divine's prestige tottered briefly, for it was a test of faith to his followers to accept the forced removal of God from his heaven by a mundane piece of paper. However, through an act of a diviner God, the Father acquired Crum Elbow as well as a handsome property on West 124 Street, and it was Daddy Grace whose triumph was now scarcely more than a hollow act of circumstance.

The Grace Temple on West 115 Street, still surrounded by the various flourishing business establishments of Father Divine, is a redbrick building plastered over with crude angelic drawings and pious exhortations. The entrance hall leads directly to a flight of descending stairs over which is the inscription GRACE KITCHEN. If you cross a narrow threshold, you find yourself in the auditorium. This auditorium is of good size, seating possibly two hundred people. The floor is a plain one of reverberating board. The seats appear new and are cushioned in red leather of good quality. The walls are blue with two foot bases painted red. At the rear, to the right, are elevated rows of seats that the choir of fifteen lusty white-robed women occupy. On a platform above them is an upright piano. At half-past seven the choir begins to drift in, and until eight they sing unfamiliar hymns grouped around the piano. Occasionally the pianist quickens the tempo into swing, and the choir sways and shuffles and beats out the rhythm with their hands and feet.

In the place occupied by the pulpit in the average church is an elevated, wooden enclosure, most nearly resembling the throne room of a Maypole queen. Six graded steps lead up to it. As the congregation drifts in, most kneel briefly at the foot of the stairs before settling in their seats. In the absence of Daddy Grace, who did not appear all evening, they made obeisance to the covered throne chair, which stood centered in the enclosure and was not uncovered at any time during the proceedings.

To the left of the throne room was orchestra space. There were a piano, a trombone, a drum, two sousaphones, and two trumpets. At half-past seven a child less than two was beating without reprimand on the drum. He played unceasingly until the orchestra members entered sometime just before eight, and the drummer smilingly relieved him of the sticks.

The auditorium filled slowly. In all, there were about seventy-five people. Most of the congregation came singly or in groups from the dining room, and many continued to munch after they were seated. There were at first no ushers. Toward the end of the evening a young man in a smart uniform with CAPTAIN written on an arm band and GRADE SOLDIER lettered on his breast, stood at stiff attention at the rear of the temple. His one duty was to admonish the half-dozen nonparticipants, a row of high school boys, not to whisper. Oddly enough, at that time the place was bedlam.

The crowd gathered informally. There were as many

young children as adults. The grown-ups visited with each other. The children played up and down the aisles. There was unchecked laughter. There were only two or three men with obvious signs of poverty and disinterest in their faces; they spoke to no one and appeared to have come in to escape the cold.

In contrast to the Divinites, who are for the most part somberly and shabbily dressed, the Grace cohorts, though apparently poor, follow their own fashion dictates. The older women were plainly and poorly costumed, but the younger women wore skillful makeup, cheap hats smartly tilted, intriguing veils, and spike heels. One young woman who came in street clothes disappeared down the stairs and returned in an ankle-length dinner dress of black taffeta. It was she who accepted the offerings that white-frocked women brought her after each collection.

At eight the choir took their proper seats, and for half an hour sang familiar hymns, with frequent interpolations of praise to Daddy Grace. The congregation meanwhile had settled and quieted. No one joined in the singing, but there was perfunctory applause at the conclusion of each song. Occasionally a member turned to look up at the choir with mild interest.

When the choir service ended, a slim light brown man in a business suit appeared. At his entrance the orchestra began to play an unfamiliar tune, a variation of four notes, in swing tempo. The man said there would be a short prayer. His voice rose in illiterate and incoherent prayer with frequent name coupling of God and Daddy Grace. At their mention, there were murmurs of "Amen" and "Praise Daddy."

The prayer concluded and the orchestra continued to play. Now the unchanging beat of the drum became insistent. Its steady monotone scraped the nerve center. The Africanesque beat went on . . . tom . . . tom . . . tom . . . tom. . . . A woman in the front row rose. She flung out her

arms. Her body was slim and strong and beautiful. Her deli-
cate-featured dark face became ecstatic. She began to chant
in a vibrant unmusical voice, "I love bread, sweet bread."
She clapped her hands in 4/4 time. Presently she began to
walk up and down before the throne, swaying from her hips,
her feet shuffling in dance rhythm, singing over and over,
"I love bread, sweet bread."

A man rose and flung his hands in the air, waving them
from the wrists. He began to moan and writhe. The monotonous beat of the drum was the one dominant note now,
though the other instruments continued to play. Others rose
and went through the motions of the woman. Children rose,
too, children of grade school age, their faces strained and
searching. A six-year-old boy clapped and stomped until his
dull, pale yellow face was red and moist.

When a shouting, shuffling believer was struck by the
spirit, his face assumed a look of idiocy, and he began to
pivot slowly in a circle. Tender arms steadied him, and he
was guided along by outstretched hands until he reached the
milling throng before the throne, where he whirled and
danced and shrieked in the whirling, dancing, shrieking mob
until he fell exhausted to the floor. When he revived, he
wove back unsteadily to his seat and helped to steer others
to the throne.

Finally both drummer and dancers were weary. The
space before the throne cleared. A big pompous dark man
in a business suit who had been sitting in one of the elevated
seats in the rear, looking on with quiet approval, descended
and came down the aisle, mounted the stairs leading to the
throne, walked to a table to the right of the throne, and put
on a gilded crown with a five-pointed star in its center. He
advanced to the front of the dais and read briefly from the
Bible. The reading concluded, he began to address the congregation as "Dear ones" and "Beloved." His voice was oily,
his expression crafty. His garbled speech played on the emotions. He spoke feelingly of the goodness of Daddy, of Dad-

dy's great love for his flock. He called them Daddy's children and urged them to obey and trust Daddy, and reminded them that they were part of a United Kingdom of Prayer. When the swelling murmurs of "Amens" and "Praise Daddy" indicated their revived strength and ardor, he bent to the woman who had first started the singing and asked in his smooth voice, "Sister, will you start the singing again?"

She rose and began to moan and sway. The orchestra took up her tune, but this time the drum did not beat, and suddenly a tambourine was heard, then another, and then another, until there were four or five. The beat was the same as the drum's had been, steady, monotonous, insidious, and far more deafening. When the open palms and closed fists slapped the center of the tambourine, these little disks jangled and added to the maddening sound.

The crowd's frenzy mounted. Their hysteria was greater than it had been before. They crowded to the space before the throne and their jerking bodies and distorted faces made them appear like participants in a sex orgy. Their cries were animal. When the young girls staggered back to their seats, they lay exhausted against the chair backs, tearing at their hair, with uncontrollable shudders shaking their bodies.

The mad dance went on for forty minutes, twice as long and twice as terrible as the first had been. When the man in the crown felt their frenzy had reached its peak, he came to the front of the platform and stood silently until their awareness of his big, overbearing presence slowed their pace, muted the tambourines, and finally hushed the auditorium.

When they returned exhausted to their seats, he immediately asked them if they loved Daddy enough to keep his temple going by the purchase of his various products. There was no attempt to gloss this bald question. When there were sufficient murmurs of "Amen" and "Praise Daddy," he blew a police whistle and up and down the aisles went the white-frocked women hawking "Daddy Grace" toothpaste, hair pomade, lotions, and toiletries of every kind. One young woman was selling the *Grace Magazine*, fifteen cents for the current issue, and five cents for back numbers.

The sales were few, and the man in the crown tried to encourage the buying by telling the congregation that soon Daddy Grace planned to open shops of every description all over Harlem, and there would be work for everybody. When the last purchase had been made, the pompous man asked the first spokesman to read the list of trinkets available for Christmas presents. The list included a cross bearing Daddy Grace's picture for one dollar and fifty cents, a combination pen and pencil for a like sum, other articles at various prices, most of them with Daddy's picture as special inducement. The devotees signified their promise to purchase these trinkets by fervent "Amens."

This business concluded, the oily tongue called for the tithe offerings. Those with tithe money were asked to form a line in the center aisle. Half of the congregation got in line. The oily tongue asked for a march. The orchestra struck one up. The whistle blew, and the marchers advanced to the front of the throne where they dropped their tithe money in the proffered baskets.

The sum collected totaled only a dollar and some odd cents. The man in the gilded crown concluded that there were some who had tithes but were disinclined to march. Thereupon he dispatched the white-frocked women down the aisles with baskets. They bent over the rows, asking persuasively, "Help us with the offering, dear heart."

When they had returned to the throne, there was a short speech about pledge money, and they were dispatched again. Again they bent down, begging as persuasively as before, "Help us with the offering, dear heart."

When the copper and silver pledges were brought for his approval, the smooth tongue asked for offerings for the House of Prayer. His voice filled with entreaty. He talked of the Grace temples in other cities and implored the congregation to gladden Daddy's heart by making this temple "the best of all." It could only be done with money, he said. His language was plain and his appeal was not garnished by any spiritual references. Rather, he fixed them with his eye and flatly informed them that the temple could not run without money, and it was money that he wanted. He then asked the pianist for a march. The pianist who was leaning indolently against the piano with his collar open and his tie loosened, said wearily, "I'm tired." One of the women in white ran down the aisle and returned with the man who had played for the choir. He obligingly swung into a march.

The police whistle blew. The people with pledges were asked to line up in the center aisle. Happily and proudly they lined up in double file. Their manner of marching was different now. It was a shuffling strut, and their arms were bent up at the elbows and held firmly against their sides. The line marched down the center to the throne, then divided, and in single file, shuffled up the two side aisles, met again at the rear of the hall, and then one after the other, went down the center aisle again and placed their pledge money in the basket.

The man in the gilded crown announced that the offerings had reached the total of $5.06. He said that he did not want to take up their time by begging since the hour was growing late, but he wondered if there was anyone present who would raise the total to $5.25. A man came forward immediately. Thus encouraged, the pompous leader asked if there was another beloved heart who would increase the sum to $5.50. The woman who had led the singing promptly gave a quarter. The leader begged for another quarter for three or four minutes, but no one came forward. Abruptly he ended his plea and announced that he would now preach the sermon.

As he spoke a woman screamed, and her arm shot stiffly up into the air while her body grew rigid. Three women laid her on the floor in the aisle. She continued to scream and moan, and then began to talk unintelligibly in a high-pitched, unnatural voice.

The man in the gilded crown announced his text. His voice grew deep and stern. "I'll tell my story about the cow and the sheep who told on the man."

He paused, and then waved his arm dramatically at the prostrate woman.

"Oh, my beloveds," he said, "sometimes I tremble in fear at the power, the wonderful, mysterious power." He shook himself in semblance of terror, but it was not funny to the congregation. They stirred uneasily.

"You must fear the power, the wonderful power," he exhorted them. "You must fear and follow Daddy. You must have fear."

A man shot out of his seat and began to moan and sob, flinging his arms around in the air. Smooth tongue looked at him with satisfaction. The congregation strained forward, a concerted sigh escaping from them. Others began to scream and moan. In a few minutes half the flock was on its feet, beginning again that stupefying, tireless dance. In a few minutes more almost every man, woman, and child was dancing, this time without music but with a uniformity of shuffling step and weaving arms.

The man in the gilded crown retired to the rear of the platform, his performance over.

The crazy dance went on. In the street the sound was audible a half block away.

*December 21, 1938*

# Deities and Their Duesenbergs

*Vivian Morris*

A wary public can always be counted upon to view the antics of cult followers in Harlem as bizarre no matter what they called themselves. Whenever Father Divine makes a public appearance, he has his followers running ahead of him shouting "Thank Father," "Father Divine is God," "God is heah reigning and ruling in de name of Father Divine." And the shame of it all is that the poor devils believe the tripe that they give voice to.

Father Divine rides in a big specially built deluxe Duesenberg sedan with a throne in the center, for "Father" to sit on. He's a great showman. When he comes into view, with his bodyguards and his followers shouting, "De body is heah." "God is heah," he quickly runs through the crowd shouting, "Peace."

The man either has no conscience, or he is mentally warped. If the latter is the case he can be forgiven. If the former is true, he should be lauded as a superpsychologist, and condemned to live like and have the simpleminded beliefs of his followers.

True, he does have stores, restaurants, and homes that have dirt-cheap prices. But, he also advocates a person entering his cult to turn their jewels, land, homes, and automobiles over to God. After all, God could keep them better than any mere mortals.

He also allows his followers to work for low wages, reducing the already low wage scale in the domestic servant field. "Father" gets a percentage of the pittance that they earn. But they continue to insist that "Father Divine is God" and who am I to tell them no?

Prophet Costonie is a younger cult leader, and he was powerful a while back as a faith-healing prophet of God, but his group has dwindled to a few hundred. Daddy Grace, the big blustering "disciple of God," extorts on a larger scale. He has dinners at sixty-five cents; his marching group buys its uniforms directly from him, and he makes over one hundred percent profit. He is siphoning off Father Divine's "gravy" at a systematic clip.

There are numerous "small fry" cults in Harlem, two and three in every block. No two are exactly the same. If the black and white members of these cults would turn their money and energy to gainful enterprises, an amazing difference would be seen in their personal economic status.

'Tis a pity that the "Father Divines," "Daddy Graces," Prophet Costonies," et al. turned their powers of leadership into such nefarious channels instead of in a constructive direction.

*January 9, 1939*

# Holy and Sanctified

## *Vivian Morris*

It was too early to be going to a joint like Dickie Wells's Cabaret on West 133 Street just east of Seventh Avenue. It was just 9:30, but I wasn't going clubbing, I was headed for the large room upstairs to hear the word of God that is served up in heaping portions at the Holy & Sanctified Church of God in Christ.

The room was made cozy by two large coal stoves—one in the front and one in the back—with stove pipes that wound up to the ceiling and came to a V point in the center on either side, dividing the church. There is a line of chairs extending from the back of the church to an elevated platform in the center front.

It was just four days before Christmas 1938.

As I sat waiting for the services to begin, the jumping rhythm of Dickie Wells's Swing Band, downstairs, was pouring out a spine-tingling jitterbug, which caused the congregation to shuffle softly in time to the music.

On the platform in back of the rostrum and seated in a chair to the left was a man dressed entirely in brown.

The front rows were taken up by the congregation and in the back seats was a collection of disinterested children of assorted ages who paid no attention to their surroundings.

Deacon Jigging, the acting pastor, lifted his shining,

cobra-shaped head in the direction of the sky. When he finally focused his eyes on his saints, he began a most effective prayer to de Lawd!

The deacon began his lengthy sermon by stretching his gray-clad figure to its full six feet and saying to one of the sisters in the front row:

"Now sistuh Nettie, read me whut de Bible seh bout 'postle Paul in dem dere Acks—you know."

Sister Nettie bellowed in a strong throaty voice that did justice to the three hundred odd pounds of flesh she carried on her busty frame: "De good book sehs heah dat de 'postle Paul toll de sailuhs aftuh fo'teen days an' fo'teen nights uh hunguh—"

"Hol' it rat dere," interrupted Deacon Jigging, cocking his head to one side and shaking a long finger at the twenty-one saints who comprised his congregation, dem's deep woids—saints . . . fo'teen days and fo'teen nights uh hunguh—go on saint, dig a mite deepuh!"

"Shipwrecked an' teared to pieces. . . . Shipwrecked," Sister Nettie says, jumping up, "an' teared to pieces! Gawd-a-mighty, think uh dat!"

" 'Postle Paul sed," moaned Deacon Jigging, who then paused.

"Stay on de ship!" said Saint Nettie.

"Stay on the ship?" Deacon Jigging asked, shifting his stance. Then he continued, "What dat mean? Now some uh y'all don' know whut dat mean? Stay on de glory ship—de Lawd's ship. Go on Sistuh . . ."

"Ef y'u wan tuh be saved!"

"Ef," Deacon Jigging said, speaking deliberately and loudly, "yo' wan' tuh be saved!" He jumped up and down now, stamping his feet, "fum de debbil!"

"Whooh!" shouted a wizened saint. "Sho' God do! Preach on!"

"Ah knows whut ahm ta'kin' 'bout," said Jigging. Then

he held one foot in the air and shook his finger in the air, saying, "An' he know whut ah'm sayin'!"

"Deed he do," seconded the wizened one.

"Now tek dat sistuh yonduh," he said, pointing to a plump, round little lady with three children surrounding her. "She 'tended to go 'way, didn't yuh, sistuh?"

"Amen, sho' did!"

"Ah know dat she felt sub'n pullin, pullin' 'gin huh and whispuhin' don' go, don' go. Dat uz me and de Lawd, saints. We fin'ally got huh tuh stay."

"Y'all sho' did pull hard," beamed the lady, "cause I had the children ready an' mah suitcase packed—an' den we didnt go!"

"Amen, dat's the powah uh de Lawd, saints—de powah uh de Lawd!"

"He's all-seein', all-heahin' an' all doin'," interposed one of the saints.

"Amen! Now le's talk 'bout Nicodemus" said Brother Jigging. "Ole Nicodemus? Yeh—Nicodemus believe in God but he didn' want his peoples to know dat he bow his head to no man," said Jigging.

"What he do, brother?" someone asked.

"He sneak 'way in de middle uh de night an' go see Jesus—sneakin' in de back way."

"No?"

"But Jesus 'buked him at the doh—an' seh, 'Nicodemus! Stop! O Nicodemus!' "

"Yeah!"

" 'Nicodemus! Stop!' Whut fo' yu come to me in de middle of de night lak a thief in de night?' Amen! Dese wonduhs which you know ah done done, is sub'n no mo'tal man could do!"

"Do Jesus!"

"No mo'tal man could do!" Deacon Jigging said, stamping his feet, wiping his sweaty brow. "Nicodemus say,

'Lawd, ah don' mean no ha'm.' Lawd seh, 'Nicodemus, ah can read y'u like a book.' "

"Amen!" someone shouts.

"An' read us lak a book," the deacon said, stamping his foot.

"Hallelujah! Hallelujah!" someone shouts out.

"An read the w'ul lak a book!"

One white sister starts to wave her hand in a fluttering, flapping motion like a bird learning to fly.

Then another sister strikes up a hymn—"Dry Bones in the Valley!" They start their hand clapping and the tempo speeds up. The saints scream and yelp, then unable to contain themselves longer, begin to hop up then down, waving their arms crazily. Acting Pastor Jiggins takes advantage of the situation to read some more from the Bible. The children gleefully join in the hand clapping and laugh and smirk at the antics of their elders.

The orchestra and pleasure seekers underneath are drowned out now by the stamping and shouting of these frenzied people.

The man on the platform with the brown suit becomes cross-eyed with religious ecstasy and dances about with a crazy, rocking rhythm, his arms flopping lifelessly at his sides.

Mid all this excitement, a little shovel-headed boy in the rear calmly draws figures of men with cowboy paraphernalia on and six-guns spitting flame (maybe a creative artist of the future) and Indians riding stick horses. The church rolls on and the tempo decreases, then a weary sister breaks out with a song consisting of only the words, "Eyes, Eyes," and she continues this ad infinitum.

Brother Jigging finally waves for silence and speaks, "A while back, some uh our saints was 'ticed 'way by some folks who tol' dem de wuz de 'real thing.' "

"True," one of the saints shouts.

"But then de debbil don' git dem 'fo' dey gits back, de'll fine out dat dey lef' de real thing heah."

"Amen."

"Wheah's de real thing?'

"Preach! Preach!"

"Sistuh Nettie, read dat passage whut says we's de real thing!"

"De followers of God who shall be saved," she says, pausing, "will be holy an' sanctified."

"Will be holy an' sanctified," the deacon says.

"Amen!" Sister Nettie exclaims.

"Dat's owah faith," the pastor says.

"Owah faith," someone repeats.

"Some uh us stan' still."

"Yeah."

"Some uh us shouts."

"Yeah."

"Ah don' condemn neither."

"Amen, amen."

"We got diffunt ways uh showin' we's sanctified."

"Amen. Dat's de trufe!"

"Now ah'll offer a li'l prayer fo' everybody."

After the prayer was over, a sister in a maroon dress jumped up and said: "How 'bout a piece uh money fuh deacon Jiggins, saints an' fren's?"

She jumped about, gobbling up nickels, dimes, and pennies and looking squarely at me, she said: 'Give us eighteen cent mo' an' make a dollah fo' de deacon fo' his evening's work.'

I dug down in my pocketbook because I had already gotten my money's worth of faith this night!

*December 21, 1938*

# Obeah

## *Ellis Williams*

Webster's Dictionary defines "Obeah" as an African religion of the Ashanti tribe that was practiced among blacks in the British West Indies. It is characterized by the use of sorcery and magic rituals, sometimes with grave or even fatal consequences. Obeah doctors are adept in the use of poisonous herbs, ground glass, and other materials in the production and fostering of fear as a means of magical influence. It was commonly practiced in black New York neighborhoods.

WPA writer Ellis Williams went to one of the better apartment houses on West 152 Street in October 1938 to interview a man from Trinidad, identified only as Mr. Crawford, to learn more about the practice.

The five-story walk-up is clean and apparently well-managed. Crawford's apartment is freshly painted but the new and modernistic furniture is in disarray, in part because the painters have recently departed and partly because Crawford is preparing for a trip to the West Indies.

The interview goes well, smoothly, in fact because Crawford is highly educated, having attended public school and St. Mary's College in Trinidad and City College in New York City. In fact, he's a newspaper correspondent, a businessman, and an amateur radio operator.

A big, imposing figure weighing around 180 pounds, Crawford is an active member of the African Methodist Church and the Police Athletic League and Boys' Clubs. Despite his sophistication, the thing he seems to excel in knowing is the practice of Obeah.

"Hello ole chap! Hello there! Come on in," he says. "What in blazes brings you over? It has been a blasted long time since I last saw you. What's new and what have you been doing?"

"I must get my supervisor some copy on folklore by Monday."

"Did you say folklore? Well, if I am not folklore itself-skippy. [I know all about it.] I could give you oodles of it but there is a but. I sail soon for home and I am busy as a bee packing and straightening out my affairs. Anyway as one good 'Iorian' [Trindadian] to another, I'll give you some stuff but what are you doing to do with it?"

"Turn it in to my supervisor who will edit and compile some in book form, which will serve generations yet unborn as a document rich in historical value."

"Are the identities of persons giving information to be made public?"

"To be truthful, I am not sure, but even if they were, there is nothing for one to be ashamed of. Persons giving information are contributing in no small way to history making."

My host loads his pipe and again settles in his seat. "Bill, have a cigarette?"

"Thanks. Here is a light?"

"Bill, what do you wish to write on?"

"Obeah," I retorted. "Is obeah folklore?"

"Certainly it is. I should say it is. You ought to know as much about it as I do."

"So true, but I'd rather use what you know about it."

"Hells bells! To anyone else I'd be scared a tiff to give them any information. Go ahead pop your questions."

"To your mind, what is Obeah?"

"Obeah is one of several cults that are merely religious systems with elaborate and complicated rituals, surpassing I would say in intricacy and symbolism most of the Oriental or European religious systems. It is strictly African. You might not know, Bill, that the basis for African religion is the unity of the Godhead or Theism. The multiplicity of angels, forces, spirits, beings, and so on does not in any way clash with the idea of Unitarianism. In most of the West Indian Islands today, there exist very vague survivals of Obeah that are due largely to the fact of the adoption of Christianity by the African."

"I want to mention also the European superstition superimposed on him. It is religious customs only which definitely survive. Consequently the 'greenies' [unsophisticated peasantry] can now be hardly imposed upon by the Obeah trickster unless he incorporates in his bag of tricks a great portion of European or American magic. This will of course include such things as candles, saints, shrines, bells, books, and so on."

"Boy, are you getting the stuff? It is rich stuff, you know. This is the kind of stuff that I get money for, you know. You are the only person I'd give this stuff to free. Come on, let us have another. I am just getting in the mood to spill (he is chuckling) what you folk call folklore," he says.

"Getting back to Obeah. There is a chap Herskovits who claims that the source of inspiration for African Obeah or voodoo is unmistakably European. That many of the Negro traits as it pertains to the practice and which many writers think are peculiar to him, are unmistakably a retention of the fifteenth and sixteenth centuries of Europe, which were imposed upon the African in the West Indies. You know I think he has got something there. Was it Mirabeau, when asked whether he believed in magic who retorted that it was very effective when given with poisons? Whatever may be the effectiveness of the Africans' knowledge of organic poisons, the fact remains that the Obeah man claims a cure for every curse. To make it clear, for every harmful effect produced from any cause, there is in the cult or wanga an antidote."

"How many wangas do you know about? Six or seven."

"Tell me something about the wangas?"

"Wangas in a great many instances are not unlike what some people call scarecrows. They are designed especially as guards to protect fruit trees against the pilferers who roam from orchard to orchard at night stealing. If you want a technical answer, I will give it to you in literary style. The construction of a wanga is based on an African concept identical with one of the doctrines of Pythagoras, an early Greek philosopher, that is, that the relation of similar forms implies the existence of other and distinct relations.

"How is that, Bill? Isn't that putting on the heat? Listen, ole man, I trust you will forgive me but I am getting packed; further my mother always hammered it in me to give, yes to give, but in little doses. If you are interested, as I am sure you must be, you will come again. Do not think I am expediting your departure but it is time for the chick to come to help me pack for the storage warehouse."

### A Second Interview: October 18, 1938

"I see you are back, Bill, much like our friends across the border who got their men. [meaning Canadian Mounted Police.] Did you bring me a copy of the last interview?

"I did. Here it is."

He reads it aloud. "It sounds durn good. Is this copy mine?"

"So it is."

"Thanks. I am going to keep it, but remember, I am
expecting you to send me a copy of the completed story.
I wish also to make clear, Bill, that in the event that it is
published I must have a copy free, gratis, and for
nothing."

"If it is at all possible."

"Getting back to my story of Obeah, the idea is seen in
many forms of European magic, as apart from symbolism,
and to my mind it is a natural though unscientific inference.
It is devilishly interesting to see how the islander of the West
Indies clings to his wanga in the hope of frightening off the
kids—those mischievous brats who in all boyish frivolity rob
for the fun of it—mangoes, bananas, alligator pears . . . and
other fruits.

"In a great measure, is he successful with his wanga?"

"No! Emphatically no. While there might be some slight
emotional reaction, the more sophisticated kids regard
wanga as a fraud and chuckle no end when they observe
them nailed to trees, displayed in a prominent place, or sus-
pended in the garden on a pole 'shrieking beware.' I once
asked a chap who had nothing floating from his garden pole
where his wanga was."

"Ah," he replied, "this is the best wanga"—pointing
to the naked pole. "Them little boys stone down everybody wanga, but when they see my pole without any
wanga—they frighten. They don't know where my wanga
is." This bloke had developed a psychological technique
to meet the incredulity of the urchins and their contempt
for wanga, for he adds mystery for whatever vestige of
fear that still lingers."

"Tell me something of the Coffin, Cocobay, Uncorked
Bottle, Cactus, and other wangas."

"The Coffin-Board wanga is what you must mean. It is
a terrifying one, as you no doubt must know. It is made
from a bit of board from which a coffin has been made. It

is draped in black and hoisted on a high pole—a candle might be added to remind you of your funeral service. All through these explanations you will note that the Pythagorean implication is true.

"The Cocobay wanga is made from a soft young calabash. If one were to dare trespass, his skin would get all the abrasions of a leper as the young calabash withers and decays. Feathers are stuck in it, but you must be careful that they are not from the body of a Sen Sen fowl, for Gede, a human subdeity, eats this bird. Sen Sen fowl is a bird that may be relied on to dig up and unearth any Obeah in one's yard.

"Wangas which very strictly follow the Pythagorean principles are the Prickly Cactus wanga and the Human Figure. The cactus will grow in an uncomfortable part of your anatomy, if you trespass, and any castigation of the human figure will be felt by the thief in the corresponding places.

"One must of necessity be filled with fear if they observe little bundles of earth hanging on trees: they have come from a newly made grave, and if you dare steal from the tree, surely there will be another newly made one.

"The Corked Bottle wanga is the most terrible of all the wangas, for the bottle will be sealed and cast into the sea. What avail it then to take a cathartic? Epson salt, senna leaves, herb teas, castor, or even croton [tropical plant] oil, cannot help you. The corked bottle is proof against all of these, and so will you be. Your belly will continue to enlarge until it pleases the offended party to retrieve and uncork the bottle.

"And to all who might read the story, and who might wish to travel through the West Indies, I attest this solemn warning: Be sure to take a large supply of aperients, for every constipated person is a suspect. Laugh it off if you may. You may argue all the scientific findings you can, but wanga will be the only verdict.

"And now, since you have got me started, I am going to do oodles of research when I get home—and if you wish me to, I will send you the data if you will pay for the air mail."

# Conjure Man

## *Vivian Morris*

Sagwa was a well-known conjure man of Harlem. The locals near his place on West 141 Street near Lenox Avenue knew him only as Sagwa or Jupiter Man. His given name was William Weiner, but no one seemed to know or cared to know anything about this West Indian medicine man's past. Sagwa's past was his own business.

The dilapidated wooden shack I visited was perched on the edge of an old junkyard just east of Lenox. It looked as if it might collapse any moment. The living room was huge, dirty, and unkempt and smelled of animal dung.

Through a partly open door that led to an adjoining room, I could see two bristling German police dogs flanked by a half dozen or more lean and hungry-looking cats. The place had an earthen floor that was damp but firmly packed, and a dank musty odor pervaded the atmosphere.

Slouched in a broken armchair was a huge West Indian man, whose skin was a sallow, dingy yellow. He weighed close to 270 pounds. His mouth was loose and sensual—his eyes, small and crafty. The thing about him that compelled my attention most, however, was his large, bloated stomach that rose and fell at intervals like some giant toy balloon. He is widely known in these streets as Sagwa the conjure man, who makes his living selling herbs and dispensing magic.

I talked with him for a long time and was spellbound by all he told me but was greatly relieved when he had finished and it was time to go. Outside the night air was sweet and refreshing in comparison to the close, ill-smelling room. But I shall never forget the things I heard. If I were a true believer in fantasy, Harlem would now appear to me like some strange, faraway city; a fascinating conglomeration of color, intriguing as the after-dark activity in a dimly lighted conjure man's den.

Lenox Avenue would be well populated with (and every side street would boast) spiritualists whose sidelines would be the peddling of herbs and the brewing of weird, seething voodoo concoctions that are veiled in mystery—a heritage from the jungles of Africa and the hot tropical climates of Haiti and the West Indies.

Even now, I am almost convinced that, no matter what your ailment, there's an herb somewhere (possibly in Harlem) to cure it. My conjure man insisted on it.

"Got an ache in your joints?" he wanted to know. "If you have, boil a few mullein leaves in a pan of water and drink a cup before meals. Your kidneys bother you? Don't let em. Boil a couple teaspoons of cream of tartar and flaxseed in a pint of water and drink it. You'll feel like a different person. Ever have trouble renting rooms or your luck go back on you? Put a handful of rice in a bag with some sycamore bark, boil and strain it, then sprinkle the contents on both sides of the doorsill.

"If your husband or wife ain't treatin' you right, feedin' you cold supper or staying out nights, buy a handful of tiny red candles, smear them with maple syrup or honey, write the person's name on a piece of brown paper greased with a month-old ham skin and burn the candles under the bed. That'll fix up everything fine.

"If your boyfriend or girlfriend leaves you, take one of their old shoes, sprinkle a little 'bring 'em back dust' on the soles, point one to the north and the other to the south.

They'll be back in a week unless somebody done used a stronger conjure than you.

"If somebody you like act kinda cool get the egg of a frizzy chicken, boil it in spring water, take it out of the shell, and beat up the yolk with a lump of sugar, starch, and Jimson weed; put it in a bag and hide it in his clothes and he'll wind up being yo' slave.

"There's a hundred different ways to bring yourself good luck or money or to put the jinx on somebody you don't like. All you have to do is cross the palm of the doctor."

All root doctors, however, are not conjure men. Take William Weiner, for instance, who operates a root and herb store and is known to Harlemites as the Jupiter Man. He is a registered pharmacist.

"I didn't know much about roots and herbs twenty years ago," he told me when I had explained my visit, "but I've learned. If I have a touch of the grippe, do you think I take some coal tar preparation like aspirin? No sir. I hurry up and take a dose of boneset. Many old black people make a tea of it. Boneset, that's one name for it, the same thing as Indian sage or thoroughwort, or sweating plant. It sets your aching bones all right. Try it next time you get the shivers.

"I guess I've got more herbs and roots in my store now than I've got regular medicine. Of course, some of the herbs they use here in Harlem are regular medicines under different names. To tell you the truth, I've gotten so I like the herb names better. Which would you rather take, cascara or sacred bush? It's the same thing.

"Some of my customers have a dozen other names for cascara, like bear berry bark, pigeon berry bark, chittam wood, and so forth. I like sacred bush better. It takes a long time to learn all the names. You have to be careful. Take bear's root. That's something else. You take that for dropsy. Some people call it Robin's rye, hair cap moss or golden maiden's hair. But poor Robin's plantain is something different from Robin's rye. Poor Robin is used for warts. It's an astringent. Another name for it is rattlesnake weed.

"If you want [something that sounds like] chinchona, you ask for quinine. My herb customers have a better name. They call it priests' bark, which goes way back to the medieval Latin, *Pulvis jesuiticus*. See, they know more about the history of medicines than most doctors.

"Most white people don't know how much they depend on herbs. There's been a widely advertised cough medicine on the market in recent years, for example. It's a good medicine. But what's it made from? Extract of thyme. Before most people ever heard of it, the people in Harlem were buying ten cents worth of thyme and making a brew when they got a bad cough.

"It's the same way with ephedrine jelly. That's a popular cure for colds. It's nothing in the world but an extract of ma houng, a Chinese herb. In Harlem, they've been using ma houng ever since I can remember. You can pay a lot of money for a widely advertised tonic laxative. People around Harlem who know about herbs could tell you to get some dandelion root, rhubarb, sacred bark, and a little mayapple root and make your own. Ten to one, if you took this home-made remedy, you'd feel much better."

And so, after these two little visits, you can readily see why I have been almost converted to the cause of roots and herbs. So much so that I am impelled to make a further, more exhaustive search for the fascinating conjure lore of Harlem.

*October 27, 1938*

# Ghost Story

## Dorothy West

Laura is a shy woman in her fifties who lives at 300 West 114 Street. A native of South Carolina, she left the South about twenty years ago and moved to Ohio, where she lived for about ten years, then she came to New York.

She brought her folklore and superstitions with her. A plump, fair-skinned woman, she is a housewife, a Presbyterian.

I went to see Mrs. Laura M., who did not want to be identified further; she is a former landlady. During a conversation that somehow got around to ghosts, I expressed the opinion that I hoped my luck would continue and that I would never see or hear anything that might be described as a ghost. Mrs. M. looked at me curiously, as if she might say something on the subject, but apparently changed her mind. A neighbor who was visiting Mrs. M. and was on the verge of going, was persuaded by the sudden turn in the conversation to tell about a strange thing that had happened to her.

In an old apartment, she had a strange experience. She had placed her baby's playpen in a corner in her living room. Soon after she had settled in the apartment, she noticed that the baby began to cry a lot; unnaturally, as if in terror. She would go to the playpen, and none of the physical things that irritate a baby to the point of crying would be apparent. The baby was in good health and there was nothing to cause the constant terrified screaming. The mother found it very difficult to understand the change in the baby's disposition as it had always been an even-tempered child. One day she mentioned the baby's behavior to her next-door neighbor. This friend listened, and then with some reluctance asked where the baby's playpen was. The mother told her. The neighbor then explained that the crib of another had stood in that identical spot. The mother of this child had died, and the family had immediately moved away. The current mother had been the next tenant to move in. The neighbor's explanation was that the dead woman, the ghost of the baby's mother, was coming back to see her child, not knowing her child had been taken away, and that it was this strange spirit that was frightening the current tenant's child. She advised the new tenant to move her baby's playpen to another corner of the room. She did and the baby's crying stopped.

After hearing this story, my former landlady's neighbor looked at me in a strained way.

Then she blurted out, "I've had a similar experience."

"Not long after we moved [she was then living with a brother] to a Hundred Seventeenth Street, I had a funny thing happen to me. It was a seven-room apartment, and I had one of the rooms on the street fixed up as a sewing room. The sewing room, bathroom, and kitchen were on one side of the hall, and the storage room and two bedrooms were on the other side. My living room was at the end of the hall and there was a bedroom off from that. Well, one day I was sitting in the sewing room when I heard a rustle in the hall. It sounded like the swish of a taffeta skirt. I looked up at the door and saw the figure of a woman go past. She had on a black taffeta dress and I didn't see any head. I called out, "Who's there?" Of course, nobody answered. I jumped up and looked down the hall. Just as the figure reached the door of the living room, it disappeared. I went in and looked around, but I didn't see anything. I went back to the sewing room and picked up my work. I just shrugged my shoulders and said I was seeing things. Nothing else like that happened for a long time.

"Then one day, a friend was sitting in the sewing room with me, and I heard the rustle again. I looked up and saw the figure again. She saw it, too. You know how she is, Mrs. M. looked at me and she said, 'Good God! What's that?' I laughed and said, 'What's what?'

"She told me what she had seen. I told her that it was just her imagination, that she had seen a reflection from the street. She insisted that she had seen the headless figure of a woman. She was nervous for about ten minutes, then she quieted down, but she kept insisting that she had seen something. She said that it must have been somebody who had died in the house, and was coming back to look for something. Well, I knew that I had seen something, so I said to myself that it must have been a good spirit since it hadn't bothered me, so I didn't worry about it any more while I was in that house.

"Then a woman who lived across the street came over and said, 'You've stayed in this house longer than the last three families.' I asked her what she meant, and she said that she had lived in the house when it was first opened to Negroes, but that she had lived in an upstairs apartment. The first family that had my old apartment in that house (it was on the first floor) had stayed there a long time, and so had the people who had lived in there after that. Then she had moved downstairs into the apartment I then had.

"She had put her bed in a certain place in one of the bedrooms and she felt like she was choking to death in the middle of the night. She didn't know what to do at first, but finally she had moved her bed to another position. After that she didn't have that choking sensation. But other little things happened, and she moved out.

"She said that the next two families had moved in and stayed a month or two and had then moved out. I'd been in that apartment about a year and a half when she told me that. She asked me if I had had any experiences in that room. I told her that I hadn't heard my brother speak of anything funny happening. She just shook her head and said it was queer.

"I used to hear sounds like steps very often. At first I thought it was my brother coming in from work. He didn't get in then until one-thirty or two in the morning. I used to call out but there'd be no answer, so I just thought I was mistaken and I'd go back to sleep.

"One night in particular I remember hearing the steps very distinctly. I thought maybe he'd had an accident, so I got up and went to the door of my bedroom and called out. There wasn't a soul there, so I went back to bed.

"Then you remember you used to hear little noises which you thought were mice. Well, some of them were and some of them weren't. I didn't want to frighten you, so I just let you think that every sound you heard was a mouse scampering around."

"I remember hearing noises in the closet of the bedroom I had, heavier than the sound a mouse makes, but I finally decided that it was Mrs. M. moving around in her bedroom next door.

"When you used to ask me what I was doing up so late at night, I gave you some kind of answer because I was always asleep at the hour you mentioned. Before you moved up with me, I had the bedroom you had. I used to hear noises in that closet, too. One night the door kept swinging and I got up and shut it. The latch clicked and I got back in bed. Before I could get the cover up over me again, the door was open and swinging a little again. Now, I know that door latch was caught.

"But I went on to sleep. There wasn't anything I could do.

"While I slept in that room, I had another experience. One night I got in bed and after a while I felt something that felt like somebody trying to stand up under the bed. It was pushing right in the center of the bed. I reached up and turned the light on and looked under the bed. There wasn't a thing there, so I turned off the light, and in a little while the pushing stopped, and I went to sleep.

"After you moved up there, I shifted the bedrooms. I took the room my brother had had, the room where the woman across the street had felt like she was choking, and my brother took the next room. I didn't ever feel anything choking me, but I did feel that pushing again.

"Again I got up and turned on the light, but there wasn't anything there. I never felt it again.

"Then once, after you moved up, I was coming down the hall—you were in the bathroom—and it felt like somebody came along behind me and blew my hair up. It felt like a breeze that a human being makes, not like the wind. Like this"—she pursed her lips and blew as one blows up a balloon. I brushed my hair down but it wouldn't stay (Mrs. M. has very light, thin hair). All of it in the back stood straight out from my scalp. I kept brushing it down but it wouldn't stay. After I had brushed it down about a dozen times, it returned to normal. There wasn't any draft, and the front door wasn't open to let air blow down the hall. And what little air comes in the cracks wouldn't have been strong enough where I was standing in front of the living room almost to blow my hair up like that. I never believed in anything like ghosts or things like that. I don't know how I feel now except that I do think whatever it was meant no harm to me, so that's probably why I didn't get frightened."

I asked her if she moved because of those experiences.

"Goodness, no. After you moved, and my brother moved, I just didn't need a seven-room flat."

*November 18, 1938*

# PART 5

# People, Places, and Things

Like any community, Harlem was an eclectic place filled with its own quirks, oddities, and personalities. In the following pieces, one of Harlem's institutions becomes the focal point of a biting commentary by the venerable Dorothy West on race relations. Even in Harlem, we learn, the long reach of discrimination can find its victims at the Apollo Theatre.

# Amateur Night at the Apollo

*Dorothy West*

The second balcony is packed. The friendly, familiar usher who scowls all the time without meaning it flatfoots up and down the stairs trying to find seats for the sweethearts. Through his tireless manipulation, separated couples are re-united, and his pride is pardonable.

The crowd has come early, for it is amateur night. The Apollo Theatre is full to overflowing. Amateur night is an institution. Every Wednesday, from eleven until midnight, the hopeful aspirants come to the mike, lift up their voices and sing, and retire to the wings for the roll call, when a fluttering piece of paper dangled above their heads comes to rest—determined by the volume of applause—to indicate to whom the prizes shall go.

The box seats are filled with sightseeing whites led in tow by swaggering blacks. The floor is chocolate liberally sprinkled with white sauce. But the balconies belong to the hard-working, holidaying Negroes, and the jitterbug whites are intruders, and their surface excitement is silly compared to the earthy enjoyment of the Negroes.

The moving picture ends. The screen shoots out of sight. The orchestra blares out the soul-ticking tune, "I Think You're Wonderful, I Think You're Grand."

Spontaneously, feet and hands beat out the rhythm, and

the show is on. The regular stage show precedes Amateur Hour. Tonight an all-girls orchestra dominates the stage. A long black girl in flowing pink blows blue notes out of a clarinet. It is a hot song, and the audience stomps its approval. A little yellow trumpeter swings out. She holds a high note, and it soars up solid. The fourteen pieces are in the groove.

The comedians are old-timers. Their comedy is pure Harlemese, and their prototypes are scattered throughout the audience. There is a burst of appreciative laughter and a round of applause when the redoubtable Jackie "Moms" Mabley states that she is doing general housework in the Bronx and adds, with telling emphasis, "When you do housework up there, you really do housework."

Next, a real idiom of Negroes is displayed when one comedian observes to another, who is carrying a fine fur coat for his girl, "Anytime I see you with something on your arm, somebody is without something."

The show moves on. The Sixteen girls of sixteen varying shades dance without precision but with effortless joy. The best of their spontaneous steps will find their way downtown. A long brown boy who looks like Cab Calloway sings, "Papa Tree-Top Tall," ending the regular stage show. The acts file onstage. The chorus girls swing in the background. It is a free-for-all, and the familiar theme song is playing. The black-face comic grabs the prettiest chorine and they truck on down. When the curtain descends, both sides of the house are having fun.

A Negro show would rather have the plaudits of an Apollo audience than any other applause. For the Apollo is the hard testing ground of Negro show business, and approval there can make or break an act.

It is eleven now. The house lights go up. The audience is restless and expectant. Somebody has brought a whistle that sounds like a wailing baby. The cry fills the theater and everybody laughs. The orchestra breaks into the theater's theme song again. The curtain goes up. A radio announcer talks into a mike, explaining to his listeners that the three hundred and first broadcast of Amateur Hour at the Apollo is on the air. He signals to the audience and they obligingly applaud.

The emcee comes out of the wings. The audience knows him. He is Negro to his toes, but even Hitler would classify him as Aryan at first glance. He begins a steady patter of jive. When the audience is ready and mellow, he calls the first amateur out of the wings.

Willie comes out and, on his way to the mike, touches the Tree of Hope. For several years the original Tree of Hope stood in front of the Lafayette Theatre on Seventh Avenue until the Commissioner of Parks tore it down. It was believed to bring good fortune to whatever actor touched it, and some say it was not the Parks Department that cut it down, but the steady stream of down-and-out actors since the Depression years who wore it out.

Willie sings "I Surrender Dear" in a pure Georgia accent. "I can' mak' mah way," he moans. The audience hears him out and claps kindly. He bows and starts for the wings. The emcee admonishes, "You got to boogie-woogie off the stage, Willie." He boogie-woogies off, which is as much a part of established ritual as touching the Tree of Hope.

Vanessa is next. She is black and the powder on her face makes her look purple. She is dressed in black, and is altogether unprepossessing. She is the kind of singer who makes faces and regards a mike as an enemy to be wrestled with. The orchestra sobs out her song, "I Cried for You," and she says, "Now it's your turn to cry over me." Vanessa is an old-time "coon-shouter." She wails and moans deep blue notes. The audience gives her their highest form of approval. They clap their hands in time with the music. She finishes to tumultuous applause and accepts their approval with proud self-confidence. To their wild delight, she flings her arms around the emcee, and boogie-woogies off with him.

Ida comes out in a summer print dress to sing that beautiful lyric, "I Let a Song Go Out of My Heart," in a nasal, off-key whine. Samuel follows her. He is big and awkward, and his voice is very earnest as he promises, "I Won't Tell a Soul I Love You." They are both so inoffensive and sincere that the audience lets them off with light applause.

Coretta steps to the mike next. Her first note is so awful, the emcee goes to the Tree of Hope and touches it for her. The audience lets her sing the first bar, then bursts into catcalls and derisive whistling. In a moment the familiar police siren is heard offstage, and big, dark brown "Porto Rico," who is part and parcel of amateur night, comes onstage with nothing covering his nakedness but a brassiere and panties and shoots twice at Coretta's feet with a stunt gun filled with blanks. She hurriedly retires to the wings with Porto Rico switching after her, brandishing his gun.

A lean dark boy playing a clarinet pours out such sweetness in "Body and Soul" that somebody rises and shouts, "Peace, brother!" in heartfelt approval.

Margaret follows with a sour note. She has chosen to sing "Old Folks," and her voice quavers so from stage fright that her song becomes an unfortunate choice, and the audience stomps for Porto Rico who appears in a pink and blue ballet costume to run her off the stage.

David is next on the program. With mounting frenzy he sings the intensely pleading blues song, "Rock It for Me." He clutches his knees, rolls his eyes, sings away from the mike, and works himself up to a pitch of excitement that is only cooled by the appearance of Porto Rico in a red brassiere, an ankle-length red skirt, and an exaggerated hat. The audience goes wild.

Ida comes out. She is a lumpy girl in a salmon pink blouse. The good-looking emcee leads her to the mike and pats her shoulder encouragingly. She snuggles up to him, and a female onlooker audibly snorts, "She sure wants to be hugged." A male spectator shouts, gleefully, "Give her something!"

Ida sings the plaintive, "My Reverie." Her accent is late West Indian and her voice is so bad, for a minute you wonder if it's an act. Instantly there are whistles, boos, and hand-clapping. The siren sounds offstage and Porto Rico rushes in wearing an old-fashioned corset and a marabou-trimmed bed jacket. His shots leave her undisturbed. The audience tries to drown her out with louder applause and whistling. She holds to the mike and sings to the bitter end. It is Porto Rico who trots sheepishly after her when she walks unabashed from the stage.

James come to the mike and is reminded by the audience to touch the Tree of Hope. He hasn't forgotten. He tries to start his song, but the audience will not let him. The emcee explains to him that the Tree of Hope is a sacred emblem. The boy doesn't care, and begins his song again. He has been in New York two days, and the emcee cracks that he's been in New York two days too long. The audience refuses to let the lad sing, and the emcee banishes him to the wings to think it over.

A slight, young girl in a crisp white blouse and neat black skirt comes to the mike to sing "Itisket, Itasket?" She has lost her yellow basket, and her listeners spontaneously inquire of her, "Was it red?" She shouts back dolefully, No, no, no, no!" "Was it blue?" No, it wasn't blue, either. They go on searching together.

A chastened James reappears and touches the Tree of Hope. A woman states with grim satisfaction, "He teched de tree dat time." He has tried to upset a precedent, and the audience is against him from the start. They boo and whistle immediately. Porto Rico in red flannels and a floppy red hat happily shoots him off the stage.

A high school girl in middy blouse, jumper, and socks rocks "Froggy Bottom." She is the youngest thing yet, and it doesn't matter how she sings. The house rocks with her.

She winds up triumphantly with a tap dance, and boogie-woogies confidently off the stage.

A frightened lad falls upon the mike. It is the only barrier between him and the murderous multitude. The emcee's encouragement falls on frozen ears. His voice starts down in his chest and stays here. The house roars for the kill; Porto Rico, in a baby's bonnet and a little girl's party frock, finishes him off with dispatch.

A white man comes out of the wings, but nobody minds. They have got accustomed to occasional white performers at the Apollo. There was a dancing act in the regular stage show that received deserved applause. The emcee announces the song, "That's Why"—he omits the next word—"Were Born." He is a Negro emcee. He will not use the word *darky* in announcing a song a white man is to sing.

The white man begins to sing, "Someone had to plow the cotton, Someone had to plant the corn, Someone had to work while the white folks played, That's why darkies were born." The Negroes hiss and boo. Instantly the audience is partisan. The whites applaud vigorously. But the greater volume of hisses and boos drown out the applause. The singer halts. The emcee steps to the house mike and raises his hand for quiet. He does not know what to say, and says ineffectually that the song was written to be sung and urges that the singer be allowed to continue. The man begins again, and on the instant is booed down. The emcee does not know what to do. They are on a sectional hookup and the announcer has welcomed Boston and Philadelphia to the program during the station break. The studio officials, the listening audience, largely white, has heard a Negro audience booing a white man. It is obvious that in his confusion the emcee has forgotten what the song connotes. The Negroes are not booing the white man as such. They are booing him for his categorization of them. The song is not new. A few seasons ago they listened to it in silent resentment. Now they have learned to vocalize their bitterness. They cannot bear that a white man, as poor as themselves, should so separate himself from their common fate and sing paternally for a price of their predestined lot to serve.

For the third time the man begins, and now all the fun that has gone before is forgotten. There is resentment in every heart. The white man will not save the situation by leaving the stage, and the emcee steps again to the house mike with an impassioned plea. The Negroes know this emcee. He is as white as any white man. Now it is ironic that he should be so fair, for the difference between him and the amateur is too undefined. The emcee spreads out his arms and begins, "My people—" He says without explanation that "his people" should be proud of the song. He begs "his people" to let the song be sung to show that they are ladies and gentlemen. He winds up with a last appeal to "his people" for fair play. He looks for all the world like the plantation owner's yellow boy acting as buffer between the blacks and the big house.

The whole house breaks into applause, and this time the scattered hisses are drowned out. The amateur begins and ends in triumph. He is the last contestant, and in the line-up immediately following, he is overwhelmingly voted first prize. More of the black man's blood money goes out of Harlem.

The show is over. The orchestra strikes up, "I Think You're Wonderful." The audience files out. They are quiet and confused and sad. It is twelve on the dot. Six hours of sleep and then back to the Bronx or up and down an elevator shaft. Yessir, Mr. White Man, I work all day while you-all play. It's only fair. That's why darkies were born.

# Almost Made King

## *Vivian Morris*

**Living in a comfortable five-room flat on West 140
Street, Wilbert Miller is a Jamaican born on that island
in the spring of 1870, who once lived in South Africa.
An interior decorator, Wilbert now lives in this well-
furnished New York apartment with his wife and a
daughter. A man with graying hair, he is an avid community organizer and an active member of the Seventh-Day
Adventist Church and the Universal Negro Improvement Association.**

**In an interview, he talked about the man who almost
became the king of Harlem.**

So you want me to tell you something about black folklore;
well, here's a story about a strapping, jet-black black man
who will live as long as folk tales are handed down from
generation to generation. To many, he was a clown, a jester
who wanted to play at being king; to hundreds of thousands
of Negroes, he was a magnificent leader and martyr to a
great cause: complete and unconditional social and economic freedom for Negroes everywhere. And had it not been
for one flaw in his plan of action, there would probably be
no more than a handful us Negroes in America today.

His name was Marcus Garvey. He was born, so the records say, on the island of Jamaica in the British West Indies

about 1887, but few people ever heard of him until he came
to New York. He was a born orator and his power to attract
and hold an audience was destined to make him famous.

I remember his first important speech.

*Wherever I go, whether it be France, Germany, En-
gland, or Spain, I am told that there is no room for a
black people. The other races have countries of their own
and it is time for the 400 million blacks of the world to
claim Africa for themselves. Therefore, we shall demand
and expect of the world a Free Africa. The black man
has been serf, a tool, a slave, and peon long enough.*

*That day has ceased.*

*We have reached the time when every minute, every
second must count for something done, something
achieved in the cause for Africa. We need the freedom
of Africa now. At this moment methinks I see Ethiopia
stretching forth her hands unto God, and methinks I see
the Angel of God taking up the standard of the Red, the
Black, and the Green, and saying, Men of the Negro
race, Men of Ethiopia, follow me.*

*It falls to our lot to tear off the shackles that bind
Mother Africa. Can you do it? You did it in the Revolutionary War. You did it in the Civil War. You did
it in the battles of Maine and Verdun. You did it in
Mesopotamia. You can do it marching up the battle
heights of Africa. Climb ye the heights of liberty and
cease not in well-doing until you have planted the banner of the Red, the Black, and the Green upon the hill-
tops of Africa.*

These, my child, were the very words of the man Marcus
Garvey, whom many called the black Napoleon. I remember
them well as you, perhaps, remember Lincoln's Gettysburg
address. He was standing there, strong and forceful before
a crowd of more than 25,000 Negroes who had assembled

in Madison Square Garden to consider the problems of the Negro race. It was shortly after the World War, August 1920, I believe.

Well that was a sight to thrill you with pride. Imagine, huge spacious Madison Square Garden, rocking with the yells of 25,000 frenzied Negro patriots demanding a free Africa, from the Strait of Gibraltar to the Cape of Good Hope—a Negro republic run exclusively by and for Negroes. Doesn't sound real, does it? Well, it happened—and it can happen again, but not until another leader with Marcus Garvey's strength, vision, and courage comes along. Some people say that Father Divine is the answer to this need. Personally I doubt it. He is a good organizer but his Divinites are not to be compared with the powerful and vigorous following once commanded by the Universal Negro Improvement Association that Garvey founded and built singlehanded. Why, he had such a magnetic personality that people flocked to see him wherever he went, and when he appeared on any platform to speak he'd have to wait sometimes five or ten minutes before the loud ovations and sounds of applause subsided. Then he would stride majestically forward in his cap and gown of purple, green, and gold, and the hall, arena, square, or whatever it was, would become magically silent.

He was always an enigma to the white people who flocked in great numbers to hear him, They couldn't decide whether to consider him a political menace or a harmless buffoon. But to his several hundred thousand Negro followers he was a great leader with a wonderful idea, an unequaled program of emancipation. He did not claim to be a great intellectual, a Frederick Douglass or Booker T. Washington, but he was certainly endowed with color and originality—so much so that he caught the fancy and commanded the solid support of the Negro masses as no other man has done before or since. He had the unusual happy faculty for stirring their race consciousness.

I can see him even now as he stood and exhorted his followers at that first organizational meeting. He read a telegram of greeting to Eamon De Valera (1882–1975), president of the Irish Republic. Wait a minute, I'll look among my papers and find a copy of it for you.

Here it is. It says: "Twenty-five thousand Negro delegates assembled in Madison Square Garden in Mass Meeting, representing four hundred million Negroes of the world, send you greetings as president of the Irish Republic. Please accept sympathy of the Negroes of the world for your cause. We believe Ireland should be free even as Africa shall be free for the Negroes of the world. Keep up the fight for a free Ireland."

After that, he spoke at length and if I remember correctly, his speech went something like this:

*We are descendants of a suffering people. We are descendants of a people determined to suffer no longer. Our forefathers suffered many years of abuse from an alien race.*

*It was claimed that the black man came from a backward people, not knowing and not awake to the bigger callings of civilization. That might have been true years ago, but it is not true today.*

*Fifty-five years ago the black man was set free from slavery on this continent. Now he declares that what is good for the white man of this age is also good for the Negro. They as a race claim freedom and claim the right to establish a democracy. We shall now organize the 400 million Negroes of the World into a vast organization to plant the banner of freedom on the great continent of Africa. We have no apologies to make, and will make none. We do not desire what has belonged to others, though others have always sought to deprive us of that which belonged to us.*

*We new Negroes will dispute every inch of the way until we win.*

*We will begin by framing a Bill of Rights of the Negro race with a Constitution to guide the lives and destiny of the 400 million. The Constitution of the United States means that every white American would shed his blood to defend that Constitution. The Constitution of the Negro race will mean that every Negro will shed his blood to defend his Constitution.*

*If Europe is for the Europeans, then Africa shall be for the black peoples of the world, We say it. We mean it.*

Following the thirty-day organizational convention of the Universal Negro Improvement Association at Madison Square Garden in 1920 more than three thousand delegates and sympathizers of the group gathered in Harlem at Liberty Hall, at West 138 Street, where they gave their final approval of the declaration of rights of the Negro peoples of the world. Delegates were there from Africa as well as the West Indian and Bermuda Islands. It was a memorable occasion.

Decorating the huge hall were banners of the various delegations. Prominently displayed also were the red, black, and green flags of the new African [Republic-to-be]. A colorful, forty-piece band, a choir of fifty male and female voices, and several quartets entertained the assembly all during the early part of the evening. Afterward, Marcus Garvey, president general of the association, announced the business of the meeting and read the declaration.

Much applause greeted the reading of the preamble to the declaration which stated: "In order to encourage our race all over the world and to stimulate it to overcome the handicaps and difficulties surrounding it, and to push forward to a higher and grander destiny, we demand and insist upon the following declaration of rights."

Then followed the fifty-four statements of rights that the

association demanded for Negroes everywhere. The first was
similar in form to the American Declaration of
Independence:

> *Whereas all men are created equal and entitled to
> the rights of life, liberty, and the pursuits of happiness,
> and because of this, we, dully elected representatives of
> the Negro people of the world, invoking the aid of the
> just and almighty God, do declare all men, women, and
> children . . . throughout the world free denizens, and do
> claim them as free citizens of Africa, the motherland of
> all Negroes.*

The first statement was greeted with loud and prolonged
applause, as were many others that followed it, but there
was so much enthusiasm, shouting, stamping of feet, and
other exhibitions of approval at the conclusion of the following statement that the chairman was forced to appeal, again
and again, for order:

> *We declare that no Negro shall engage himself in
> battle with an alien race without first obtaining consent
> of the leader of the Negro peoples of the world, except in
> a matter of national self-defense.*

Another statement which met with popular fancy was

> *We assert that the Negro is entitled to even-handed
> justice before all courts of law and equity, in whatever
> country he may be found, and when this is denied him
> on account of his race or color, such denial is an insult
> to the race as a whole, and should be resented by the
> entire body of Negroes. We deprecate the use of the term
> 'nigger' as applied to Negroes and demand that the word
> Negro be written with a capital N.*
> *We demand a free and unfettered commercial [re-*

*lationship] with all the Negro peoples of the world.
We demand that the governments of the world recognize our leader and his representatives chosen by the race to look after the welfare of our people under such governments. We call upon the various governments to represent the general welfare of the Negro peoples of the world.*

*We demand that our duly accredited representatives be given proper recognition in all leagues, conferences, conventions or courts of international arbitration whenever human rights are discussed.*

*We proclaim the first day of August of each year to be an international holiday to be observed by all Negroes.*

The thing that makes this ambitious adventure all the more remarkable, my child, is that all these strong resolutions and gigantic plans were conceived entirely by this one man, Marcus Garvey, who, in the beginning, was just another underprivileged West Indian boy; a printer's apprentice. Fired with the idea of welding the divided black masses of the world together, however, he became an entirely different and revolutionary personality.

Garvey worked his way to London and studied, at night, at the university. His education was supplemented by travel and observations in the different European countries. He did not get to Africa but listened attentively to many fellow ships' passengers who told of the cruelty inflicted on the natives in many districts. Later, Garvey worked on freighters that touched several of the West Indian, Central, and South American ports. He had many opportunities to observe the exploitation of the black workers of quite a few different countries who created vast fortunes for their white bosses while they lived in abject poverty. Once he is quoted as having said: "Poverty is a hellish state to be in. It is no virtue, it is a crime."

And so, it was this knowledge of unfavorable working conditions for black men everywhere that fired the wandering, giant Negro with his idea of a separate country and homeland for these oppressed peoples: a country with a civilization second to none. Africa, he felt, was the logical country. Thus was born the "Back to Africa" movement.

Nineteen-seventeen saw the actual beginning of the Garvey movement, but not until the spring of nineteen-eighteen did Marcus succeed in officially organizing the Universal Negro Improvement Association. Later, in the fall, he established his own newspaper, *The Negro World,* and began a systematic appeal for contributions to the movement. It was also his medium for preaching his doctrines to the out-of-town public. Week by week the paper's editorial pages aired his opinions.

Soon, money began pouring into the coffers of the association, and it was not long before Garvey organized a steamship company, known as the Black Star Line, scheduled to operate between the West Indies, Africa, and the United States. During the winter of 1919 alone, more than half a million dollars' worth of stock was sold to Negroes. One Negro college in the state of Louisiana was reputed to have raised seven thousand dollars for promotion of the scheme. Three ships, Garvey said, had been bought from the entire proceeds of the national fund: *The Yarmouth,* the *Maceo* and line *Shadysiah.* Another, the *Phyllis Wheatley,* was advertised weekly in the Negro World. It was claimed that she would ply between Cuba, Saint Kitts, Barbados, Trinidad, Demerara, Dakar, and Monrovia. The only hitch was the date of sailing never came. In fact, the mass inspection of the *Phyllis Wheatley* that Garvey kept promising his followers never came. Certain doubters in the organization then began to wonder whether there was any ship at all and they went even further than that. They sent a delegation to His Highness, the President, with a demand to see the boat. Garvey, always at ease in the face of any difficult situation, told them that he would attend to it the next day. When the next day came, he put them off again. And so it went from day to day.

This difficult situation arose during the famous "first convention" that was held in August 1920 and lasted for thirty days. There was a grand and imposing parade through the streets of Harlem and the colorful, regal mass meetings were held at Madison Square Garden and Liberty Hall. Garvey said he was busy. There was nothing for the delegates to do but wait. The publicity that the movement received during this gigantic display of marching legions and blaring trumpets skyrocketed the circulation of the *Negro World* to the unimaginable figure of 75,000 in the field of weekly Negro journalism. It was one of the instruments that made Garvey the most powerful black man in America at that time. Harlem and black America were literally at his feet.

Garvey then bought a chain of grocery stores, restaurants, beauty and barber shops, laundries, women's wear shops, and a score or more of other small businesses. He instituted a one-man campaign to completely monopolize the small industries in Harlem and drive the white storekeepers out. His one big mistake came, however, when he printed and issued circulars asking for additional purchasers of Black Star Line stock and assuring prospective buyers of the financial soundness of the company. This was too much for the delegates who had been asking for a detailed accounting of the Association's funds throughout the entire convention only to get the run-around. They immediately petitioned the U.S. Post Office Department of Inspection to investigate the company's books. When the true state of affairs was brought to light, Garvey was immediately indicted for using the mails to defraud. The investigation also brought showed that Garvey had collected thousand of dollars for his so-called "defense fund."

Well, to make a long story short, by June 1924, instead of perching majestically on his golden throne in some faraway jungle clearing, being waited and danced attendance upon by titled nobles, the erstwhile Black Napoleon and Provisional President of Africa found himself sitting, disconsolate and alone, in a bare cell of the Tombs prison. It was the culmination of a twenty-seven day trial in the U.S. District Court. The jury, after listening to testimony and arguments for practically the entire duration of that time, brought in a verdict of guilty. Marcus, the great, had been duly and officially convicted of using the mails to defraud.

Loyal officers of the movement had a bail bondsman on hand, ready to secure the release of their idol, but the Assistant U.S. District Attorney foiled this move by asking that Garvey remain in prison without bail. His request was granted when the Court was told that Garvey's African Legion was well supplied with guns and ammunition and would probably help their chief to escape.

And so, in the midst of heavily armed U.S. Marshals and a detachment of New York City policemen, the "Leader of the Negro Peoples of the World" was marched off to the anything but comfortable and homelike atmosphere of the Tombs. Later he was transferred to Atlanta. With him went his dreams of a great Black Empire, his visions of a final welding of all Negroes into one strong, powerful nation, with himself as dictator and his favorite supporters as elegant lords, princes, dukes, and other personages of high-sounding title: like "High Commissioner," "His Highness and Royal Potentate," "Minister of the African Legion," "The Right Honorable High Chancellor," "His Excellency, Prince of Uganda," "Lord of the Nile," and so on.

Yes, there's no doubt about it, Garvey had grandiloquent ideas. Conceiving and attempting to put over big things was his specialty. But like most dreamers, he dreamed just a little too much. He was too little the realist. Otherwise, his story might have been different. As it was, few of his dreams ever came true; not, mind you, of their lack of soundness. I still feel that he was a great man, honest and sincere. But he was not practical. Conducting a business enterprise according to established rules meant very little to him. That was his undoing. But there was no denying that he was a colorful personality. The way he thought up such grand titles for his subjects was only one manifestation of it. In defense of conferring these titles, by the way, Garvey said: "It is human nature that when you make a man know that you are going to reward him and recognize and appreciate him for services rendered, and place him above others, he is going to do the best that is in him."

Garvey also called attention to the fact that the conferring of degrees by colleges and universities adopted from European customs is only parallel to the conferring of titles by the Universal Negro Improvement Association. The only difference being that one is scholastic, the other political. And perhaps he was right.

*October 20, 1938*

# Cocktail Party

## Dorothy West

**The era of alcohol prohibition had been over for six years when Dorothy West chronicled a night out she experienced in January 1939. In this piece, she offers us a glimpse inside a Harlem house party.**

The party was on the fifth floor, but even as we entered the lower hall, we could hear the shouts and laughter. It was a successful party then, for judging by the volume of voices, the four-room flat was packed. That meant that all invitations had been accepted. The elevator bore us up and let us out. Our smiling hostess stood in her open door. Behind her was a surge of varicolored faces, the warm white of fair Negroes, the pale white of whites, through yellows and browns to rusty black.

We brushed cheeks with our hostess, and our mutual coos of endearment fell on the already false air. We entered the smoke-thickened room, brushed cheeks with a few more people, shook hands with some others, and followed our hostess into the bedroom.

A visiting Fisk professor, already bored with the party, had got his length somehow into a boudoir chair and sat pulling on his pipe. He could not leave because he had come with his wife, who would not leave until all the important people had come. Gloomily he uncoiled himself when we entered and, after greetings, assured his hostess in sepulchral tones that he was perfectly happy.

We laid our coats as carefully as we could on the pile of wraps on the bed. Our hostess fingered a soft brown fur. "Mink," she sighed. "Real mink." She blew on it for our inspection, then rubbed a fold of it over her rump. "The closest I'll ever get to it, I guess."

She was on the city payroll, had graduated from a first-class Negro college, belonged to a good sorority, had married respectably, and was now entrenching herself in New York Negro society. There had been one or two flamboyant indiscretions in her past, and so every once in a while, to assure herself and her hometown that she had lived them down, she entertained at a lavish party. She was not yet sufficiently secure to give a small affair. And of all the people lapping up her liquor, hardly one would have come to an intimate dinner. As yet it was necessary for her to give large, publicized affairs so that everyone felt bound to come out of fear that it might be thought he was not invited.

As we returned to the main room, a woman in cap and apron shuffled up inexpertly balancing a tray of cocktails. We had not known that our hostess had a maid. Yet the woman's harassed dark face was familiar. We remembered that once before, while we visited with our hostess, there had been a ring at the door and a voice had called that it was the janitor's wife with a package, and presently this woman's face had appeared.

Our hostess found places for us on the already populated divan. We sat among acquaintances, balancing our drinks. To our left were a public school teacher; two Department of Welfare investigators; two writers, one left and one right; a "Y" worker; a white first-string movie critic; a white artist and his wife. To our right were two Negro government officials, two librarians, a judge's daughter, a student, a Communist organizer, an artist, an actress. There were others. In this room and in the inner room were crowded fully sixty incoming and outgoing people. With the exception of the Communist organizer, all of the Negroes were members of Harlem society. Some of their backgrounds began with their marriages or their professions. One or two were the unimportant offspring of earnest men who had carved small niches in the hall of fame. Two or three were as celebrated as their fathers. Some of them were well-to-do, most particularly where both husband and wife held well-paid jobs. Others had fallen on lean times, but family connections and Home Relief [welfare] kept them in circulation.

The women in general were light-colored, one of the phenomena of Negro society. Their dress was smart, their makeup skillful. The men were varying colors and soberly dressed. Our hostess had no reputation as a conversationalist, and our host, of better reputation where social talk was concerned, was already in his cups. There was no attempt by either to marshal their guests into interesting groups. The crowd was too unwieldy, and our hostess had only probed beneath the surface of a half-dozen men who thought her pretty. She could only dump a newcomer into whatever space was available, and introduce him to the nearest of the sitters. Whereupon the ensuing conversation was either polite or flirtatious, depending upon sex and preference. When a friend found a friend's face in the crowd, navigation was too difficult, and the greeting was confined to a shouted, "How are you?"

We listened to the conversation around us. A tall unattractive girl on our right had assumed an affected pose. She languished on the divan and blew puffs of smoke through a cigarette holder. Her large foot pivoted on its ankle. She surveyed it dreamily. Her father was a man of importance, and although she had neither beauty nor charm, she had constituted herself the year's number one Negro debutante.

A young leftist writer was talking to her around our backs. He had brought her to the party. Generally one of the artist group squired her. They were indifferent to her lack of prettiness and liked her father's liquor. She boasted of her escorts to her sorors who expressed no envy. They were quite content with their younger beaux who were marrying men.

The writer said, "Will you serve as a sponsor for the dinner then? Your name will look good on the stationery. I can come up tomorrow and go over a guest list with you." She smiled at the toe that protruded through the space in her shoe for its protuberance. "I've two other dinners that week, you know. Three will give me such a crowded calendar. But for you—and your guest of honor is quite celebrated, isn't he?"

"Very," he said enthusiastically. "He's been in the papers a lot. The critics rave about him. I'm going to read his book as soon as he gives me the copy he promised me."

"I'll expect you tomorrow night," she said, "Come at dinnertime. Father will want you to sample his latest concoction. Keep the rest of the evening free, will you? My sorority is—ah—having a dance at the Renaissance. There's no tax. Maybe you'd like to look in."

"I'd love to," he exclaimed, "but I can't! I've a meeting at nine, important. Anyway," he added helpfully, "I haven't got a tux."

Her eyes returned to her toe, but this time they were sorrowful. Cocktails, little sausages on toothpicks, black and green olives, cheeses with crisp little crackers, two-inch sandwiches went in continuous file around the room. Our hostess had a fine array of liquor with impressive labels on the improvised bar. Once she had recommended her bootlegger to us, but we had stopped his visits when we found his labels were often not yet dry and no two like bottles had similar tastes. Since most of the people were connoisseurs no more than we were, they eagerly drank the badly cut liquor and got high.

The actress, from a chair-backed hassock, surveyed the room with disdain. She was playing in a downtown hit! Her hair went up and her nose turned up, and even her lips was slightly curled. She was light-skinned and lovely and remote as a queen among her subjects. Ten years ago she had been a gamin and her accent had been Harlem. Now offstage she was indistinguishable from a throaty Englishman.

We bent to flick our ashes in the tray she was holding in a graceful hand, our mouths open for a pretty compliment. She withdrew her hand in horror and we let our ashes fall on the floor. Her eyes asked us elegantly, "Have we met?"

The white movie critic started toward her, the white artist's wife on his arm. The actress smiled and smiled.

The woman said, "My husband and I saw your show last night. We thought you were marvelous."

"How kind!" said the actress.

"My paper gave you quite a plug," said the movie critic proudly.

The actress smiled and smiled again. All of them beamed at one another.

"I'm so-o-o sorry," the actress murmured, "that we haven't been introduced. May I have the pleasure of your acquaintance?"

The movie critic told her his name and introduced the artist's wife. In a moment they were as chatty as old friends.

We had come at a late hour, and when it was an hour past the scheduled time for the party's end, the crowd gradually began to thin. Our hostess's hair-up had drifted down and her trailing gown had been trampled on. She struck a graceful pose at the door, and her meticulous phrases sped each departing guest.

We had not seen our hostess in several months. She urged us to stay for a little chat. When the last guest had gone, she dispatched her husband and the janitor's wife with borrowed chairs and hassocks and end tables and ashtrays to various flats in the house. She sat down, shook her shoes off, and pulled the rest of her hair down. She lifted her arms and wrinkled her nose.

"I put four on the card, cause I know colored folks, and I knew they'd start coming around six. I didn't even plan to take my bath until five. I start sweating so quick. And then at four sharp here come two white folks. I forgot they don't keep c.p. time. Well, I jumped into this, and did my hair and face, and I know they thought my party was a flop, because nobody else came until around five, and they left before six."

We said it was the best attended party we'd been to in a long time.

She fanned herself under the arms.

"It was kinda nice, wasn't it?" she agreed. Then she chuckled softly.

"You notice how Dr. Brown's wife kept looking at me? She knows he likes me. She only came to keep her eye on him. She'd have to go some to keep her eye on me! You notice that good-looking chap with his wife, one wore the sleazy green dress?" She smiled meaningfully.

"Well, she's just up for the holidays, but he's here for the winter."

The janitor's wife came back. She was frankly dragging now. Her cap was at a comic angle, but she did not look funny. She stood respectfully before our hostess. I could see that one of her shoelaces was black and the other was white, ink-stained black.

"I'll see you Saturday," said our hostess to her cheerfully, though this was Sunday. "That all right? I won't have a penny until then. Pouring liquor down all these darkies cost a lot. They'll talk about you if your drinks are scarce. Saturday noon, I'll see you, Flora."

The woman covered her embarrassment with a painful smile. "That's all right," she said.

She turned to go. When she reached the door, our hostess jumped up suddenly, called to her to wait, rummaged in her bathroom, returned, and thrust some silk pieces in the woman's hands.

"Will you do these for me, Flora? I'll pick them up Saturday when I pay you."

When the door shut behind Flora, our hostess came back and said triumphantly, "I'll give her a few cents extra, and I'll save a dollar's washing. We're going to two affairs this week, and that dollar'll mean taxi fare. I hate to come home late at night in a subway with a lot of funny-looking derelicts."

We said we hadn't been anywhere in weeks and hoped that she'd have a good time.

Our hostess said we ought to get out more, and she tried to interest us in the affairs she was planning to attend. One was for Spain, the other for China, both causes worth supporting. She spoke with feeling of the pogroms in Germany [against Jews]. It was obvious that she kept abreast of the international situation.

We asked her what she thought of the Gaines decision. She said she hadn't seen any reference to it in her paper, and she read the paper daily. We said it had been given front page space in the Negro weeklies for the past two weeks. She laughed and answered that she only read the society pages of the Negro papers because of their poor journalism. The society reporters were no better, but at least you kept up with what the darkies were doing. As an afterthought she asked us what the Gaines decision was.

We explained that it was a Supreme Court decision whereby a Southern state must either admit a Negro student to its university or build a university of equal standards for him.

She laughed and said she hoped they'd build one. She was tired of her present job and she was a qualified teacher. She'd like to go South and teach a group of good-looking male students.

Her husband returned. It was obvious that he had had

another drink or two in somebody's flat. It had made him hungry.

"Any food, female?" he addressed his wife. "None of these scraps." He surveyed with distaste the dainty sandwiches. "Got any greens left?"

"Greens and spare ribs, have some with us?" she asked.

We thanked her but said we really should go.

Her husband looked at us a little belligerently. He was born in the South, and he said that he yearned for it, but he never got any farther than his government job in Washington even on holidays.

"You don't like colored folks' cooking?" he asked.

We said that we loved greens and spare ribs and named all the other Southern dishes and said that we loved them, too.

He smiled at us paternally and said that he wished we were all down South, celebrating the New Year right, with black-eyed peas and hogshead.

"My mother," he reminisced happily, "would turn her house inside out for my friends. You folks up North got a lot to learn about hospitality. You all buy a quart of gin, a box of crackers, and a bottle of olives, and throw a couple of white folks in, and call it a cocktail party."

Our hostess stood in her stocking feet and drew herself up grandly. "You're drunk," she said coldly. "Go and eat."

Gravely he bade us good night and walked away with unsteady dignity.

Our hostess went to the door with us in her stocking feet. Again we thanked her for a lovely party.

She surveyed her tumbled rooms complacently. "I'll clean up and take a bath, and turn on the radio and do my paper. I'm speaking Wednesday at the Young Matrons' meeting. I'm going to talk on the evil of anti-Semitism. There is some anti-Semitism in Harlem which should be scorched at the start. How you like that for a subject?

We told her we didn't think there was any anti-Semitism

in Harlem as such. There was only the poor man's resentment of exploitation by the rich. It was incidental that in this particular instance that one was black and one was Jewish. Black workers and Jewish workers did not hate each other.

"Maybe," she said brightly. "But I still think it's a good topic for a paper. Last month some dumb cluck read a paper on child care. Who can afford to have a child now anyway? I want to give em a paper on something current."

We urged her to go and put her shoes on before she caught cold. We brushed cheeks all around. When we got home, we wondered as usual why we had gone to a cocktail party.

# Cliff Webb and Billie Day

## *Frank Byrd*

In 1934, the Broadway team of stalwarts, producer
Charles Dillingham and director Leonard Stillman
launched a successful variety show at the Fulton Theatre
that they called *New Faces*. The original production fea-
tured comedian Imogene Coca, who would later become
a television star with Sid Ceasar.

Originally presented in Pasadena as *Low and Behold*,
Stillman's production would run on and off in six subsequent productions over an eighteen-year period between
1934 and 1952, featuring various new talents. These
included such soon-to-be luminaries as Coca, Stillman
himself, Henry Fonda, and future film director Charles
Walters. So, it is noteworthy that this long and varied
cast of characters included two perfomers who had been
well-known in Harlem entertaiment circles when they
were drafted to appear in a 1938 production of this
long-running talent showcase. It would be Dillingham's
sixty-second and final Broadway musical.

When Charles Dillingham's Broadway production of *New
Faces* opened last season, the show played to admiring, capacity audiences for many months. In it were two faces that
were once well known in the vicinity of the Park Avenue

Market in Harlem—Cliff Webb and Billie Day—who at one time provided almost all the after-dark entertainment for the street peddlers in the Latin Quarter.

In a little basement cabaret in East 111 Street, people gathered nightly to hear these two croon their plaintive Negro, West Indian, and Spanish songs to the accompaniment of an out-of-tune piano and a battered but tuneful guitar. Cliff played the piano and Billie accompanied her own singing with the guitar obligatos. Occasionally there was dancing. Then these two vivacious kids acted as chorus and orchestra for the pleasure-seeking peddlers. It is surprising that they were able to earn a living solely on the tips they received owing mostly to their popularity. They never received a definite salary. In fact, it was very peculiar how they even happened to get the job.

The two kids had a habit of wandering from one little restaurant or cabaret to another, singing their songs, dancing (if asked) and passing the hat (if the proprietor had no objections) and filing out as quietly as they had appeared. One night they went to the Casa Diablo, the small basement place in West 111 Street, and were such a huge success with the peddlers and other transient guests that the owner of the place, a Puerto Rican whom everyone called El Gato, asked them to come in every night and sing for tips. The only incentive offered them was all they wanted to eat and drink. They stayed.

Not long afterward, the place became quite popular, and one night some friends of Leonard Stillman, the director, stumbled in accidentally. They listened to the two rollicking youngsters and tipped Stillman off to their whereabouts. He engaged them for his show and they were an immediate success. The very first night they stopped the show and were forced to take curtain call after curtain call. The blasé first-nighters were simply mad about them. They were so new, so fresh and unspoiled.

El Gato's place remained the favorite retreat for the market peddlers but the atmosphere was never the same after Cliff and Billie left. Night after night, the peddlers used to sit around talking about the good times they had when these two kids were about and how different it was without them.

*January 19, 1939*

# Matt Henson Retires

## *Theodore Poston*

There was little work being done on this special morning in the chief clerk's office of the U.S. Custom House downtown. The first man to reach the North Pole was retiring.

The whole staff had gathered around the desk of the genial and unassuming little man who had worked there for twenty-three years. For Matt Henson, sole survivor of Admiral Robert E. Peary's dash to the North Pole, was retiring from government service that day—on a clerk's pension.

A few reporters had dropped in to record the occasion. Friends from Harlem and other parts of the city had come down also. One by one they assured the bald-headed but erect one-time explorer that they would continue the fight for Congressional recognition of his deed. And Matt Henson thanked them and turned to bid the staff farewell.

The reporters asked questions. Reluctantly, Henson answered. He displayed no bitterness against a government that had heaped undying honors on the late rear admiral and completely ignored the only other American to reach the pole. Of the proposed Congressional pension, repeatedly denied him, he said: "I could use the money. I think that I deserve it. But I will never ask the government nor anybody else for anything. I have worked sixty of the seventy years of my life, so I guess I can make out on the $87.27 a month pension I've earned here."

Black leaders had not been so philosophical, however. For a quarter of a century they had demanded official recognition and a commensurate pension for Mr. Henson. Through their efforts six bills had been introduced in Congress. All died in committee.

Congressman Arthur W. Mitchell resurrected the fight in 1935. Scores of prominent Negroes appeared before the House committee to support the bill, which asked for a gold medal and a $2,500 pension. They pointed out that the late Rear Admiral Peary had been awarded a $6,500 pension and a Congressional medal. They recalled that Henson had twice saved Peary's life. They charged that Henson's race was his only barrier to recognition.

The House passed the bill. The Senate killed it. At the prompting of the reporters, Matt Henson again described their arrival at the North Pole on April 6, 1909, the culmination of a nineteen-year struggle on their part. Together he and Peary had made eight expeditions into the Arctic regions, and five unsuccessful dashes for the pole. Twice a helpless Peary had been brought back to civilization by his black companion—once when his feet were frozen and again when he was stricken by pneumonia.

For the last time in the Custom House surroundings, Mr. Henson recalled the climax of the final dash that had started July 8, 1908. As trail breaker for the party, which included the two Americans and four Eskimos, the black had been the first to arrive at the pole.

"When the compass started to go crazy," he recalled, "I sat down to wait for Mr. Peary. He arrived about forty-five minutes later, and we prepared to wait for the dawn to check our exact positions. Mr. Peary pulled off his boots and warmed his feet on my stomach. We always did that before going to bed up there."

The next morning when their positions had been verified, Peary said: "Matt, we've reached the North Pole at last."

With his exhausted leader looking on, Henson planted the American flag in the barren area.

"That was the happiest moment of my life," Mr. Henson said. Henson's early life fitted him admirably for the hardships he was to undergo with Peary. Born in Charles County, Maryland, in 1866, he was orphaned at the age of four. When he was nine, he ran away from his foster parents and signed up as a cabin boy on the old sailing vessel *Katie Hines*. A few years later, the *Katie Hines* was ice-bound for several months in the Baltic Sea.

"That was my first experience with bitter cold, he recalled, "and it sure came in handy later."

Peary met Henson in 1887 when the latter was working in a store in Washington. Informed of the youth's love of travel, the explorer offered him a job on a surveying expedition in South America. Henson accepted and for twenty-two years, the two men were never separated.

Criticized for taking a black with him on his dash to the pole (his critics held that he was afraid that a white man might steal some of his prestige), Peary once said: "Matt was a better man than any of my white assistants. He made all our sleds. He was popular with the Eskimos. He could talk their language like a native. He was the greatest man living for handling dogs. I couldn't get along without him."

Despite this tribute, however, and a glowing forward to Henson's book, *Black Explorer at the North Pole*, Peary never publicly joined the forces that fought for Congressional recognition of his black assistant, Henson recalled.

"Mr. Peary was a hard man like that." the assistant said. "He didn't want to share his honor and his glory with anybody. He wanted everything for himself and his family. So, according to his lights, I guess he felt justified."

The Chief Clerk came over and shook his hand, his fellow workers gathered around to present him with several small mementos, and Matt Henson bade his friends farewell.

When he walked from the room, he had ended the only recognition the government had given him for his deed. For President Taft had appointed him a clerk in the Customs Service for life.

*Sometime between 1938 and 1939*

# Race Horse Row

## *Vivian Morris*

Now "Race Horse Row" is not a swanky bookmaker's establishment where the landed gentry places thousands on a horse's nose and scarcely flickers an eyelash as their choice runs second in a photo finish.

Oh no, to the contrary, it is the three blocks between West 135 and West 138 streets on the west side of Lenox Avenue. "The Rows" are tall unkempt, overcrowded, exorbitantly priced apartment houses that seem to scowl down at passersby like evil ogres.

There we will find a few of the vast army of Harlem's unemployed chancing their nickels, dimes, and quarters in a desperate last-ditch gamble trying to raise the rent or food.

The stores here lure prospective buyers with flaming red signs, shouting out "bargains" in meats, most of which is unfit for human consumption. The groceries are old and stale; the eggs listed as "fresh from nearby farms" are sold from cold storage holes kept hidden elsewhere in the building. There are vegetable stands and cut-rate stores with everything cut but the prices.

The block between West 136 and West 137 streets on the east side of Lenox Avenue facing "Race Horse Row" is Harlem Hospital.

The casual observer, on this warm sunshiny afternoon

sees a stream of toilers, domestic workers, with roomy bags containing their working paraphernalia; the coal worker sprinkled with flecks of the grimy material with which he labors; professionals with their brief cases all wending their way, presumably to their homes.

The keen eye detects more; it sees neatly dressed, furtive-looking men walking hurriedly up and down the blocks, in and out of stores, glancing quickly at pieces of paper and writing as they scurry. One of the men passes close to a hopeless-looking woman and hands something to her and whispers from the corner of his mouth, the way movie star Humphrey Bogart might, saying "Yo hoss was secunt—even money. What cha want in 'd' nex'?"

"Dig me later," the woman says. "Got a li'l figgerin to do." She goes around the corner followed by five or six other women. The runners hurry on their way dropping a word here and there to persons who have placed bets with them. You can tell by the expression on each face whether the wearer has won or lost.

I watched the women until they had secluded themselves in a doorway and then I quickly made my way to that same spot. They were dividing the winnings. The little woman who had collected the bet was saying, "Mary—your dime gits you twenty. Macie, your quarter gits you fifty. Your dime gits you twenty, Mae Lou, and let's see, Kitty your thirty gits you sixty, an' my nickel gits me ten. Where the hell did I git this extry dime?" She puzzledly held a dime in her palm. A little woman of about sixty snatched the remaining dime snorting, "Ah 'clare Mae Lou, you fuggits me evah time. Ah b'lieve you got sup'ma'gin me! 'clare, Ah does."

"Honey you ain' nevuh been so wrong. How you 'speck I got sup'm a'gin you w'en you is de one whut giv us de hunch to play de hoss an' save us all," said Mae Lou with a hurt expression on her thin face.

"Yo' dream bout yo' dead gram'ma sho' brung us luck," opined one. "Ah us dead set on dat fav'rite, Dead Ready."

"He's dead aw'rite—an' ready fo' de glue fact'ry."

"Who we gwine play in the nex' race?" asked Mae Lou. "I walk way up in de Bronx t'day—didn' git no job. On'y had one nickel. Thought I'd play today and git sup'm. Nickel ain' nuthin'."

"Yeh, les git together," another said. And they dug into their bags and pulled out newspapers with the varied and vague selections of the so-called leading handicappers. Their brows take on heavy frowns as their lips move and they slowly mumble the names of the horses.

"Well ah think we oughta play White Hot," said Macie slowly. "Das a good name."

Mae Lou thought differently, "I think we ought to play Veiled Lady cause I et pig feet las' night and dreamed some funny, crazy things. I dreamed dat I was at a fewn'al an' some mo' crazy mess. But y'all know dat w'en yo' dream bout fewn'als dat dey's got to be ladies an' w'en dey's ladies at a fewn'al dey got to have veils w'en dey's moanin', aint dey?"

"Mae Lou's right," chimed one. "Dat dream is clear as day. Veiled Lady is de hoss all right."

"Come on y'all," said Mae Lou quickly putting her paper back in the bag, "better get our bets in. Near pos' time—thirty-eight de pos'. Hits thirty-three now. Come on."

"Y'all kin play who y'all laks but ah lak White Hot," said Macie. "An' Ah got fif' cent an' Ah'm gunna put it on his nose." Macie left them to place her bet.

"Kin ya bet dat," said Mae Lou. "D'as de way hit is wid some people—w'en she had huh li'l quarta she was glad to play in wid us. Now she gut nuff to play by huhse'f, she gits real independent. We still got nuff to bet 'tween us. Les play Veiled Lady in de belly to run second."

A runner heard a low whistle and looked up. A woman leaning precariously out of a window on the top floor dropped something down wrapped in a piece of paper, which was deftly snatched as it fell by the bet taker. He gave her a knowing nod.

The next ten minutes seem to be an eternity as far as the betters were concerned. Some of them shifted their feet nervously, others blinked and twitched spasmodically, some paced.

Macie came back, but got the cold shoulder from her buddies.

"If dis'n wins—a pot o' greens and po'k fo' me," said Mae Lou cheerfully.

"If he doan win—whut?" asked Macie.

"I won't ast you for a looie" [cent] said Mae Lou angrily. Her buddies nodded agreeably.

"Y'all bes' stop stabbin' [playing long shots] an' play hosses dat figger. Dat White Hot don' win his las' two races an' kin win a'gin," said Macie philosophically.

The runner breezed by. The women waited with bated breaths. He almost passed these women, who looked after him with sinking hearts. He saw Macie and stopped, "Ah— you had a half on 'White Hot' did'n you?" He starts giving money to her first, some change, then two crumpled bills. " 'Leven-foty [eleven dollars and forty cents, for two dollars] de win. Git cha two-eighty for fifty cents."

Mae Lou asked timidly, wetting her lips, "Veiled Lady git second?"

"Nuthin'—out de money," he answered cruelly as he went on his way.

"Ah sho' lakked dat White Hot," said Kitty. "Ah com' nigh playin' him ef it had'n been fo' Mae Lou an' her Veiled Lady."

She looked angrily at Mae Lou, and the ones who lost their last thoroughly agreed with her, because they "sho' lakked that White Hot." They left Mae Lou.

The runner caught up with them as they were moving. "What cha want in de nex'?" The little woman who had been the first to attack Mae Lou, asked Macie sweetly, "Whut we gwine play, honey? Ah got a thin."

"We ain' gwine play nuthin," said Macie. "Um thu, you better tek that thin an' buy yu'se some hog ears—or sup'm else to eat."

They blended in with the other passersby and were quickly swallowed up.

*March 22, 1939*

# Harlem Hospital

## *Vivian Morris*

The woman sat down on the opposite bench, looked around, and made general complaints to the public within hearing. Possibly this general public thought she was "a little off," or possibly just another of those "sorry" cases that filled the waiting rooms of Harlem Hospital (at Lenox and West 135 Street), because those who heard her looked but didn't stop. The nurses simply didn't look. She caught my eye, and considering me an audience, pegged me with her conversation.

"O, Lawd, how I feels bad! I can't make out how I evuh come t' see daylight agin. Thought I was done fo' this time. Thought I'd nevuh git up," the woman told the worker, who showed no signs of reacting. Not that she wasn't convinced, she was nonplussed. She verified her puzzled head shaking with an almost wistful string of: "No, no, no."

The woman sat down on the bench, opposite me, looked around, began complaining again. "M'am, thought I was gone fur good now. Ain' been wukkin fur years now exceptin' on odd n' end jobs. Cleanin' wuk an' cookin' wuk. I been feelin' sick fum my rheumatism fur so long an' it's been worse all th' time. I picks up a job cleanin' las' week. Been sick when I took it, but I hadda take it. I wuks through th' day feelin' in pain an' faint. Then I git home t' fix up my house an' then it happens. Listen, I ain' no bad woman.

No, mam, I nevuh drinks. So help me Lawd, I nevuh takes a little drink. They foun' me lyin' ona floor unconscious. I can't remember much but I does remember my gittin' up ona ladder, all th' way up about eight feet so's to take a valise down, an' then I feels faint an' falls. Lawd, was I there stretched out! Stretched out as large as life.

"No, ma'm, don' think I hadda drink. I ain' no drinkin' woman. Somebody foun' me sprawlin' an' unconscious. I was hurt plenty. See, ma'm, I'se hurt here ona side, and aroun' my waist.

"Sure I been here befo'. I comes on Wednesday all weak an' sick an' was tol' it's too late. Here I was sick an' in pain an' they says no. Same thing an Thursday. I ain' got no treatment as yit.

"Third time I been here. Yuh shoulda heard how they talks t' me aroun' here. No respect fur age or illness. Y' comes an' gits cut up an' yelled at an' y' goes home.

"O, Lawd! Trouble wit'em is they don't know Jesus. If they did they wouldn' ack like they does. Jus' like a lotta cattle they acks t' us poor colored folks. Them white folks in nis hospital is gittin' nasty. I don't say nuthin' against white folks in gen'ral. I likes em all—cullud an' white n' they makes no diff'rence t' me. Only if they's kind n' got Jesus teachin'.

"I wukked fifteen years fur a gentleman in Charlotte, No'th Carolina. He was good t' me an' my daughter an' he built us a house nexta his. That's nice. But they's many that ain' nice. O, Lawdy me! Them that hires cleaners an' cooks an' servants. They ain' so nice, no ma'm. They wuks yuh t' death like you ain' no human. See whut's happened t' me? Me fallin' in a faint.

"An' I ain' nevvuh had a drink, ma'm. I tell yuh agin I'm a hard-wukkin' woman. I'm a good woman. So help me, Lawd. It pains me all aron' here. An' I ain' nevvuh took nuthin'. 'At's whut they seems t' think aroun' here. A little mo' of Jesus is whut's needed. Mo' of His teachin' in their hearts. We black folks always have suffered ever since I kin think back. We always have sufferin' wit' us.

"Whut kin we do, huh? I don' like t' be talked to this way. I'm good an' clean an' God-fearin' an' I nevvuh takes t' anythin' 'at's bad. Leastwise drinkin'. I tells yuh th' God-hones' fact. Lady, take me ovuh to th' desk, please. Yuh kind an' bless yuh. Take care a yuhself."

*June 6, 1939*

# Angelo Herndon

## *Theodore Poston*

Angelo Herndon, a black twenty-year-old Communist from Ohio, was arrested in Georgia on the strength of an allegation of inciting insurrection after he took part in a demonstration against economic conditions in Atlanta. Herndon told the story of what happened to him in his autobiography, *Let Me Live.*

He was convicted by an all-white jury and sentenced on January 19, 1933, to serve a twenty-year term on a chain gang under an old Georgia law that had been used to prevent slave uprisings. In his autobiography, *I Wonder as I Wander*, Langston Hughes said Georgia authorities used the antebellum statute against Herndon and his fellow demonstrators by simply calling it a "rebellion." Herndon was freed on fifteen thousand dollars bail and traveled to New York and elsewhere to publicize his harsh sentence.

Herndon's appearance followed the example of others who were considered political prisoners. The most famous of the era was the Scottsboro, Alabama, case in which nine black men were accused of raping two white women on a Southern freight train.

Like the Scottsboro case a few years earlier, the Herndon story was a major news story while the WPA Writer's Project was collecting folklore in the early 1930s.

He was tired. Very tired and very sick. His sagging muscles, pallid face, drooping shoulders and nervous fingers proclaimed it. And as the train headed for Pennsylvania Station where six thousand people waited impatiently to hail him, Angelo Herndon turned wearily to the reporter who had met him at Manhattan Transfer.

"Oh, *The Amsterdam News*, I remember it. It was one of the five papers which came to me regularly at Fulton Tower prison. They never let me read *The Daily Worker*, *The Amsterdam News*, *The New York Times*, *The Atlanta World* and *The Wall Street Journal*." He smiled slowly. "No, they wouldn't let me read even the *Wall Street Journal*. They poured ink on it."

"How was prison?" the reporter asked. "How did they treat you?"

"It was hell." He answered simply and shrugged his thin shoulders. After a pause he continued: "They tortured me. Oh, they tried to be clever about it. They insisted they were giving me 'special attention,' but they did things to me under that pretense. They cooked up that lie that I tried to escape. They searched my cell twice for steel saws. They found some rusty bits of tin that had been in there for years, and used this as an excuse to move me into a damp cell where water dripped from the ceiling.

"I pointed to the water and told them I was sick. (He looks tubercular.) They said: 'We don't give a damn if you drown,' and left me there. Later they put me in the death cell. They put special guards near my door. They taunted me."

"Didn't they give you regular treatment?" the reporter asked. "There was a letter in *The Nation* from a young white woman who said she visited you and found you were treated all right. She said you looked fine."

"Regular treatment?" he smiled again, wearily, fleetingly. "They took my medicine away from me."

He looked down at his thin bloodless fingers. "Do I look fine? I remember that young woman. They let her in to see me. I wasn't allowed any other visitors, except my lawyers. I think she was fine. She was a Socialist though. [Herndon is a Communist.] As she was leaving she said: 'We are so far apart.' "

Was there a demonstration when he left Fulton Tower prison? What did the other prisoners and guards say? Were they surprised?

"The authorities were dumbfounded. They never expected that we could raise the money. That's why they made the bail fifteen thousand dollars. The boys were surprised too. They were glad to see me go. They wished me good luck. The turnkey said: 'Hope to see you back soon—for good.' "

"We left quietly. There had been some talk about a lynching. They are conducting a campaign throughout the state against Communists. They didn't bother us though."

"If the United States Supreme Court reverses your conviction," the reporter asked, "and you are freed at a later trial, will you continue to work in the South?"

"Why not?"

"Won't the publicity attendant on your case make it impossible for you to continue there? Won't it be too dangerous?"

The wry smile again. "It's dangerous to be a worker anywhere—if you're trying to better your condition."

The train was pulling into Pennsylvania Station. Bob Minor, the grizzled Communist leader, was the first to reach Herndon. Awkwardly he threw his arms about the youth's frail shoulders and kissed him. James Ford, Negro candidate for the Vice Presidency of the United States in 1932, was second. He too kissed Herndon clumsily. Ruby Bates, one-time accuser but later chief defense witness in the Scottsboro case, was next. She hugged him and held her cheek to his.

Milton, Angelo's young brother, stood a little to the side. The two boys gazed quietly at each other. Silently they shook hands and embraced. On the upper level, six thousand persons, mainly white, strained against the police lines and yelled for their hero.

Angelo Herndon had come back from Georgia.

*August 7, 1934*

# Swing Clubs

## *Vivian Morris*

**Tom Mooney was a twenty-two-year-old labor activist who was arrested in 1916 in connection with a bombing in California during a Preparedness Day incident in San Francisco. Mooney was pardoned on January 7, 1938, by Governor Culbert L. Olson. Mooney was revered by labor groups. Like many activists, he traveled the country, promoting the causes of the working-class people he represented.**

The Harlem Swing Club has a dance every Sunday night on the ground floor of a big, spacious hall at 41 West 124 Street. Bright decorations of red and green crepe paper have been used to help create a festive appearance, and on the night I attended the club, there were various posters on the walls saying CELEBRATE THE FREEDOM OF TOM MOONEY," etc.

On the wall, directly behind the bandstand, is a placard with the words A BLUEPRINT FOR DEMOCRACY written boldly on it. Other decorations included drawings made by children who attend the Neighborhood Children's Center held in this hall daily. The Harlem Swing Club gives a dance and Jam Session every Sunday night during the winter season in this hall. The musicians who provide the excellent swing music are all members of Local 802, American Federation of Musicians—and the people who attend the club regularly are of all types and ages, the majority being young black girls and boys who love to dance the Lindy, the Tutti Fruitti and the Big Apple. Because the price of admission is very reasonable, they come here Sunday after Sunday, and forget their problems, their tedious jobs or lack of jobs, in the joy of dancing to the rhythmic beat of drums, the muted trumpets, and the wailing saxophones.

The club is now in its third year of existence, and is growing steadily more popular and more widely known. Lovers of swing music, intellectuals from Park Avenue and Greenwich Village, well-known band leaders and musicians, frequently drop in to listen to the music and watch the dancers. The atmosphere is friendly—anyone is welcome who behaves properly. Best of all, it provides an evening of happy entertainment for the young people of the neighborhood, both white and black who dance tirelessly, number after number, from 10 P.M. until 2 A.M., when the Swing Club closes its doors.

The club is near Mount Morris Park North.

While dancing is the main attraction, the club is also a place where black and white workers congregate and have a bit of Sunday night pleasure by resorting to the terpsichorean art or relaxing in the chairs lining the walls and delving deeply into these serious economic and political crises that are staring us in the face today. They realize that it's a dog-eat-dog existence despite the seemingly carefree air of the people who make up the Swing Club. Sometimes, one feels that the smiles are artificial; the brains behind them are restless, seeking solution to the unfair tangled state of things.

The dancers glide over the cozy hall floor with an agile tread and seem to feel the spine-tingling music that the Swing Club orchestra sends forth. One notices the ease with which the individuals in the orchestra handle their instruments, the finesse with which the piano player coaxes the tones from his piano. Some of the greatest musicians of our

day are before you—the personnel of the Harlem Swing
Club Band are men from the great name bands of national
and international fame. The men drop in and play a while
and if they have other engagements they leave and join their
band, but if they have the night off they usually spend the
evening at the Swing Club, where there is such a friendly
tone in the surroundings that everyone feels at ease.

The band plays some torrid swing music and a little
brown man, a scant four feet tall, proves to be the most
phenomenal, untiring dancer on the floor. His partner is a
young lady with an engaging personality who tops him in
height by about four inches. The little man dances with
abandon. He runs the gamut of the latest swing crazes; the
perspiration sticks to his back but he doesn't let up.

A pretty girl, with an aquiline nose, joins hands with her
tall, loose-jointed partner and they give a dance exhibition
with such scintillating ease that it gives the impression that
anyone could emulate them.

The room becomes warm and fills with cigarette smoke
as the music ceases and the dancers find seats or drift toward
the walls and stand together earnestly talking in little groups.

A brawny man with a booming voice walks to the center
of the floor and asks for silence. With flowing adjectives and
tremor in his voice he introduces a speaker whose greatness
and worth to the working class could not be explained, even
with all of the superlatives in the English language. He is
Angelo Herndon, a living martyr. There is ear-splitting applause! Herndon is an idol of the working man. He's the
fearless young black man who was remanded to an Atlanta,
Georgia, chain gang, for life; he dared to interfere with the
shameless infringements by Southern law enforcers, demanding the Constitutional rights of black and white
workers.

Herndon appealed to the Georgia Supreme Court, but
it broadly winked at justice and upheld the Atlanta court's
decision to lock him up for life. But Herndon was not to be

so easily daunted—he appealed to the U.S. Supreme Court, which saw the joker in the case and said, "Free Herndon."

Herndon is a clean-out, softspoken man, who incessantly puffs on a cigarette. His physique doesn't lead one to believe that he could stand the physical and mental brutalities that were heaped upon him. A man's heart must be elephantine in proportion for him to calmly state, in the face of almost certain death, as Herndon did while in that filth-ridden prison in Georgia, "I am not one, I am millions; if they kill me, a million more will rise in my place." He's a man.

Herndon's speech is about another martyr—Tom Mooney. Mooney was released from a California prison yesterday, after serving over twenty-two years on a trumped-up charge. Those two men have something in common—Angelo and Tom. Herndon modestly spent his speech extolling the amount of courage and spirit it took Mooney to survive his experiences. Herndon's speech was short but packed with working-class, political dynamite and he was cheered.

Then Herndon introduces some other heroes, Americans who served in the Loyalist lines in Spain are in our midst. "Let's give them a hand," we are told. "They are men, every one of them. Give a moment's silence for the boys who did not return from Spain." There is a deafening silence.

The music begins afterward and the dancers resumed dancing; I slip out of the Harlem Swing Club, feeling pleasantly surprised.

*January 1939*